Fear and Violence
on the Job

Fear and Violence on the Job

Prevention Solutions for the Dangerous Workplace

Steve Albrecht, M.A., PHR

CAROLINA ACADEMIC PRESS

Durham, North Carolina

Copyright © 1997 by Steve Albrecht
All Rights Reserved.

Library of Congress Cataloging-in-Publication Data

Albrecht, Steve, 1963–
    Fear and violence on the job: prevention solutions for the
dangerous workplace / by Steve Albrecht: foreword by Joseph A.
Davis.
        p.   cm.
    Includes bibliographical references.
    ISBN 0-89089-658-5
    1. Violence in the workplace. I. Title.
HF5549.5.E43A35   1997
658.4'73--dc21
                                                            97-3617
                                                            CIP

Printed in the United States of America

CAROLINA ACADEMIC PRESS
700 Kent Street
Durham, North Carolina 27701
Telephone (919) 489-7486
Fax (919) 493-5668
www.cap-press.com

This book is dedicated to "Boots," who continues to amaze me with her incredible beauty and fearless intelligence, and to Matthew, whose strength lies inside his kind and gentle nature.

TABLE OF CONTENTS

FOREWORD

BY JOSEPH A. DAVIS, PH.D, LL.D., A.B.F.E., A.B.F.M.

Unfortunately, violence in American society has reached epidemic proportions. The emerging threat of violence perpetrated in the workplace can no longer go unnoticed as a rare occurrence and isolated incident. Furthermore, as the workplace setting provides yet another venue and opportunity for many individuals to express inappropriately their problems, corporations and businesses, large or small, continue to operate in the dark without adequate personnel training or planning.

Businesses, who operate without an absolute understanding that violence (of any kind in the workplace) can happen at any time to any enterprising company, must carefully recognize that without appropriate education, research, training, and planning, a crisis situation and a potential disaster is waiting to happen.

The aftermath of such violence is usually traumatic and catastrophic. Like most workplace problems, violence on the job in most all cases, could have been prevented, defused, remedied, or completely avoided if evaluated, assessed, and screened by properly prepared and trained personnel.

Steve Albrecht, a seasoned investigator, professional educator, trainer, author, and researcher, is not only an experienced and knowledgeable industrial-organizational consultant regarding interpersonal violence, he is a very talented writer and lecturer on the subject.

Steve's book, *Fear and Violence on the Job,* is more than just another text on the subject of workplace violence. His work is thoroughly researched, written and designed for the executive, manager, supervisor, director, security officer, trainer, professor, or student of this subject.

In fact, Steve's research and experience accurately pinpoints, isolates, and addresses many of the problems found in workplace settings today. He effectively communicates his knowledge in an easy to understand manner. I find his thoughts to be very insightful, reliable, and valid on a variety of workplace issues, particularly when addressing personnel matters, prevention strategies, and intervention planning. Steve's knowledge of this subject, in its many forms, is sought out by many of the Fortune 500 companies.

Fear and Violence on the Job: Prevention Solutions For the Dangerous Workplace addresses many of the critical issues and controversies sur-

rounding this subject and provides timely and useful solutions to problems that can potentially lead to the possible self-destruction of companies if the leaders, managers, supervisors, and employees are not properly informed, trained, and prepared.

Once you complete Steve's book as I did, you will walk away with a
higher degree of confidence as a *direct* result from being taught by this
book to address and manage the most difficult employer-employee scenarios facing business today.

Additionally, two of Steve's other books, *Crisis Management for Corporate Self-Defense* (AMACOM, 1996) and *Ticking Bombs: Defusing
Violence in the Workplace* (Irwin Prof. Publ., 1994; co-authored with Dr.
Michael Mantell), are both critically acclaimed and acknowledged as com-
prehensive works in the field. My impressions find that both books are
just as insightful and make additional readings a must once you have completed this fine work.

Dr. Joseph A. Davis

JOSEPH DAVIS, PH.D, LL.D., A.B.F.E., A.B.F.M., is an internationally recognized expert in forensic psychology, forensic mental health, and law. He
is the Director of the Center for Forensic-Behavioral Sciences in San Diego,
California.

PREFACE FOR READERS

I come to this textbook with an admittedly eclectic background. From a business standpoint, I have been a management consultant and seminar trainer since 1989. In 1994, I co-wrote *Ticking Bombs*, the first nationally published business book on violence in the workplace. In this book, I interviewed a convicted workplace murderer and used his accounts to help solidify my understanding of this subject.

I have been associated with law enforcement since 1984, both as a regular police officer, now as a reserve sergeant, and currently, the only reserve investigator on the San Diego Police Department.

My Masters Degree is in the new arena of security management. While the subject of formally protecting employees and company property is certainly not new, a post-graduate degree program in this subject is a recent addition to the field.

Lastly, I continue to teach the subjects of workplace violence prevention and domestic violence in the workplace awareness for private sector firms; government and law enforcement agencies; schools, colleges, and universities; the military; and as part of my work as an adjunct professor with two colleges.

Since the problem of occupational violence is difficult to categorize, I'm pleased to have this written forum to help bring the varied fields attached to it under one umbrella.

The subject of violence in the workplace is hardly new. About 20 people are killed per week while at work, by people who are total strangers to them, or by those they know, work with, or who purport to love them or have had a physical relationship with them at some previous point. The numbers of employees threatened, assaulted, or battered while at work each year ranges from the hundreds of thousands to the millions, depending upon whom is asking the questions and how.

You can assume that the true statistics for this organizational-societal issue vary because it is at heart, a "shadow" problem. Few workplace cases short of homicide make the newspapers. The vast majority of non-homicide employee-upon-employee, employee-on-manager, or the more rare, manager-on-employee violence crimes go unreported to the police. Obviously, this does nothing to raise the arrest rates for workplace crimes of violence.

Since the subject usually only receives outside or public attention following some horrific workplace tragedy, we have to rely on our understanding of parts of the puzzle, since the totality of the problem today is still not entirely clear.

History has long recorded many cases of workplace violence when an employee injured or killed his boss following a dispute over pay, working conditions, presumed mistreatment or a termination. Even more employees have been injured or killed at work by disturbed customers or most commonly, criminals. But while this type of violence has been around for generations, it has intensified, both statistically, and in visibility in the last five to seven years.

We have come a long way in our understanding of this subject and yet not so far. Violence has always been one solution to workplace conflict for that percentage of highly enraged, immature, emotionally disturbed people in our midst who believe they cannot cope with their work or life situations in other positive ways.

For all our accomplishments, our society has not evolved too far past the Wild West days, where men pulled guns from their vest pockets or holsters and shot their rivals, enemies, or perceived tormenters. And while assault weapons were still in the imaginations or on the drawing boards of a few gunsmiths at the turn of the century, they exist in full power today.

You'll notice my frequent and purposeful use of the male pronoun to describe the actors in violent episodes. Occupational violence has been and is a male practice, completed by males and largely against male victims. Women, for all their past and recent attempts at workplace equality, have thankfully avoided all but the most rare cases of workplace violence. So when I say "he" and "his," it is with the understanding that male perpetrators overpopulate the subject of workplace violence.

Recent literature does document the occasional disturbed female employee who has injured her boss or co-workers or even more infrequently, committed homicide in the workplace. As our police and prosecutors will attest, more women today have shown they are capable of street crimes including armed robbery, driveby shootings, or carjackings. But these too are rare, especially in comparison with male perpetrators, whose crime activities dominate their gender.

More specifically, while women are not often the perpetrators of workplace violence, they are its victims. During my speeches and presentations, I hear the gasps in the audience when I mention that statistically, the leading cause of death for women at work is murder. That our society and our business people accept this fact with a weary shrug says volumes about how far we have to go.

And it's not just women who are injured or killed at work by angry co-workers, robbers, or disturbed customers or trespassers that is so disconcerting; it's those that are killed by people whom they know, and in most cases, supposedly love or loved them.

This book will discuss also the newest workplace violence phenomenon, which is how and why domestic violence has crossed over (or "spilled over" as the newest term has been coined) from the home into the workplace. While the number of stranger-upon-stranger homicides is increasing (as the case clearance rate is decreasing), women continue still to be killed by enraged former or current boyfriends or spouses. We see more indications that the stalking boyfriend or spouse has few qualms now about bringing his rage and his gun to his partner's workplace, both with tragic results. Here, home problems have become work problems and management intervention into one has to include the other.

In terms of my use of language, other points remain. My use of the collective "we" is on purpose. I'm assuming that you come to this book as a new or returning college or university student, either with no or limited job experience or with plenty. I'd like you look to the future a bit and put yourself in the role of the manager or supervisor who must face similar employee behavioral problems discussed in the book.

At opportune points, I have inserted my own experiences into the text in order to illustrate a point properly. This is done with editorial license in mind, not for commercial self-promotion purposes.

Further, as I believe occupational violence is an employee behavioral issue, I refer frequently to the perpetrator as "disturbed." This is less for psychological reasons and more for writing convenience. This term works if we can agree at the start that any employee, customer, vendor, or criminal who threatens or attacks anyone working in an organization is by proxy highly irrational and disturbed. Their behavior is not normal, safe, or justifiable, regardless of the circumstances.

This is more than just a textbook about specific workplace violence incidents. It's not filled with arcane governmental research reports, meaningless employment statistics, or psychological treaties about what makes the workplace murderer tick. Further study of the psychology of human behavior, and more specifically criminal human behavior, would swell the pages of this book and distract us from the message, which is: occupational violence is both a human resources issue inside the organization and a behavioral issue in society. Preventing these events requires an understanding of both realms.

Steve Albrecht, M.A., PHR
San Diego, California

A NOTE TO THE INSTRUCTOR

This book will show instructors, readers, and students how to recognize potential problem employees; dangerous or violent customers, students, or patients; identify specific warning sign behaviors; change those behaviors legally and safely; and protect the entire organization and its valuable assets from the real, costly, and even deadly hazards of workplace violence.

The author is nationally known as an expert on this subject. He has helped many executives, managers, and supervisors intervene at all levels and recognize and deal with problem people before they explode into violence.

The book will serve as a complete college/graduate level guide to the subject. Along with defining the issue, it discusses safe hiring practices, discipline procedures, termination policies, and management intervention steps that will help solve existing problems and prevent potential disasters.

Other topics covered include domestic violence in the workplace; obsessive or stalking behavior at work; new personnel and HR intervention methods; and updated security management solutions.

This book also examines the growing number of workplace violence incidents from an organizational security perspective. The student/reader will review the spectrum of workplace violence from covert threats to homicide, and recognize solutions to the problem using internal and external resources.

Students/Readers will:

- understand workplace violence from various social, psychological, and historical perspectives.

- review cases of workplace violence homicide, including a case study discussion in the Appendix of a workplace/domestic violence murder, in an effort to understand patterns, profiles, and warning behaviors.

- analyze current human resources practices pertaining to legal and effective hiring, screening, and interviewing methods; counseling and employee assistance referral; and effective discipline and termination methods.

- learn the knowledge, skills, abilities, and resources needed to help solve or prevent these kinds of problems.

This book has been designed for professors, instructors, and students of university, college, and community college undergraduate and graduate-level courses in business management, human resources management, personnel, criminal justice, security management, sociology, criminology, and human behavior in the organization.

It covers a subject that is timely, current, and filled with hidden hazards. Workplace violence is a growing "underground" problem for business, not just in the 90's, but well into the new century. This textbook will help to fill an existing gap, since many business or security college-level texts now only mention the subject in a few paragraphs or at best, a few pages.

This book will educate instructors, students, and readers and change their understanding of the problem, and teach them strategies for business protection and survival.

Fear and Violence
on the Job

1

Fear in the Workplace: Productivity and Performance Issues

KEY POINTS TO THIS CHAPTER

- The impact of workplace fear
- Associated connections to employee performance, productivity, stress, and morale
- Financial risks to the organization
- The need to send the right message

The subjects of occupational violence and specifically, workplace homicides, cry out with more questions than answers. "Why does this happen?" leads the list, followed by "What can we do to prevent these cases in the future?"

Answers to either query are usually long, complex, and unfulfilling, giving little comfort to surviving victims, witnesses, or far-off observers of these incidents.

This dissatisfaction surrounding the issues is coupled with our collective inability to grasp the actual reasons why an individual would bring a gun into a place of business and use it to injure or kill one or more employees, customers, vendors, or other bystanders.

Our perceptions of injury or death on the job are often clouded by misperceptions based upon well-meaning but incorrect assumptions. Any adult even a bit familiar with our criminal justice system knows instinctively that America is constantly becoming a more dangerous and violent place in which to live. Now this conclusion has made its twisting, turning way into the places where we work.

The media has helped to shape most of our views about violence in the workplace by focusing on the most spectacular, horrific, and ominous crimes. From a national level, these incidents used to be noted as "Page One" news; now they might get a brief mention, buried somewhere in the back of the newspaper, along with other street crimes that cause people to shake their heads and wonder what has become of our nation.

Real or perceived, the public, or more importantly, the *corporate* view of workplace violence is that it only involves homicides, i.e. the well-storied, frequently-quoted "Disgruntled Ex-Employee Returns With A Gun, Slays Two."

What does *not* make the newspapers, on any page, is the fistfight on the loading dock, the anonymous phone threats to the worried supervisor, or the feelings of dread and anxiety that plagues intimidated employees who stand in the parking lot and hesitate to go inside their office buildings for fear of encountering their tormentors.

And it is this misperception that occupational violence is only about homicidal maniacs that more than distorts the view of the problem as a whole.

As a new or continuing student of this subject, you have the opportunity to learn about violence in the workplace from a wide perspective, taking in the various constituencies surrounding the problem, understanding some of the motivations of the perpetrators, and reviewing the possible solutions as they become apparent.

This book seeks to change your perception of this problem as something that doesn't just "happen to other people in other companies," but as one that serves as a mirror for the problems of violence in our society as well.

Models and Concepts

Two iconic images come to mind when considering the problem of violence at work. One is the onion, which, although it appears solid, is really comprised of many thin layers attached to other thin layers that make up the sum of its parts. In other words, as we can determine from our review of individual occupational violence cases or the problem as a whole, there is more to all this than meets the eye. And with the obvious connections to onions and shedding tears, the problem causes much grief for all the participants, witnesses, and company leaders even at its least violent levels.

The other icon is the stone thrown into the pond, causing the proverbial ripple effect, as concentric circles flow outward from the center. If we will admit from the start that workplace violence is both vexing and complex, we also must agree that the ripple effect is literal.

Problems that begin at the center of an organizational relationship, i.e. between an employee and his supervisor, will reflect outwardly and touch many other workers, their colleagues, various family members, other departments, and the civil and psychological health of the company.

And as the stone-in-the-pond idea illustrates, a disruption at the center of any otherwise smooth system, in this case, the organization, causes many people to act or respond in ways that take them far outside their usual comfort zones.

It's hardly groundbreaking news to suggest that managers and supervisors dislike conflict, confrontation, or the imposition of having to correct the behavior of others. Even the moderately disturbed or disgruntled employee, customer, vendor, or trespasser can create much anxiety in the manager who must intervene in what is largely a problem between human beings rather than mistakes on a balance sheet or a production run.

As such, though an employee (or customer) may go about making scenes, proffering threats, or otherwise creating problems in an organization, there is usually a hope from the people in charge that somehow he will (in a yet to be determined way) leave, move, quit, retire, transfer, or otherwise self-correct himself.

In their efforts to avoid confronting unethical, unsafe, illegal, emotional, or potentially violent behavior, most managers and supervisors will look for the least difficult problem-solving method. And all too often, as they wait for the "right moment" or the "right" policy, procedure, guideline, or law to appear, the employee, customer, or other troublemaker in question does irreparable harm to the organization's people, reputation, or psychology.

The reason for this forced apathy parallels the causes of workplace violence in the first place: fear, of both the known (people *have* been shot and killed at work) and fear of the unknown (what do *I* do about this person and the problem so that I am not injured or killed, right now or sometime in the indeterminate future?).

It's human nature to choose the convenience of stereotypes when we don't understand a person or a problem. And it is this sense, fueled by the often media-created themes that workplace violence is really only about so-called "nuts with guns," that leads so many managers to feel less than comfortable about their understanding of the problem.

Coupled with this theme is the ill-considered idea that occupational or employee violence "won't happen here because our firm is not...," and here people will fill in the name of the industry, type of business, or organization more likely known for its exposure to this problem. Since one organization comes to mind immediately, it's worth exploring its connection to violence in the workplace.

Blaming the Messenger

Pity the poor United States Postal Service; most people do. It serves as the most notorious organization in America, tagged with the perception of being the "birthplace" of workplace violence. And thanks to so much like-minded publicity every time a homicide or other incident of employee-related violence strikes a postal facility, the flywheel begins spinning all over again.

This organization of over 750,000 employees who go about the business of getting nearly 175 billion pieces of mail into our collective hands can get no break from us.

And following each new workplace violence event involving a postal employee, the suggestion rings out each time that somehow our post offices are a new "killing field." And it is a sad truth that the phrase "going postal," i.e. choosing violence, losing control, blowing your top, flying off the handle to the nth degree, etc., has made it into the mainstream of our business vocabulary.

Comedians pepper their monologues with jokes about the Postal Service, hammering on everything from gun-toting employees to high stamp prices and ill-mannered clerks. Cartoonists create strips where postal workers are shown as homicidal, incompetent, or ignorant. Moviemakers have also made the USPS fair game, as the satiric comedy "Naked Gun: 33 1/3" demonstrated by opening up with a scene of postal workers armed with assault weapons.

To say all this is in the name of plain old fun is wrong. For the people who work at the Postal Service, those depictions are hurtful, mean-spirited, and continue to perpetuate the stereotype that the post office is both an urban hunting ground waiting to explode and a vacation spot for retired-on-the-job layabouts just waiting for their pension checks.

During a meeting with Postal Service officials in one west coast city, the director of personnel, the head of HRD, and the director of employee safety each told me the same thing: "All the jokes and comments really hurt our employees' feelings and damage their sense of pride in the work they do and in their organization. Our internal and external image is a big concern for each of us."

Author and Northeastern University professor James Fox points to a number of related items. "It's a combination of factors," he told an Oprah Winfrey audience in 1993. "The post office is typically seen as a high-stress working environment where the employees face constant, never-ending deadlines. And our society doesn't appreciate the work these people do. We caricature them in TV shows like 'Cheers'." Clearly, the hapless know-it-all mailman Clifford Claven is hardly a role model for the post office. Yet, thanks to his unflattering representation on such a widely-viewed and popular television program, it's hard to imagine many children look to their parents and say, "Mommy and Daddy, when I grow up I want to be a letter carrier."[1]

Some outside observers believe the job lacks dignity and is usually correctly perceived by most people outside it as blue collar work. In reality, the postal service job is something certain people gravitate toward, probably because of the relatively high pay, the excellent benefits won by the powerful postal labor unions, and because the job has a certain civil service steadiness to it. The chances of being fired are still quite slim — as long as you do your job adequately — and most people, once they settle into the routine of the work, can make a career of it. There are few jobs like it in the government's workforce; it's unique. And there are few private sector jobs that match the pay for the type of work involved.

But back to this idea of image management, most people still make the easy association between the Postal Service and workplace violence. The sad fact that the themes and concepts surrounding workplace violence have been inextricably linked to the Postal Service really belies the facts. There have been approximately 44 postal worker homicides in the last decade. While that sounds like too many (and even one is tragic), most people don't realize that 14 of those deaths happened in 1986 in Edmond, Oklahoma when postal employee Patrick Sherrill killed his co-workers and then himself.

A painful paradox follows the Postal Service when it comes to the rare workplace violence shooting on its premises. We have become so accustomed to any form of homicide that what used to be frontpage news, i.e., "Worker returns to pickle factory and kills two," has now been relegated to page 26, bottom of the fold. Many people — in business or otherwise — now take workplace violence cases for granted. Even homicides in the workplace, which are the smallest but most visible part of the problem, get short attention, except when they happen at the post office.

In May 1993, two postal homicide incidents took place on the same day—one in Dana Point, California and the other in Royal Oak, Michigan. Within days, we saw bold articles in *The New York Times, USA Today,* and a host of other national magazines and newspapers. All the stories were keyed around the central theme, "What's the problem with these postal people? Why do they keep killing each other?"

---

1. Fox, James. "The Oprah Winfrey Show." May 27, 1993.

The two easiest answers to these questions are: workplace violence inside the Postal Service mirrors workplace violence in the rest of our society and any organization with over three-quarters of a million employees (which makes it the largest civilian government employer) is bound to have the same problems as the rest of the adult population and workforce.

The Postal Service is not unique in its employee problems, just more visible. It only took a few shootings before journalists began to think they had uncovered a trend. And then unfortunately, every incident that followed built upon this supposed legacy of homicide that people think however incorrectly, that plagues the Postal Service.[2]

Precursors to Workplace Violence

To put the stone-into-the-pond model back into play, consider that, besides being a hazard of post office duty, many people still view occupational violence within the narrow confines of workplace crimes such as robbery or murder. Still others don't make this connection too well, seeing these unfortunate events as somehow not related to the subject or distracting from their impression of the subject as only the "disgruntled ex-employee with a gun."

Upon reading of yet another shooting death of a store clerk late at night, some people will comment, "That's not *really* workplace violence is it? It's more like a robbery and a homicide, a series of street crimes, right?"

For those people either not personally affected by these kinds of crimes, or who do not work in the industries where they are more prevalent, it's easy to dismiss the incidents as not really "workplace violence" in its purest definition.

Indeed, even one of the most recent fact-finding studies on occupational violence — the July 1996 report from the National Institute of Occupational Safety and Health (NIOSH), lists the most "dangerous" jobs by rate of homicide incidence as cabdrivers, armored car drivers, police patrol officers, and store clerks.

Using circular reasoning, many people in business therefore honestly believe that if they neither work in those industries nor hire, manage, discipline, or terminate the people who do, then they are somehow immune

2. Albrecht, Steve. *Crisis Management For Corporate Self-Defense: How to Protect Your Organization In a Crisis.* New York: AMACOM, 1996, pp. 67-69.

to the threat of workplace violence. This perception suggests the attempted use of a corporate security blanket made from imaginary cloth.

To a disgruntled or highly disturbed employee, who is the most powerful man in any organization? The CEO? The president? The Chairman of the Board?

No, to the enraged employee, the most powerful person in an organization is himself, when he brings a gun to work. He can make all of these important people or their subordinates feel very afraid by his words, actions, or mere armed presence. Today, the disturbed employee says to all who will listen, "People better not mess with me. If something bad happens to me, I just might take someone out. I'm deadly serious. If you don't think so, just look at what happened at other places where a good man was fired for no reason and came back with a gun and did what he had to do."

Are these statements threats? Without question. Are these threats legitimate? Possibly, but while we may not have enough information to make a rapid intervention decision right now, there is certainly enough to initiate an immediate investigation into this person's problem.

Today, more and more company leaders are beginning to understand that these threats often serve as a stepping stone for future violence. And they're learning that the earlier they can intervene when they recognize or hear about these early-warning signs, the better opportunity they have to lessen the impact.

The High Cost of Fear On the Job

If you stopped reading this text at the close of this chapter, this last section will at least finally set you on the right track about what occupational violence is and what it is not.

It is not just about disgruntled employees, former or current; it's not just about crime at work, committed by outsiders, that injures a victim-employee; it's not just a problem that happens at the United States Post Office; it's not only about homicides that occur at or near the workplace; and it's not something that only happens at other companies.

Workplace violence is about fear, and who uses it as a weapon to make other employees feel afraid, anxious, intimidated, or unable to work. This fear can come in the form of psychological or physical threats, threatened or actual attacks, and can cripple a victim-employee even if he or she is never touched by the perpetrator.

Understanding that fear exists in the workplace will help many people inside and outside an organization to deter potential episodes of violence. Managing the presence of fear in the workplace starts by intervening when behavioral problems erupt, by creating policies that deter fear, and by implementing safety and security procedures that lessen employee anxiety.

Managers and supervisors who ignore the presence of employee fear diminish the real anxieties of their employees. The fact is that fear, like other emotions that create a normal and standard "fight or flight" stress response, is an authentic human feeling that shouldn't be explained away as irrational or unreasonable.

Events or actions will create feelings of fear in different people in different ways, especially those tinged with the potential for violence. In other words, what scares one employee into hand-shaking inactivity may not bother another employee at all. But the level of intensity or the reaction of the victim should not be the primary concern.

Just like episodes involving sexual harassment, what bothers one woman may not bother another, but that doesn't make the violation of this company (and federal) policy acceptable just because there is a sliding scale of reaction or concern. Harassment is harassment, even if the impact upon the victim is minimal; the impact upon other co-workers, managers, and the organization may be significant.

The perpetrator-employee who threatens to batter one employee but not others has committed a policy violation that affects the safety and security of every person in the organization, including customers, vendors, or visitors. Management's attempts to minimize one victim-employee's reports of threats or potential violence places the rest of the organization's employees at risk. This is why managers and supervisors need to intervene and investigate every fear-creating incident that they discover, witness, or gets reported to them. The true victim of feelings of fear created by threats of workplace violence is the entire organization, not just the reporting employee.

Management's failure to respond, either by not creating policies that help to relieve employee fears, not investigating incidents immediately, not taking any threats aimed at employees seriously, or by failing to administer sanctions for this behavior, may find this apathy to be a central feature of a civil court case.

When one bullying employee threatens to punch out anyone who tells the boss he is stealing tools, everyone in the vicinity of this action becomes afraid. Each of the witnessing employees gets victimized by this threat and feels fearful (at various levels or degrees), even if he or she was not named or targeted specifically. If the threatening employee's supervisor fails to intervene and correct this problem once he or she is notified of it, any one of the surrounding employees can claim that the organization allowed a dangerous or hostile workplace to flourish, despite being put on notice.

At a minimum, fear distracts; its presence helps to prevent employees from getting their work done to the best of their abilities. Its existence in a company hovers like a toxic cloud over the interactions between co-workers and their desire to work without anxiety.

Fear damages performance in the organization because its victims can't concentrate on their work. It diminishes productivity both for the primary victim-employee and those co-workers who must relay on that person's work output.

The female secretary in an office who is involved in a domestic violence relationship and who fears her ex-husband may stalk her at work, may not be able to answer the telephone, type correspondence for others, or sit at her desk for even short periods without bursting into tears. Her fear problem becomes, like it or not, the organization's fear problem.

The employee who is told by a co-worker, "If I ever catch you alone, I'm gonna beat your face," may find himself so afraid that he cannot work alone, enter the facility by himself, or stay late.

One case I recall involved an employee so fearful that a co-worker would shoot him that he actually bought a bulletproof vest from a police equipment mail-order house and wore it under his shirt and suit at work. He had received death threats from the co-worker and had learned from others that he had shown them a gun and may have kept it at work. Only after the terrified employee's manager found him weeping in his car in the employee parking lot did the organization recognize the seriousness of the problem and quickly intervene.

Fear, left unstopped, affects employee morale and can destroy the positive culture that may have flourished inside the organization. Employees who are fearful of each other may not want to work together, despite cajoling from management. The influence of fear may lead to partial or even total employee inactivity, apathy, or complete paralysis.

Unchecked fear of violence in the workplace may cause enormous financial risks, employee hardships, huge legal fees, court appearances, court costs, lost work time for many employees, and the potential for huge monetary settlements.

It's very difficult to put an actual dollar-figure for costs and losses due to organizational violence. Different studies and reports have measured these numbers in unique ways, either quite specifically or more general. One widely-quoted figure from Joseph Kinney and Dennis Johnson's 1992 report on workplace violence from their National Safe Workplace Institute suggested as much as $4.2 billion is lost per year due victim injuries and lost worktime. Other figures have been more conservative, but most experts agree that with over 1,000 workplace homicides per year and hundreds of thousands of violent or near-violent incidents, a benchmark figure is at least $1 billion per year.

Victim-employees who file suits either alone, or as part of a class-action against the organization, may reap million-dollar awards for their emotional losses and pain. The National Council on Compensation states that the average stress-related disability claim costs over $20,000 per claim; and that figure has surely risen since this report in 1993.

Cases involving the threat of workplace violence may appear in labor law, workers' compensation, disability claims, stress claims, or other civil court proceedings. As long as the physically or emotionally injured plaintiff(s) can prove in court that management either knew or should have known of the resulting threats or actual violence and failed to intervene with an immediate investigation, policy changes, security additions, or discipline or termination for the perpetrator(s), they probably will prevail.

Lastly, left unchecked, fear in the workplace sends the wrong message to a wide viewing audience inside the organization. It suggests to victim-employees that the company doesn't care about them, their concerns, or worse, their physical safety.

It may help witness co-workers to feel that instead of reporting threats or incidents, they should keep their mouths shut. It could intimidate them into silence, both because they fear retribution from the perpetrator or condemnation by other employees or their supervisors. And if they see other employees' fears go unabated, they may hide their own concerns if, in the future, they are victimized by violence themselves.

For those highly-disturbed employees who see no intervention from management, no sign that they are concerned about workplace violence, no use of security measures to protect others, fear becomes their most powerful weapon, short of a gun.

Company leaders who ignore fear or are themselves to afraid to take the proper intervention steps tell perpetrator-employees that they can in reality, get away with a variety of acts that terrify, harass, intimidate, threaten, or injure frightened co-workers without much sense of deterrence, sanctions, punishment, fear of termination, or even arrest.

It's time to change this perception and start enforcing the rules of the organization and the laws of society. Every normal employee, who doesn't choose to use threats, fear, the potential for violence, has the right to a safe, secure workplace and protection from those perpetrators, who either work in the same company or attack it from the outside.

REVIEW/SUMMARY

Workplace violence is not just about disgruntled ex-employees with guns, problems at the United States Post Office, or hapless clerks killed during convenience store robberies; it's really about fear, and who creates and uses it to influence negatively the work behavior of others.

The hidden cost of workplace violence fears — individual and class action lawsuits, stress cases and worker's compensation claims by other scared employees; damage to the physical, psychological, and human assets of the company, etc. — must be identified and dealt with before they cause violence, litigation, or even the demise of the company.

DISCUSSION QUESTIONS

1. What key words or phrases shape your own perceptions about workplace violence?
2. How has the media portrayed this subject? Has this depiction been fair and accurate?
3. Discuss the connection between the United States Postal Service and workplace violence.
4. Why is fear the driving force behind workplace violence?
5. What post-incident actions drive up the costs of a workplace violence episode for an organization?

2

The Changing Workplace:
The Age of Entitled Disgruntlement

KEY POINTS TO THIS CHAPTER

- The growing prevalence of workplace violence
- Anger and entitlement at work
- Changing employee rights
- The impact of off-the-job problems
- Violence in society

The World As We No Longer Know It

It's no great revelation to suggest that we live in the most violent country in the world. We have come to accept this inference as a sign of the way things are, as part of our history and heritage, the legacies of our involvement in wars, the development of the handgun as a protection device, and the continuous rise in both crime statistics and criminal acts.

But when many people shake their heads in disgust and dismay and chalk all this up to the state of the nation, it's often from the perspective that we have "lost" the war on street crime.

Additionally, there continues to be much debate as to the overall impact of the "war" on drugs. Even the most optimistic crimefighters will usually admit that we've done little to stop the flow of drugs into the U.S., not made much of a dent on the consumption of illegal drugs, nor had much to say about why people make, take, or sell narcotics for, to, or with each other.

Again, there seems to be a sense that people have thrown up their hands and tacitly accepted their realities of the crime and drug situation. And for many people, who live in the suburbs or better protected neighborhoods in large cities, crime as personal reality is largely an arm's length exposure.

Most people's exposure to street crime is either anecdotal (something that happens to others or that they hear or read about), or they are victimized by disheartening, inconvenient, or occasionally violent events. They have been mugged on the street (still a rarity outside most high-crime inner

15

cities), had their homes burglarized, or suffered through the bothersome ordeal of reporting their stolen cars.

Otherwise, crime, as a subject to be reckoned with personally, is usually something that happens to "other people in other places."

This mindset lies at the heart of what makes workplace violence so difficult to categorize and so disturbing to consider. In a phrase, crime in the streets has now become crime in the suites. The problems of the "real world" have crossed long-established and seemingly crystalline lines of demarcation.

What disturbs us now is that our workplaces, those once protected enclaves where crime never shed its burning light, is now subject to the same violent vagaries of the streets. Crimes of violence no longer recognize the boundaries of the workplace.

Thanks to the national wire services, it's difficult to pick up the local newspaper in any city, or a national daily like *USA Today* and *not* see at least a passing reference to some version of the well-storied template "Disgruntled Man Goes On Rampage At Office, Shoots Two."

Other than the actual events themselves, two things make this growing problem more distressing—first, as mentioned previously, that the problem of occupational violence is now becoming more commonplace and is intruding into an area we once thought was immune. Secondly, that the subject gets play, not on Page One, above the fold, as in months or even years past, but is now relegated to a space on page 26 where the national news is thumbnailed for quick review.

In speeches, lectures, and media interviews, I'm constantly asked why we see now so many episodes of workplace violence. This well-meaning question seeks a single, simple answer to an obviously complex and difficult issue.

In a phrase, violence in our workplaces is simply a mirror of violence in our society.

Why Are We So Upset?

The subtitle of this chapter is a play on words from the phrase we see so often in the media, especially when featuring stories covering workplace violence homicides or other sad events where an angry current or former employee brings a firearm to work. Its roots come from the "entitled" employees, who feel certain they should be subject to many more rights and privileges where they work and the oft-used "disgruntled" employees, who feel certain their life, home, and emotional problems are somehow work-related or worse, work-sponsored.

Two of the more common phrases found in our workplaces today seem to be, "It's not my fault," and "Who can I blame for my problems?"

A short story illustrates this idea: A colleague was having coffee late one night at a fast-food restaurant. Seated at the table behind him were two young men, clearly working in the construction trades from their conversation. My friend couldn't help but overhear the following exchange:

"Did you take that power drill you have in your truck from the company?" said the one man to his associate.

"Yeah, I did," replied the other.

"Why did you do that? It's not right. It's stealing."

"Hey! Screw that company and those people. I'm entitled to take something from them now and then."

"Yeah? How come?"

"For a lot of reasons. For one, because I deserve it. Those cheap [expletives] won't give me a raise. And besides, you know what a [jerk] my boss is..."

At issue in this conversation is not just the disturbing specter of employee theft, but the *right* to steal from the company, which is perceived somehow as reasonable by the employee.

The word "entitlement" even came up during the discussion, in which the one man clearly felt uncomfortable that his friend had taken a power tool from their employer. Suffice to say that nothing probably came of the conversation. It's hard to imagine the man's discomfort with his associate's ethical misconduct would have much of a deterrent impact upon the man's desire to steal. He still saw it as part of his "right" as an employee working from a disadvantaged position against the management of his firm.

Parenthetically, theft by employees from their employers is a serious, expensive, rarely discussed issue in the U.S. More goods, nearly twice as much, are stolen from companies by employees than outsiders. In their book, *Are Your Employees Stealing You Blind?* (Pfeiffer & Co, 1994), authors Edwin C. Bliss and Ismau S. Aoki estimate that fully 75% of workers steal from their employers at least once. In a 1995 report, the National Retail Federation (NRF) said that overall, thieves pilfered $14.7 billion in goods from stores across the country, up from $6.4 billion in 1993. This fact, euphemistically called "internal shrinkage" by the retail industry, accounts for higher costs of goods to the consumer and higher protection and inventory costs for the seller.

As one retail security expert puts it, "We have our store surveillance cameras pointed in the wrong directions and at the wrong people."

Putting all this into the context of the tool-stealing construction worker, we can argue that the theft of company property, i.e. merchandise, equipment, supplies, etc., can serve as individual acts of revenge, intimidation, and vengeance against the firm in general and against certain employees, managers, and supervisors specifically.

Workplace violence can best be described as a spectrum of events, ranging from "silent" activities, like anonymous letters, e-mail, or vandalism of an employee breakroom; to more confrontational behaviors, like overt threats, intimidation, or damaging personal property as a warning to one or more co-workers; and finally, more violent behaviors, assaults, batteries, assaults with deadly weapons, to murder.

Animals in nature, when threatened, use a variety of pre-attack postures, threatening gestures or movements, or other attention-getting and signal-sending activities. These "warm-up" maneuvers may or may not lead to an actual physical confrontation or attack with an enemy, but the mere presence of these behaviors should serve as a definitive warning to stand clear.

Similarly, humans exhibit similar postures that display their anger, aggression, anxiety, rage, or capacity for imminent violence. Some people in the workplace have decided that, short of physical violence, they will attempt to send other harmful messages to the company, i.e. "I'm upset. I'm not happy with my life and my work, so I plan to take it out on everyone around me. I deserve better, so until I get it, I'm going take what I feel is mine and do what I feel I need to do to protect my ego or my dignity."

And while these phrases may or may not come out verbally, they certainly act as internal, below-the-consciousness level drivers for certain employee behaviors.

A Swinging Pendulum:
Employment At Will Versus the Right to Work

To understand better this idea of employee entitlement, it helps to look at two important concepts related to human resources and labor law: employment at will versus the right to work. The differences between the two are both striking and polarizing at the same time.

In the United States, we have always operated under the principle of

---

1. Sherman, Arthur W. and Bohlander, George W. *Managing Human Resources.* 9th edition. Cincinnati, OH: South-Western Publishing, 1992, p. 531.

labor law known as "employment at will." (This doctrine exists as a result of a 1908 U.S. Supreme Court decision, Adair v. United States.)[1]

In essence, this decision states that the employer has the right to hire and fire employees at his or her own discretion, i.e. at will. There is no guarantee of employment, no implied permanent or guaranteed employment, or no concept of "lifetime" employment, as might be found in certain companies in Japan. Under this doctrine, the employer can terminate the employee at any time, with or without cause.

In practice, however, most employees are rarely fired without cause. Most forward-thinking (and lawsuit-aversive) firms practice a concept called "progressive discipline." (This will be discussed in detail in Chapter 12.) Under this approach, employees who are removed for behavioral reasons, not laid-off for business reasons, i.e. downsizing, bankruptcy, plant closures, failing sales, etc., are taken through a step-by-step process that increases in severity at each stage. Examples include: a verbal warning, an informal counseling session, a formal session with a note added to the employee's personnel file, a probationary period, a paid or unpaid suspension, and finally, outright termination.

In association with this idea is that the employee also has the right to leave the employer for a better job, higher wages, or for any other reason he or she does not have to share.

Under the employment at will doctrine, it is the employer who makes the decision as to which employees to hire, at what wages, and for how long. While this practice has had its problems in the past (abusive employers, horrific working conditions, uneven discipline, etc.), it exists to protect the rights of the employer as the primary decision-maker, wage-payer, and final hiring/firing authority.

With that in mind, let's look at the other end of the spectrum: the right to work, or as it is also known, the "job-as-property" doctrine. This concept is less concrete than employment at will. It suggests that while management has the right to hire and fire, there are many employees who feel that the loss of a job has serious economic and personal consequences. Therefore, employees should be entitled to legal protection under due process. This includes the right to progressive, fair, defensible, and appealable discipline; the right to know the expectations and requirements of the job; and the right to fair and equitable treatment by management.

And while proponents of the right to work viewpoint don't expect a guarantee of lifetime employment, they do suggest that the employer-employee work relationship is indeed a contract, with rights, duties, and responsibilities on both sides.

In some cases, entitled employees think they shouldn't be fired for even the most egregious behavior, shouldn't be let go for poor work or bad work habits, or shouldn't be terminated for breaking work rules, violating company policies and procedures, or worse, breaking the law while on the job.

There's a saying in business that states, "A strength, taken to an extreme, becomes a weakness." Under an extreme view of the right to work doctrine, the entitled employee says, "Not only am I entitled to this job, I'm entitled to act any way I want because I'm so underappreciated, underpaid, or underutilized. In other words, I'm owed a living." (In most cases these employees leave out the personal descriptions "underachieving," "unmotivated," and "unneeded.")

And while we still operate under the employment at will doctrine, the dockets in labor law courts are filled with cases of employees who feel their employers are wrong in their interpretation of what is and is not employment.

Some labor and human resource policy experts suggest that the pendulum, which has long swung toward protecting the sanctity of the employment at will philosophy, is now careening toward more of a right to work approach, especially in light of plaintiff-employee court case filings and new policies regarding such employee-favorable legislation as the Americans with Disabilities Act, the Family Leave Act, and Equal Employment Opportunity laws.

As we will see throughout this text, there now exists a plethora of frivolous law suits against firms who have fired perfectly terrible employees and were sued for trying to make the firm a better place to work for the remaining co-workers.

To put these two doctrines into an occupational violence perspective, some employers now feel hamstrung by their desire to operate using employment at will, that is, hiring based on need and ability to meet the job requirements and firing those employees who can't or won't cooperate, work, or follow the rules.

In the most extreme cases, employees who have assaulted or injured managers, supervisors or co-workers later filed suit in labor law court, arguing that draconian management practices somehow drove them to react violently.

And not only do they suggest that they are the true "victims" in the organization, they are also entitled to get their jobs back, with full pay, and no punitive sanctions.

In one case, a mentally disturbed employee pointed a gun at a co-worker and pulled the trigger. It was only because the gun failed that he did not kill the co-worker. He was arrested and later charged for the crime, although the story does not end there. In a sad twist to the employment at will versus right to work controversy, he was able to convince a labor union arbitrator that he deserved his job back after completing a psychological counseling and substance abuse program. Imagine working side by side with this employee, knowing that in the past, he had attempted to murder a co-worker.

Downsizing Realities

If the United States of the 1980's was the decade of rising capitalism and the era of mergers and acquisitions, the 1990's has been the decade of the corporate pink slip.

Consider the November 1996 announcement by self-professed company rescuer Sunbeam CEO "Chainsaw Al" Dunlap. Following a similar course he had swathed at Scott Paper, he took over the venerable toaster and blender maker, and in his usual blunt manner, closed factories, disbanded entire product lines, slashed costs, and cut the payroll to half its prior size. This process, otherwise known as "downsizing," "reengineering," or "human asset reallocation," is best called what it is—layoffs.

His firm is far from the only major U.S. employer to announce widespread changes in the company labor pool. AT&T began a process to cut nearly 40,0000 jobs throughout 1995 and 1996; the Big Three automakers—Ford, General Motors, and Chrysler hire and layoff, hire and layoff, and hire and layoff in a continuous cycle; Apple Computers, facing continuously difficult economic times and uneven sales, has had to layoff even longtime employees; and even once-secure IBM, which has seen its market share eroded by the flood of personal computer clones, has given up on its long-lived policy of "reassigning" employees to other IBM departments or divisions, and has had to join the layoff parade.

All this is not to drag these firms over the human resources coals for these downsizing actions. The economic realities of the day guide publicly-held companies and their leaders, who must make difficult decisions in an effort to maintain profitability and serve their true employers—the shareholders.

The victims and their families and other supporters, who have had to bear up under all of these acts of seemingly harsh job-cuttings are understandably short-sighted and introspective when it happens to them. They are more concerned with their economic futures than the reasons why their former employers have had to take these drastic steps. It is, in reality, the responsibility and duty of the CEO, and by proxy, the firm's board of directors, to serve the best interests of the company's stockholders.

Much of this requirement is lost to the downsizing company's managers and supervisors, under the strain of having to vacate large numbers of people from their positions. The remaining company employees may in fact understand the need to downsize, either as a practical course (to save their own jobs) or intuitively (they may agree with the need but disagree with the approach or the process). But as the bearers of the bad news, they are often the targets of the terminated employees' rage. When this rage turns violent, people can be killed or injured.

Speaking about the connection between layoffs and workplace violence on the "Oprah Winfrey" show, Northeastern University criminology professor and *Mass Murder* author James Fox suggested that, "We don't take enough time to fire people. We need to conduct our layoffs with more compassion. We spend a substantial amount of time and effort hiring these people, only to fire them in the middle of the week at the beginning of their shift. 'Clean out your desk by noon' has become the 'downsizing' model of today."[2]

He and other researchers into the subject of organizational violence continue to make the link between the psychologically unstable, potentially violent employee and an inhumane, abrupt, or humiliating termination event. We will examine the volatile issue of so-called "safe" terminations in Chapter 12.

Personal Problems Come to the Job

Were it possible to employ only robots in our workplaces, perhaps we would not see any incidents of occupational violence, save for the occasional dented machine when it gives an irate customer the wrong product or incorrect change. After all, robots are not human and therefore are not cursed with the foibles of humanity.

As this world doesn't exist, we are faced with the fact that some employees bring their non-work related problems with them to our workplaces. Various human resource associations have studied this issue of off-the-job problems and have suggested that at least 20 per cent of employees come to the workplace with significant problems that seriously affect their ability to work productively and with acceptable performance.

---

2. Fox, James. "The Oprah Winfrey Show." May 27, 1993.

In this context, the definition of what constitutes an off-the-job problem is loose enough to include those personal circumstances that interfere with the employee's ability to concentrate fully on his or her work tasks. This is not to suggest that employees become so fixated at work that stray thoughts of home don't intrude from time to time; these are a natural part of life. The issue is whether off-the-job problems are so pervasive, monumental, damaging, or bothersome that the employer is not getting a full day's work from the employee for a full day's pay.

Examples include the woman who sits trembling at her desk, fearing that the next time the phone rings it will be her abusive ex-husband; the woman who wonders if her battering boyfriend will confront her as she crosses the employee parking lot at lunch; or the man whose illegal drug or alcohol problem has reached not only job-threatening proportions but life-threatening ones as well.

This issue gets much coverage in the following chapter, so at this point, suffice to say that off-the-job problems constitute one of those difficult gray areas in the employer-employee relationship. Managers and supervisors wonder when and if and how to intervene and employees can become obsessed with keeping their "secrets lives" separate from the workplace.

Or in even more difficult situations, the troubled employee attempts or succeeds in bringing difficult, expensive, time-consuming, or even threatening problems into the workplace. This has the unpleasant side effect of creating an environment where the employer becomes the "problem solver of last resort" for the employee.

Our Culture of "Acceptable" Violence

Lastly, when we consider the causal factors for workplace violence, we cannot deny that our society exhibits, encourages, and even relishes violence as both a fact of our existence and sadly, as entertainment. We live in a culture that deems widespread national or international violence not as a frightening phenomenon, but as an unavoidable reality.

Where do we see most of our violence in this country? It's everywhere, but television offers the most available source. It's also in our movies, series shows, and on the network and local news programs.

We live in a TV and movie-driven culture where we see numerous examples of people who solve their problems with their fists, or more significantly, with guns. The movie screens are filled with American cultural icons

like Arnold, Bruce, and Sylvester (no last names are even necessary to identify them).

Studies abound that tell us children are the most willing recipients of
television and entertainment violence (video games, computer games). For
hours at a time, they get stimulated by colorful 3-D images that help them
blur the lines between reality and fantasy.

Where do our children learn about how to handle anger? From watching TV and interacting with other kids who have observed that the TV
offers unique solutions to life's more vexing problems. There are few opportunities for them to learn formal, practical and beneficial anger management techniques. Chances are remote that they get any formal training in
schools. There is not much demand or even student or parent interest for
grade school, middle school, or high school classes on stress management,
conflict resolution, or anger control.

Where do children learn how to get along with each other and adults
without resorting to violence? By reviewing the behaviors and responses
to stress and marital strife of adults who grew up in abusive homes, there
is a better likelihood the learned violence will continue into this next gen-
eration. When children grow up in homes where their father hits their
mother on a regular basis, and the mother allows this behavior to occur
without sanction, they begin to see this as somehow appropriate, acceptable, or worse, behavior to be modeled.

Hollywood threat assessment expert Gavin de Becker says it best, when
discussing loner-type people who become extremely violent as a result of
their lack of proper socialization. "Our country," he says, "makes more of
these kinds of people than any other nation in the world."

REVIEW/SUMMARY

This chapter examined the changing culture in the workplace that often
says, "It's okay to hit your boss" or the employee who says, "This company *owes* me something and if I don't get it, I'm going to act out with my
frustrations."

Our society has a long and undeniable historical connection to the use
of violence as a seemingly viable problem-solver. This culture of violence
has made its way into one of our last protected enclaves—the workplace.

Like children who hit their teachers, employees who assault their supervisors or co-workers don't feel the same social stigma anymore. In this era
of the entitled employee or the newly-terminated who are also disgruntled,

company leaders will need new protection strategies to help themselves cope.

DISCUSSION QUESTIONS

1. Explain the parallels between street crime and violence and workplace violence.
2. What rationalizations motivate the so-called "entitled employee"?
3. Explain the differences between employment at will and the right to work. Which is most prevalent and what is the trend?
4. How can business organizations improve the way they conduct widespread or massive employee layoffs?

3

Off the Job Problems:
Crossing the Line

Key Points to this Chapter

- Problems crossing the boundaries between home and work
- Stress causal factors
- Impact on the organization
- The need for management recognition and intervention

In days of old, perhaps more specifically prior to the 1980's, we asked our employees to come to work, check their personal problems at the door, and give us an honest day's work for an honest day's pay. What worked as an operational guideline 10 to 20 years ago is now less secure.

Today, the symbolic line between home and work is less visible, especially when it's supposed to serve as a barrier between those things that interfere with an employee's productivity and those that he or she can control without company assistance.

This point brings up a highly-charged issue between two opposing factions: employers and employees. The bosses argue that they have the right as employers to demand their employees' full attention to their work. For their part, some of the employees suggest, through their actions or their requests, that the employer becomes, by proxy, in large capital letters, "The Problem Solver Of Last Resort."

Any student of decision-making and problem-solving tools will remember the old 80-20 rule, where 20 percent of anything affects 80 percent of something else. Coined in design by the 19th century economist Vilfredo Pareto, for our discussion, most managers and supervisors will heartily agree that 20 percent of their employees cause not only 80 percent of their workplace attitude and behavioral problems, but burn up 80 percent of their time on administrative correction steps.

In the best case and at the lowest end of the annoyance/bothersome scale, an employee with a noticeable behavioral problem is at least distracting to others around him. In the worst case, he is violent, dangerous, and potentially homicidal.

A Horn of Plenty:
Listing the Top Off-the-Job Problems

On any given work day, there are those people who may fall into the "having a bad day" category. Still worse, there are those that place in the "Having a bad week or month" strata. Lastly, there are those people who appear to be "having a bad life." It is this last group that demands our attention, from a work productivity perspective and from a behavioral one as well.

We can look at this list of 10 personal problem areas in two contexts. One viewpoint must start by saying that many of us have experienced similar difficulties in our personal lives and it has certainly affected our work performance.

So to avoid a suggestion along the lines of "Let he who is without sin cast the first stone," suffice to say that the author and readers alike have stared down at one or more of these life-tightening problems. And as in most things in life, some may have worked themselves out to such a degree that we worried in vain. Others may have required considerable pain, time, money, or suffering before a solution allowed us to regain our equilibrium.

And to be fair, some of these issues qualify as constant sources of worry or even anxiety in most adults. We are all concerned with our family, marital, personal, and work relationships. All but a few carefree types think about economic necessities, especially when we are engaged in the workplace activities that are supposed to earn our compensation.

Now for the second context: Some people cannot escape these off-the-job, work-damaging difficulties, to the point where the degree of intensity makes their problems multiply exponentially. In other words, their off-the-job problems may reach a rolling, boiling, point of no return. It is at this critical juncture between life and work success and life and work failure that they can become very dangerous.

In interviews and as part of the research for this book and my other workplace violence business book, it became clear that the people who could not hold their lives together along a variety of fronts were the most at risk to choose violence as a solution. And for those rare individuals who could not keep a tight rein on their personal problems, and in some manner lost hope, they were able suddenly to make that highly illogical leap from the thought of violence to a firing gun in their hands.

This list follows a rough scale of commonality with employees, with the most common problems near the top. The purpose of this collection is to offer some possible trigger points as to why some employees have chosen violence as a solution.

As you review the list, keep in mind that it's more common for several of these problems to hit the employee at once. While one problem may become the focal point for the employee, there are often more sub-surface issues as well. This is important when we consider intervention methods and violence prevention techniques throughout the remainder of the book.

Marital or Love Relationship Problems

This problem leads the list because it is so intertwined with many of the following problems. Relationship difficulties are caused by some of those on the list below just as well as they can cause some of them. Few people are able to distance themselves from problems with their personal-sexual relationships.

These include: overall relationship discord, escalating arguments, physical fights, the threat of infidelity, separation, divorce, child custody battles, related financial divisions, and even the decision to get engaged or married.

In serious cases, where one partner threatens to or actually leaves the other, takes the children, or otherwise jeopardizes the relationship, the potential for violence can escalate dramatically. Worse yet are the incidences where the home problems become visible at work, affect the performance and productivity of the employee and co-workers, or threaten the employee's future with the company.

Here, the stakes rise for the disturbed employee, especially when he loses his relationship and job within a narrow time period. Certain perpetrators, with nothing to lose at home and no job to go back to, may chose murder-suicide solutions, either at home or the workplace.

Domestic Violence or Related Behaviors

Let's preface this by reiterating the reason for the use of the pronouns "she" to describe the victim and "he" to describe the perpetrator. The numbers from police cases indicate the ratio of female victims and male batterers to be near the 85%-15% range. While this should not suggest that males are not the victims of domestic violence—we know they can be assaulted, battered, threatened, harassed, called, stalked, injured, or killed—the statistics lead us to conclude that the suspect has historically been male.

The issue of domestic violence ending up in the workplace gives many managers queasy stomachs. This physiological response is not unlike that of most field police officers, most of whom despise these calls for their emotional content, deadly potential, and seemingly unsolvable nature.

When a woman comes into her workplace with a black eye, red welts on her arm, or fresh tears, few managers see this scenario as a welcome invitation to ask questions and intervene. They fear appearing "too nosy," re-starting the emotions in the victim, or retribution from the suspect, who in some instances, may work at the same facility as both the victim and the manager.

As with other workplace violence-related issues, domestic violence ranges in severity. It may include everything from a brief marital spat that makes the victim fear for her future more than her safety, to a one-time incident of battery which may or may not have received police intervention, to an on-going pattern of physical and psychological abuse, to telephone or voice mail threats, restraining order violations, to outright stalking behavior.

Obviously, these can cause many related problems in the workplace. Besides the danger factors—that the victim could be injured or killed at home or work by her disturbed current or former partner—there are the issues of work performance, productivity, and co-worker impact again.

The employee grapevine can be a powerful communication device. In small workplaces, where a group of people may work closely in one facility, it's difficult (and embarrassing) for the victim of domestic abuse to keep her problems inside. Not only may her visible injuries or emotional demeanor reveal the problem, but her abuser may bring it to light by confronting, threatening, cajoling, or crying at the victim's workplace.

In cases where the victim-employee has changed her home telephone number in order to cut off contact with her abuser, he knows he can reach her nearly any time he wants by dialing her work number. He may choose to make phone threats to her or her co-workers, knowing this behavior usually gets short attention from management or the police. If so, he can successfully impair an entire office just by making the phone ring.

Each time a call comes in, the victim-employe and her co-workers have no way of knowing if it is the abuser on the line until they answer. This can make everyone very apprehensive each time the telephone rings, whether it is a valid customer or not. Worse yet, by calling intermittently, i.e. every day for weeks and then not again for months, then every day for weeks, the perpetrator can terrify an entire workgroup by *not* calling. Here, he discovers he can wield just as much power by planting the intrusive thought, "When will he call again? Will I be the one he threatens if I answer?"

Keep in mind that many states now recognize same-sex domestic violence relationships as valid. In California, for example, the spousal abuse law — that usually requires either cohabitation, parents of child together, or marriage — has been retrofitted to include live-in same-sex partners. In the past, cases of gay males or lesbian females involved in sexual relationships and domestic violence were culled out by police officers or investigators as non-domestic violence related. It's important to recognize the possibilities that the suspect and victim in domestic violence cases that crossover to the workplace may be of the same sex.

Situations involving the threat or actual domestic violence demand management intervention at the earliest stages. As we will discuss again and again in this book, the company needs to bring the power of other "employee services" departments, i.e. Employee Assistance Programs, Human Resources, Personnel, Security, Legal, etc. with the interventions provided by law enforcement, social services, and psychologists, therapists, and counselors.

Money Worries

In reviewing those occupational homicide cases where a recently terminated employee has returned and shot one or more co-workers, it's easy to get distracted by the act of termination as a possible reason for the outburst.

Most observers of workplace homicides begin their focus on the relationship between the suspect and his boss or co-workers, looking for some hint that a breakdown in communication somehow led to the killings. This path, while valid, ignores a more base reason for the act—as a twisted response to the economic reality suddenly faced by the suspect.

During my prison interview with convicted workplace murderer Robert Mack in 1993, he revealed that some of his rage toward his employer (General Dynamics) and superiors (his victims were his direct supervisor and a labor relations manager) were motivated by problems with his paycheck.

During the weeks before Christmas in December 1991, Mack was placed on an unpaid administrative suspension from the missile plant where he had worked for nearly 25 years. A three-day suspension somehow deteriorated into three weeks as the Personnel Department, his work department, and his shop steward assumed someone else was handling his paperwork. As Mack fretted at home, waiting to go back to the only job he had ever held as an adult, more and more administrative paperwork mistakes left him in the dark.

As result of the General Dynamics bureaucracy, he missed two paychecks over the Christmas holiday. By the time he received a letter in the mail telling him he was terminated for his attendance and absenteeism (the tip of the iceberg for other developing work performance problems), he was out of both money and hope.

One week later, Mack took a gun to his formal termination hearing at the plant, with predictable results. During a break in the proceedings, he shot and killed the labor relations manager assigned to his case and shot and wounded his direct supervisor.

So while it's not safe to generalize that money problems are the root cause of some outbursts of workplace violence, neither is it necessarily true that failed work relationships are primarily to blame. In cases where the perpetrator is terminated for either performance or behavioral problems or as a part of general layoffs or downsizings, the answer for his response may lie in the economic impact. In other words, money, or the lack of it, motivates some people to do very desperate or uncharacteristic things.

In a widely publicized workplace homicide case in March 1995 in Montclair, New Jersey, a postal worker went into his own facility near closing time and robbed the employees of several thousand dollars in cash. He shot and killed four people and wounded one before he fled.

Later, his landlord thought it was unusual that one of his tenants—who owed several months back rent—was able to pay him completely off with a large wad of cash. Hearing of the post office murders and knowing his tenant worked at the same facility, the landlord called police. During his statement, the suspect told investigators that he was deeply in debt and desperately needed the money to pay his bills.

Since we know anecdotally that people will kill *themselves* over their debts, it's no stretch to suggest that a sudden termination for a person living on the monthly money edge—mounting bills, creditor threats and phone calls, bankruptcy proceedings, divorce divisions, or property repossessions—might prompt a violent outburst.

Family Problems

These issues are similar to domestic violence problems or money concerns because they instill a similar sense of helplessness in some employees. Those who feel their home lives are out of control and who carry these problems into their workplaces can feel intense stress in both locales.

This may exhibit itself during emotional outbursts on the job or on the telephone between the employee and a family member, frequent absenteeism, or other homelife difficulties with the employee's children or stepchildren, elderly parents or in-laws, or former spouses.

Related issues include: custody battles, which in the worst cases, deteriorate into hostile parent-oriented stolen, kidnapped, or missing children cases; alcohol, drug, violence, or psychological problems within the family or caused by the employee himself or herself. In these latter instances, family members may attempt to intervene in the employee's life with counseling, rehabilitation, or medical treatments.

In cases where the employee is causing or creating the family problems, there may be some transference between feelings of guilt, anger, rage, or anxiety at home and those same feelings in the workplace. This person may take offense if well-meaning co-workers try to intervene in their personal lives or if the boss takes on a role that appears too "parental" to the employee.

As with marital problems and the complexities of domestic violence, home problems that the employee feels jeopardizes his job may put co-workers, bosses, or family members at risk of outbursts of frustration-based violence.

Boss or Co-worker Hatred

People who work in proximity with each other develop friendships and what might best be called "dislikeships" or in the extreme, "hateships." Beyond normal dislike, these are co-worker or supervisor relationships that degenerate to a point where not speaking to each other is a possibility, along with certain passive-aggressive behaviors like petty theft of co-workers' property, personal property vandalism, or company property destruction.

In more extreme incidences, where one employee seeks to blame his boss or a co-worker for real or perceived slights, the feelings of hatred may escalate to the use of threats, intimidation, or actual violence. Certain disturbed employees may become so obsessed with the actions or comments of co-workers they begin to describe conspiracies and conspirators everywhere. In the twisted view of the disturbed employees, these people are seeking to steal credit for their great ideas, make sure they look bad in front of others, or help get them passed over for promotions.

When examining hatred of other employees or a supervisor, consider a few caveats. In our society, it is fashionable to blame the victim for what the perpetrator has done. We see this in many forms along the criminal justice system, e.g. sexual assault cases ("she shouldn't have worn that outfit"), drunk driving accidents ending in manslaughter ("It was the bartender's fault), or robberies ending in homicide ("He should have just given me the wallet when I asked for it and I wouldn't have had to shoot him.")

And in the workplace, the lament is similar: "I punched my boss because he is a jerk," "I hit my co-worker because she told my supervisor I came in late. If she had kept her mouth shut, I wouldn't have had to do it," or "I pulled the trigger because all those people were out to get me. If they had only left me alone and not always tried to steal credit for my work, this never would have happened."

Co-worker hatred is surpassed only by supervisor hatred. Because managers and supervisors are in obvious power positions, disturbed employees may see them as the root for their psychological discomfort, low pay, unfair or singled-out mistreatment.

There is much historical symbolism in the boss-employee relationship. It's hard for most normal people not to feel as if this association is always a "one-down" position. Even where both parties get along well, where they have a long-established friendship, the supervisor still exerts legitimate power, which may or may not border on being coercive.

The abnormal employee sees himself as a victim of this longstanding employer-employee relationship. Using transference, he may blame his supervisor for all his work and personal failings, especially if he is able to point to one or more incidents where he was somehow victimized by the organization, not given credit, ignored, embarrassed, or punished by the company and its leaders.

It's important to stop at this stage and express the idea that we should never blame the victim for the outrageous or violent actions of the actor. If the boss is truly an unchangeable jerk, quitting is a more viable option than punching. We should be careful not to buy into rationalizations, excuses, or finger-pointing as a justification for the wretched behavior of a violent person.

When a man returns to a company following his termination and shoots and kills several co-workers, it is he who loaded the gun and pulled the trigger, not them, regardless of their work behavior or their treatment of him.

In a recent tragic case in California, a 36-year-old graduate student shot and killed three of his professors on the campus of San Diego State University. He was supposed to present his masters thesis to them for review. Having failed to convince this committee once before, the graduate student planted a handgun inside a wall-mounted classroom first aid kit and waited for his instructors to convene their meeting with him. Minutes into their discussion of his work with him, he retrieved his pistol and gunned the three professors down as they tried to hide behind desks in the room.

Defense attorneys preparing his case suggested that the shooter was "under tremendous stress" because of the demands placed upon him during his graduate work. This effort to shift the blame directly off the shoulders of the suspect and somehow on to the professors for being tough taskmasters is unconscionable.

So when we examine the interactions between a potentially violent employee and his bosses or co-workers, the environment, however unpleasant, cannot and should not ever justify homicide.

About the only good thing you can say about toxic employees who hate their boss and/or their co-workers is that they rarely keep their feelings to themselves. The enraged employee usually exhibits many manic, discomforting, or threatening behaviors that are rarely kept secret from the other employees. The presence of these kinds of activities and statements, i.e. "Everyone here hates me," or "My boss is out to screw me," should serve as early-warning signs for more immediate management intervention.

Workplace Coping Problems

These are trying times. The economic realities of today suggest there are few guaranteed jobs, no more lifetime employee, and not much hope that some people in some jobs are not two weeks' notice away from a layoff, downsizing, or a termination.

The phrase "do more with less" permeates throughout most organizations. This means more people are asked to do more work with less help, for the same or less pay. This can create the kind of stress that the well-described Type A people thrive on and other employees who are less driven find destructive.

The employee who has problems coping with the schedules, workload, or time demands that are part of the work or the organization exhibits many of the same stress-induced behaviors as the employee who hates a co-worker. Only in these cases, the anger is most often directed at the organization as a whole, "I hate this place," "These people [collectively] don't understand the kind of problems I'm having," or "This company would be better off if they..."

In Chapter 10, we will discuss management awareness and the need and ability to interpret these kinds of emotional warning signs.

Alcohol or Drug Abuse

The presence of alcohol and drugs in the workplace is currently in a state of flux. We can all agree that the use of illicit substances by employees has received much publicity.

Coupled with the growing use of urine tests (and now, hair testing), this subject is now common enough to warrant policies and procedures, enforcement sanctions, more forgiving legislation (like the Americans with Disabilities Act), and rehabilitation opportunities through employee assistance programs.

Yet, for all these possibilities for job-saving treatment, matched with the threat of termination and even law enforcement intervention, few human resources managers would suggest that we have a drug-free workplace.

A December 1996 report authored by the National Institute on Alcohol Abuse & Alcoholism (a division of the National Institute of Health), states that up to 9% of the total adult population is alcoholic by definition (medically and clinically addicted to alcoholic beverages).

Workplace drug use, while harder to pinpoint with exact statistics, certainly must parallel national drug use figures. In former drug czar William Bennett's book *The Index of Leading Cultural Indicators: Facts and Figures on the State of American Society* (Simon & Schuster; 1994), he says, "Approximately 25 percent of drug users consume 75 percent of the illegal drugs in the United States, and these hard-core users are the most resistant to anti-drug use strategies."[1]

Some experts suggest that people who abuse drugs and alcohol to extremes do so in response to various psychological problems. They have convinced themselves that they are smarter than their bosses or co-workers and they can use illegal substances without getting caught for it. This begs the question: Is it possible to be a "functioning" alcoholic or illegal drug user? Yes and no.

Many employees can tell stories about "ol' Bill" in Sales who comes to work with the proverbial rheumy eyes, beery breath, and warm glow to his

---

1. Bennett, William. *The Index of Leading Cultural Indicators: Facts and Figures on the State of American Society.* New York: Simon & Schuster; 1994, p. 39.

face, and yet who still manages to complete his work without complaint for years and years. Because alcohol use and alcoholism are both so socially prevalent, we tend to look away when we see employees who come to work impaired.

Conversely, however, we can recognize the drug-using employee early into his or her experiences because the physical side effects are much more severe. And since illegal drug use typically affects the body most at the ingestion points, i.e. needle marks in the arms and legs, nasal burns and internal damage, heavy coughs, these signs are visible even to the untrained eye.

The addicted heroin, cocaine, or methamphetamine user can't keep up the pace of these chemicals and do good work as well. So if it's possible for the maintenance alcoholic to continue to work and drink, it's less probable that the maintenance drug user will be able to function at work without drawing management attention.

The point to this is that statistical research, interviews with criminals, and even workplace killers tell us that drugs and alcohol often played an important part in their activities.

There's no denying these chemicals can provide the kind of courage, rationalizations, or motivations many people need to engage in violence. Like the other off-the-job problems, the use of drugs and alcohol often masks other issues in the employee's life. Disturbed, angry, or highly aggressive employees who impair themselves at or prior to arriving at work may offer potential warning signs for future violence.

Psychological Illnesses

Mental health professionals say that clinical depression affects at least 10 percent of the adult population at some point in their lives. From a statistical standpoint, this figure suggests that certain employees in our workplaces are suffering from depression in some form as well.

The insidiousness of depression is that it takes different forms in different people. Symptoms like spontaneous weeping or intense sadness found in some depressed employees will not manifest themselves in others.

There are no easy answers to psychological problems in people, save to say that like the abuse of alcohol or drugs, mental illness are not part-time afflictions. Employees may enter the workplace with bipolar disorders, manic depression, obsessive-compulsiveness, schizophrenia, or psychotic, violence-possible behavior.

As some of these problems exacerbate, the employee may feel out of

control, may lose hope, or become completely dysfunctional without immediate intervention from a mental health professional.

While it's not safe or fair to say that people suffering from mental illness
are all homicidal or even violent, these behaviors found in certain highly-
disturbed employees should serve as a forewarning for potential productivity, collaboration, or authority-figure problems.

Housing or Transportation Problems

An employer relates the following story: A newly-hired warehouse
employee had worked without problems for about a week. One morning,
he failed to show up and his boss did not receive a call from him to explain
the absence. Finally, about 10:00 a.m., the employee called his boss to say
that he had car problems. "I don't feel like taking the bus," said the employee. "Will your company pay for a cab from my house to work?"

The fact that the employee worked about 30 miles from the plant made
this cab trip far from economic (more than the employees' daily wage).
Still, the boss agreed and paid the hefty fare when the cab arrived with
the tardy employee.

After counseling the employee to get his transportation needs in order,
the boss went back to work. As you might guess, at day's end, the employee asked his boss to pay for the cab trip home. He became quite upset
when the boss refused, and suggesting that he was "entitled" to the fare
(a belief we discussed in Chapter 2). The boss agreed to pay his cab fare
home and gave the employee his pink slip for his stubborn ways.

This human resources conundrum illustrates the reality that some employees have a tremendous difficulty keeping body and soul together. In transient industries with low pay and high turnover (fastfood, assembly, retail
clerking), some marginal employees may be one missed paycheck away
from becoming homeless. Others may have continuing difficulties getting to
work, either because they have highly unreliable transportation, refuse to
use public transportation, or aren't responsible enough to develop a practical system for getting to and from the workplace.

While some of these employees may simply be going through hard times
and will rebound with some support and consideration from management,
others are caught in a continuing cycle of bad personal relationships, lousy
cars, and unstable housing. And it is this last group that may — as with
the cab-requesting employee above — blame co-workers or more likely,
their bosses for their plight.

The more manipulative employees may use guilt, pity, or even techniques of pseudo-extortion to connive their co-workers or supervisors into "helping" them get on their feet. And in cases where either or both of these two reluctant support groups fail to provide the proper amounts of assistance, the employee falls back on the disgruntled entitlement defense.

All these struggles to keep within sight of Maslow's hierarchy of needs can lead the troubled employee into what Thoreau reminded us are "lives of quiet desperation." When circumstances put the basic needs of shelter and reliable transportation into doubt, the employee may become desperate enough to try anything, i.e. steal from the company, from co-workers.

If their work performance falls or they are docked, suspended, or terminated for attendance problems or other work rule violations, their economic health is suddenly seriously jeopardized; the potential for violence against managers or co-workers rises to meet their frustrations.

In cases where current or suddenly-terminated employees feel they have no hope in their lives and they cannot keep even the barest of necessities together, they may be candidates for suicide or, in instances where they blame the organization for their life failings, workplace homicide.

Criminal Justice System Contact

There is an old motto in police work that says cops and crooks go together like refrigerators and magnets. The attraction between these two highly-interactive groups is unmistakable.

This is why the man with 20 kilos of cocaine in his car drives with a tail light out at night and quickly gets pulled over by a police officer and taken off to jail. Despite his best intentions, he attracted unwanted attention from law enforcement.

Some employees who are having a number of the above-mentioned personal problems, also seem to have frequent contact with law enforcement or the court system. They get traffic warrants for failing to pay their tickets, their cars get towed out from under them for 15 parking violations, they get arrested for public drunkenness at sporting events, or they must spend their mornings and afternoons in court, explaining to a judge or jury how they were in the wrong place at the wrong time with the wrong people.

The results of all this criminal justice interaction means that the employee may not show up for work, may be arrested by the police at work, or may look to the employer for help in these problems, i.e. bail money, legal advice, a pay advance, more time off, etc. The impact upon the workplace is obvious, as it is with the remaining co-workers and managers, who must compensate for the employee's absence or off-the-job problems that get dragged to work.

And as mentioned several times throughout the discussions of these problems, some highly distraught employees may reach the end of their ropes. When they lose hope, or they feel they have been humiliated beyond repair at work by their bosses, co-workers, or circumstances, they may lash out with the kind of violence that suggests they have absolutely no concern for the consequences of their actions.

Determining the Impact

If we agree that all employees must deal with some form of personal problems while at work, and some handle them better than others, the remaining factor lies in the word "impact." Before we can apply prevention solutions to these problems, we have to first understand that the measure for any intervention by a manager or supervisor starts with an answer to these two questions: "Do one or more of these off-the-job problems cross over into the workplace and affect that employee's work performance, productivity, ability to follow work rules, or ability to get along with supervisors and co-workers? Or do any of the employee's problems affect the performance, productivity, and physical or psychological safety of the supervisors or the co-workers?"

If the answers to either are "no," then the manager does not have the right, nor the duty to intervene in the employee's life. Many people have marital, financial, family, or other problems that don't succeed in affecting their work performance to a degree where management should be overly concerned.

Realistically, however, the sheer magnitude, complexity, and difficulty of one or more of these off-the-job issues can't help but worm its way from the personal life into the workplace life of the employee. As such, these problems demand management intervention, for the good of the troubled employee, management, and co-workers, who should not have to suffer by proxy or be victimized by the problems of the troubled employee.

Managers are quick to raise the issue, "I'm not a (FILL IN THE APPRO-PRIATE CHOICE: marriage, drug or alcohol counselor, financial, career, legal, or psychological) counselor! Why should I have to intervene in these problems, even if they affect my workplace? What am I supposed to do?"

The answer to the first question is succinct. Management has a legal obligation to intervene in employee behavioral problems that have the potential to create an unsafe, dangerous, threatening, hostile, or violent work environment. Courts now require the organization and its leaders to exhibit due diligence in cases where an employee calls attention to himself through highly inappropriate behavior. Courts and judges now hold the company to a higher standard, in terms of correct, legal, and immediate intervention into behavioral situations.

The answer to the second question is just as concise. If success in real estate is all about location, location, location, then dealing with employee problems is all about the ability to refer, refer, refer.

Once managers or supervisors recognize certain employees' behavioral problems that affect their performance and productivity or the safety of others, they have the same requirement not to attempt to administer a quick-fix solution, i.e. "I think you're right. You *should* get a divorce."

Their duty lies in finding the appropriate confidential referral source, either as part of an internal employee assistance program (EAP), or external social services support. The majority of the manager's initial problem-solving duties end when he or she gets the problem employee to a professional problem-solver or resource. As an example, the employee who disturbs his co-workers by speaking frequently of suicide and showing signs of despondency will certainly not have much energy for work. Upon recognizing the extent of this difficult problem, the manager should make an immediate and confidential referral to a qualified mental health professional and assure that the employee actually makes personal contact with the therapist.

At this point, the manager should document his or her activities and wait for the therapist to confirm that the employee is out of danger or requires more help. There is no need to handhold the employee through what can be intensely personal and private pains. As with similar off-the-job problems that cross over into the workplace, the manager's initial referral is the best first step.

REVIEW/SUMMARY

The once-solid wall between home problems and work has been blurred by circumstances. This chapter identified the early-warning signs of a potentially-disturbed employee. It offered a detailed list of the most common and debilitating off-the-job problems that some employees bring to work, as well as possible internal referral sources, outside resources, and intervention methods.

DISCUSSION QUESTIONS

1. Discuss why many managers and supervisors are reluctant to intervene in their employees' off-the-job problems.

2. What should be the primary criteria for management intervention?

3. What is the most powerful tool for managers and supervisors to use when faced with an off-the-job problem outside their areas of expertise?

4. Which outside agencies in your city or county might be able to assist an employee with an off-the-job problem related to drugs or alcohol abuse ?

5. What internal departments inside the organization should get involved in a case where a female employee is being stalked by her ex-husband? Which outside agencies should be called in?

4

Perpetrators of Workplace Violence: Categories and Classification

KEY POINTS TO THIS CHAPTER

- Workplace violence perpetrators
- OSHA Workplace Violence Categories
- Recent incidents of workplace violence

It should come as no surprise that the subject of occupational violence is hard to grasp. Getting a handle on the dynamics surrounding any serious and potentially violent human behavior problem requires an understanding of the actors. In other words, before we can understand the "whys" of occupational violence, we need to determine first the "whos;" that is, who are the perpetrators of these acts?

Perpetrators of Workplace Violence

As mentioned in Chapter 1, as of this writing, the National Institute for Occupational Safety and Health has conducted the most recent federal study on workplace violence.

This study reviewed the incidents of violence and homicides by looking at a variety of demographic, psychographic, and geographic factors. And in this latter factor, from 1980-1992, the South and the West led the nation in the highest numbers of homicides per 100,000 workers (4,819 and 2,278 deaths, respectively).

And because the state of California has had many high-profile workplace violence injury and homicide cases, legislators have attempted to tackle parts of the problem with new laws and employer policies. This state has led the nation by developing some of the most aggressive legal and law enforcement intervention methods.

Some of these have been added to the California Penal Code — outlawing "terrorist" threats, creating tougher restraining orders, and drafting the nation's first anti-stalking law. Other laws and policies were attached to the Labor and Civil Codes and much groundbreaking work has been done by the California Occupational Safety & Health Administration (CALOSHA).

From my perspective, one of the most helpful developments in understanding occupational violence came when CALOSHA categorized the perpetrators of violence. These participant dividers helped me get a better grip, by applying figurative and literal bookends, around this highly-complex subject.

As you review this list, consider both the people who use violence and their targets. This grouping list is not completely inclusive; there is some room for the addition of other types of participants. It includes not just violence-prone employees, but other perpetrators who chose the workplace as their targets.

CATEGORY 1 WORKPLACE VIOLENCE PERPETRATORS: PERSONS WITH NO LEGITIMATE RELATIONSHIP WITH THE ORGANIZATION OR ITS EMPLOYEES

These incidents involve suspects who have no verifiable connection to the workplace. This category typically involves outside participants who use violence, the threat of injury or death, or who actually kill during their interaction with employees.

This includes criminals who come into the workplace, i.e. an armed robber who kills a store clerk, or those who encounter employees in the streets as a part of their job duties, i.e. an armored car driver killed while transporting money to his truck. Other cases might include a school teacher beaten and raped by a non-student trespasser in her classroom, a late-working employee shot during a burglary attempt, or a disturbed suspect who shoots people at random in a restaurant.

This category is purposely broad enough to include such varied perpetrators as store, plant, or office robbers, commercial burglars caught in the act, rapists who assault female employees in or near their workplaces, trespassers who confront or are confronted by employees, i.e. a security guard who stops a man loitering in a company parking lot and is injured or killed during a struggle.

What makes this category unique is that there is no apparent link between the perpetrator and the workplace or the employees. In these instances, a person with criminal motives or who suffers from psychological illness may come on to company property and become assaultive.

The connection between the Category 1 attacker involves his predatory nature and his need for money, attention, or revenge. We must improve the facility's security policies; tighten access control procedures; improve the visibility of the employees to other co-workers, security officers, or the police; protect the employees from attack by using physical and psychological barriers; and work harder to keep the firm's assets—cash, property, equipment—out of the hands of criminals.

CATEGORY II WORKPLACE VIOLENCE PERPETRATORS:
CUSTOMERS, STUDENTS, PATIENTS, PASSENGERS, OR VENDORS
OF THE ORGANIZATION OR ITS EMPLOYEES.

These incidents involving customers, patients, or vendors of the organization, i.e. an irate customer who attacks a store manager, a patient who batters a doctor or a nurse because they deny him narcotics, or a delivery driver who fights with a warehouse employee. Other cases include those where a customer, patient, or vendor physically sexually harasses a female employee.

In these cases, the connection to the workplace is peripheral, but it is stronger than in the previous category.

Examples include the bank teller who is verbally threatened or intimidated by an irate customer who just had his account closed; the telephone customer service operator who is verbally harassed or assaulted by a disgruntled caller; or the high school teacher or college professor who is battered by a disturbed student, non-student, or parent of a student.

Ours is now a service-driven economy, so some highly disgruntled customers feel empowered to attack service employees for real or perceived problems in the relationship. It's not unusual for telephone representatives at power and gas companies, cable or local network television firms, or actual or quasi-governmental agencies to receive death threats, bomb threats, obscene calls, or other telephone terrorism activities.

In the educational example, the onset of campus violence has changed the dynamics of a once-staid environment. For years, most junior high, high school, community college, and university administrators, departmental managers, and teachers and professors have believed that the school campus served as a safe zone from the perils of street or workplace violence.

The reality today is that most school environments are plagued by the same kinds of crime and violence that affect our communities. The presence of metal detectors on high school campuses, the rise of driveby shootings targeting students or teachers, and the escalating number of confrontations between students and teachers, non-students and teachers, students and students, and parents and teachers leaves many who see the classroom as a barrier to all that is bad in the world to change their views.

Violence can strike a school district or college campus in many ways, including: workplace incidents involving threats or attacks from disgruntled school employees, disturbed students, non-students, trespassers, gang members, or others who seek to attack the people who work there or attend classes.

And domestic violence—long thought to be an "off-the-job" or "off-campus" problem—has made its way on to campus. Battered employees or students may require counseling, security protection, or other necessary interventions most administrators or managers may be reluctant to make.

In the healthcare setting, the potential for violence is complicated by the public, "open all night" nature of hospitals and medical clinics, the usual presence of narcotic or psychiatric drugs, and the highly unusual emotional state of patients, their families, or friends of patients (as we have seen when gang members or their rivals converge on a hospital emergency room in search of information about a gunshot victim).

Healthcare and hospital employees must deal also with psychologically disturbed patients, either prior to their admission in a lockdown psychiatric care facility or while housed there. And family members of patients may use violence to express their frustration about what they perceive is a lack of effort or concern for the health problems of their loved ones.

In December 1996, a man who once had assaulted a nurse at New York City Hospital who was treating his daughter for leukemia nine years ago returned to the same facility and injured five people. The man's daughter died of her disease in 1991 at the age of 12. He had been incarcerated in a mental hospital from 1985 to 1995 for the attempted murder of the nurse. He returned to the hospital and slashed his daughter's former physician and four other people. He attempted to cut his own throat and wrists at the scene before he was arrested for this latest attack.

The healthcare industry offers several government and industry-funded studies about the inherent dangerousness of this environment for physicians, nurses, and staff employees, especially in the emergency room. This includes the presence in the e.r. of domestic violence or stalking victims, sexual assault victims, or child abuse victims, who incur the continuing wrath of their attackers at the hospital. We have seen many disturbing cases where irate husbands or boyfriends have continued to assault or even kill their wives or partners inside the hospital.

Because most hospital security guards are unarmed (and often untrained in the dynamics of workplace and domestic violence), they may become victims of the perpetrators of this violence as well.

Another perpetrator category is nearly as broad as those involved in healthcare: passengers of public or private commercial transportation systems. Here, CALOSHA defines these actors as those who assault, injure, or kill employees of passenger airlines, trains, taxicabs, limousines and similar shuttle/jitney services, ocean liners, and bus services.

The precedence for these attacks on these specific locales is sadly in place. As we know from the recent NIOSH report, not surprisingly, that the most vulnerable occupations involve isolated customer-employee relationships and the exchange of cash. In the transportation industry, taxicab drivers run a higher than average risk of occupational violence, most specifically homicide.

On December 7, 1987, a terminated employee of a large California-based airline used his ID badge to go around the typical X-ray machines and metal detectors installed at an airport security checkpoint. He waved his badge at the security personnel and passed unchecked around them. Had they looked carefully, they would have noticed this man's employee badge had expired. Had they forced him to go through the metal detector and send his briefcase through the x-ray machine, they would have noticed he was carrying a large handgun.

Angry with his supervisors, this former employee boarded his flight and waited until the plane was 30,000-plus feet in the air before he made his move. Drawing his hidden gun, the man shot and killed several people on the plane, most importantly, the pilot, the co-pilot, and other members of the flight crew. The plane crashed and 43 people lost their lives in this modern-day, large-scale workplace violence disaster.[1] In December 1996, national newspaper stories featured airline flight attendants reporting a discouraging increase in the number of in-flight confrontations between argumentative passengers or between passengers and flight crews. According to American Airlines, there were almost 900 cases of verbal and physical abuse against its flight crews. This figure represents a threefold increase from 1994 to 1995.[2]

Most airlines offer new flight attendants some formal training on how to handle on-board behavioral problems. This includes dealing with disgruntled or drunken passengers, those with psychological problems, or those who refuse to follow FAA flight safety rules.

To combat the rising tide of passenger problems, the larger airlines are requiring even more flight attendant in-service training in anger management, conflict resolution, and behavioral control.

Federal, state, and local governmental organizations are often the targets of distraught people willing to confront and kill employees who are

1. Mantell, Michael and Albrecht, Steve. *Ticking Bombs: Defusing Violence In the Workplace.* Burr Ridge, Illinois: Irwin Professional Publishing, 1994, p. 170.

2. Staff written, "Public Eye." The San Diego Union-Tribune. December 12, 1996.

merely doing their jobs. In September 1996, a man walked into an office of the South Carolina Department of Social Services and shot three state employees to death. He was upset because one of his children had been placed in a foster home.

In another September 1996 case, a man entered a courthouse in Mobile, Alabama and shot and killed one security guard and wounded another. He was killed at the scene by police.

This incident parallels numerous other acts of violence at federal and state welfare offices, unemployment and job training offices, tax centers, and military installations.

Lastly, the relationship between the organization's vendors demands new attention. While many managers and supervisors don't pay much attention to the interaction of vendors into the organizations, it is possible they can cause significant damage.

In January 1996, a Portland, Oregon deliveryman, fired from his job, returned to an office building where he serviced accounts and took four hostages. He shot and wounded two employees before he surrendered to police. He told authorities that he was angry at some of the women in the building and blamed them for his termination.

These perpetrators may include salespeople who service company accounts on a daily, weekly, or monthly basis. They may have frequent customer contact as well as employee contact, and their on-site presence can create difficult safety and security issues should they become disgruntled.

Again, the precedence has been set for issues involving vendors using inappropriate, threatening, or violent behavior. In one notable case, a man who started stalking a female grocery store employee actually went out and got a job for the same potato chip firm that serviced the store, just so he could see her on a more regular basis and for ostensibly valid reasons. It was only after she made the connection between his threatening and unwanted contact outside the store and his new and frightening presence inside it that she notified management. Her bosses were able to intervene with a restraining order and a successful request that the man be fired from his employer.

In my seminars, I ask managers how they would respond to an in-house case of sexual battery, that is, an unwanted sexual touching, just short of rape. Their response is almost always within the usual guidelines for a proper, legal intervention. This includes: conducting an immediate and full investigation, interviews with the complainant, any witnesses, and the alleged perpetrator, counseling, discipline, including sanctions, arrest, or termination for the guilty party.

However, when I change the scenario, their answers get more disjointed. "How would you handle the same situation," I ask again, "if the perpetrator was the man who comes in once per week to fix your copy machines?"

Now the answers change to, "Gee, uh...isn't that the responsibility of the copier repair guy's boss? Are we supposed to enforce our sexual harassment prevention policies against people who don't actually work for our firm?"

The correct responses are no and yes. The victim-employee has the right to demand complete investigations, interventions, and legal sanctions or punishments applied from *both* organizations. Examples might include, if the case was severe enough, a police report for the crime of sexual battery, arrest and prosecution of the suspect, termination from his employer, and in case few or none of these approaches work, the victim-employee's company can help her initiate a civil suit against the suspect.

With Category 2 perpetrators, we must monitor the relationships between them and the organization and the connections between individual employees who may become targets for threats, intimidation, abuse, assault, or attack.

CATEGORY 3 WORKPLACE VIOLENCE PERPETRATORS: CURRENT OR FORMER EMPLOYEES; CURRENT OR FORMER SPOUSES OR PARTNERS OF EMPLOYEES.

This category is clearly the most visible, largely from media reports of specific incidents where highly disturbed current or former employees have entered or returned to the workplace to commit acts of violence. Most of the instances that draw the attention of the media involve horrific homicides, with multiple fatalities or injuries. These represent the worst of this subject—people who kill other people where they work.

As we will discuss in the next chapter, the impact of this kind of violence is varied and traumatizes many people related to the victims, perpetrators, eyewitnesses, and co-workers.

These cases often end in the murder of one or more employees or in murder-suicide cases where the suspect kills his spouse, other employees, or himself in the process.

Examples of this kind of unforgivable violence abound. Here is a collection of incidents that took place over 1995-1996:

- In December 1996, a recently-terminated mail handler returned to the U.S. Post Office facility where he had worked in Las Vegas, Nevada and shot and killed his former supervisor. His former supervisor had represented the USPS in a May 1996 arbitration hearing. The ex-employee learned he had lost his appeal three days before the shooting.

- Also near year's end in 1996, a former employee of a Vallejo, California McDonald's returned just days after he was told twice by telephone that he could not have his old job back. (He originally lost his job because he had to serve a sentence for armed robbery.) Entering the restaurant near closing time, he shot three former female co-workers, injuring two and killing one.

- In August 1996, an employee who had worked at the Plymouth Township, Michigan Ford Motor Company plant for 30 years walked into the security office and shot and killed a security supervisor and then himself. Three months later in November, a man seeking to kill his estranged girlfriend, entered a Ford Motor Company plant in Wixom, Michigan and started shooting. Armed with an AK-47 assault weapon, he shot and killed a Ford manager and wounded three others. The woman, who was not at the plant at the time, had rejected the killer's marriage proposal. He was arrested after being found hiding in a nearby drainage ditch.

- In February 1996, a city maintenance employee, who had been fired one year before, returned to his old workplace at a City of Ft. Lauderdale, Florida crew trailer and shot five of his former co-workers to death before killing himself.

- Also during February 1996, a Honolulu, Hawaii man who had been fired from his job two months previous returned with a shotgun to hold five former co-workers hostage. He shot and wounded his ex-supervisor before being killed by police.

- In December 1995, an enraged Boston man, angry at his wife's divorce lawyer, confronted him outside his law office and opened fire, killing him, wounding a nearby police officer, and then killing himself.

- In July 1995, a man who had worked for the U.S. Postal Service for 22 years shot and killed his supervisor after an argument at the City of Industry, California mail facility.

- Also in July 1995, a Los Angeles city electrical worker, angry over his poor performance evaluation, shot and killed four of his bosses with a handgun he had brought to work.

- New York City Police shot and killed a man who brought a shotgun, a handgun, and more than 200 rounds of ammunition to a Brooklyn Social Security Administration office. He was looking for his former girlfriend, who was an employee at the site.

- Distraught military personnel and civilian employees who work for the military have resorted to violence after conflicts at work.

In November 1996, a former Marine from the Vietnam era went into the San Mateo, California offices of his congressman and shot himself to death in front of a receptionist.

In March 1996, a Camp Pendleton, California marine sergeant shot and killed one of his commanding officers and wounded another after he said they had insulted him.

In March 1995, on the other side of the country in Arlington, Virginia, a civilian employee of the United States Navy shot and killed his supervisor and then himself. The victim was much younger than the perpetrator, who fired on his boss because he felt he did not respect his military background.

It is at this stage and within this category that most people match their own perceptions of occupational violence.

In fact, of these three above categories, which is the most common statistically? Based on our understanding of this subject from a mass media perspective, we would certainly guess Category 3 participants as the most prevalent. We would be wrong. Category 1 incidents are the most common.

The high public visibility and graphic nature of Category 3 workplace assaults and homicides committed by employees are not close to the actual number of crimes, assaults, and homicides committed by strangers.

To quote from the most recent NIOSH report again:

> "The circumstances of workplace homicides differ substantially from those portrayed by the media and from homicides in the general population. For the most part, workplace homicides are not the result of disgruntled workers who take out their frustrations on coworkers or supervisors, or of intimate partners and other relatives who kill loved ones in the course of a dispute; rather they are mostly robbery-related crimes."[3]

However, while these results and the accompanying statistics are what they are, it's important not to lose sight of the broad spectrum of workplace violence. The non-homicidal acts include threats, intimidation, targeted vandalism, harassment, inappropriate use of anger, actual violence, and serious injuries that involve employees, managers, or even customers of the company.

---

3. VIOLENCE IN THE WORKPLACE: RISK FACTORS AND PREVENTION STRATEGIES. U.S. Department of Health and Human Services, National Institute for Occupational Safety and Health, June 1996, p.10.

In other words, just because no one dies at work doesn't mean a company does not have serious behavioral problems related to occupational violence.

The misperception between speculations about the false prevalence of Category 3 cases versus the realities of Category 1 crimes is troubling for more than a few reasons. Due to the national media coverage concerning workplace violence and the way occupational homicides are portrayed at the United States Post Office or a government agency, or a fastfood restaurant, or an assembly plant, employees at other places may not see themselves or their place of work as even remotely vulnerable to this problem.

By studying where suspected violence perpetrator fits into each of the three CALOSHA-supplied categories we can help to answer two critical questions: Where is a company most vulnerable? And who will be most likely to victimize the business and the employees?

Managers and supervisors need to look to their own firms with an eye toward the highest likelihood of occurrence. Category 1-vulnerable companies include nearly every public or private firm engaged in business with outside customers, from offices and retail stores to taxicabs and gas stations.

Category 1 incidents point to the need for better security measures; more use of security guards; the use of security devices like closed-circuit TV cameras, locks, alarms; more crime prevention techniques; tighter access control policies; safer moneyhandling and transportation policies; more employees working in pairs or teams instead of alone; more interaction with law enforcement; and better manager and employee observation of people who don't have legitimate business with the firm.

Category 2-vulnerable firms include all the above and most specifically, retail firms (especially high-volume cash and carry business); banks and credit unions; schools, colleges, and universities; hospital and medical office facilities; transportation firms; and companies where there is a high incidence of interaction with vendors or other service alliance partners.

Category 2 incidents point to the need for most of the same protection devices, measures, and policies as with Category 1 problems, save for the inherent proximity issues. In this category, some of the people who do business with these firms are out to do it or the employees some kind of harm. Managers, supervisors, and security professionals need to understand the dynamics of positive versus negative customer interactions.

In this era of the consumers' misguided belief that "The Customer Is Always Right," some disturbed people feel they have the right to threaten, harass, embarrass, intimidate, assault, or attack company employees for not meeting their needs immediately.

One security manager for the California-based Wells Fargo National Bank has a good solution for outraged, overly-aggressive customers who threaten his bank tellers. As you can imagine, some people take great offense to a bank bouncing their checks or charging them fees for services. If he hears repeated reports from tellers or branch managers about a customers' unacceptable behavior, he calls them and informs them he has just closed their accounts. It's cheaper for the bank to lose one bad customer than to risk the assault or injury of one of its employees or customers.

Schools and educational administrators must recognize that the usual open design of their facilities breeds trespassing by people who may have more then just higher learning on their minds.

Hospitals administrators and hospital security directors recognize the need for sensitivity to the emotionality that surrounds their interaction with patients and their families. Access control is a critical issue, along with the protection of employees in vulnerable areas like the pharmacy and the emergency room.

Transportation industry operatives must continue to provide protection devices and procedures for employees who work with money and supposed customers whom they know absolutely nothing about.

And all managers, supervisors, and their employees must monitor constantly the interactions and relationships between the company and any outside vendors. They must report or act upon any inappropriate, sexually harassing, threatening, or violent behavior with representatives from both firms.

Lastly, Category 3-vulnerable firms include any company with more than one employee; those with a high percentage of female employees, some of whom may be involved in domestic violence relationships with their partners; firms with historically high turnover (hourly jobs in retail sales, convenience stores, low-tech assembly or manufacturing, telemarketing, or warehouse work); or those firms that may lack the necessary security measures to exclude former employees or disturbed spouses or partners from the premises.

These three categories help us put the subject of occupational violence into a contextual framework. While all this is not to say that occupational violence has overtaken every workplace, it is an organizational and behavioral reality worthy of more study and more aggressive management and law enforcement intervention methods.

Each of these three categories can encompass workplace stalkers and those obsessed with certain employees of an organization, office, factory, or store. But as with all things related to criminal or violent behavior, there are no absolutes.

REVIEW/SUMMARY

This chapter defined the victims and perpetrators of workplace violence; the types of companies, facilities, and locations where these events take place; and how one state (California) has classified workplace violence in three distinct formats. Each category was described and discussed, with examples.

Chapter Appendix

A Case Study: "Invisible" Stalking in the Workplace

Companies and their leaders have a duty of security and due diligence for those cases of workplace violence threats, domestic violence crossover, or other types of fear-inducing behavior that reach their collective or individual attention. But what about those they don't discover until it's too late?

In his bestselling book *Mindhunter: Inside the FBI's Elite Serial Crime Unit* (Scribiner; 1995), former FBI Special Agent John Douglas documents the case of Kris Welles, a woman who worked for Conlans Furniture Company in Missoula, Montana.

She had started at the firm as a sales manager and by 1985, she was the general manager. While she worked in the office area, a man named Wayne Nance worked in the furniture warehouse. He was quiet, nondescript, and one of the hardest workers among the warehouse crew. Ms. Welles had what could be best described as a passing acquaintance with Nance; she was polite and friendly to him, but their relationship was strictly employer-to-employee.

She also believed that Nance had some temper-control problems and could be moody one day and pleasant the next. While these behavioral issues did not appear to interfere with his work performance, she did worry about Nance's personality swings.

What she and her husband, Doug, a local gun dealer, did not know was that Wayne Nance was stalking her in his own way. He watched her daily at work and had a cardboard box full of pictures he had taken of her, memos and letters she had written at the office, and some of her personal property.

Further, Nance was also a murderer and a child molester. In 1974, he had sexually molested and stabbed a five-year-old girl, a crime that he apparently had gotten away with over the years. And later, authorities discovered he had bound, gagged, and shot several other women in other Montana counties surrounding his home. As Douglas writes:

> "Kris Welles didn't know any of this until the night Nance broke into her and Doug's home outside of town...Armed with a handgun, he shot Doug, tied him up in the basement, then forced Kris upstairs into the bedroom where he tied her to the bed so he could rape her. She obviously knew him well and he made no attempt to hide his identity. Meanwhile, in the base-

ment, Doug had managed to wriggle free from his bonds. Weak and on the verge of unconsciousness from pain and loss of blood, he staggered over to a table where a rifle loader from his store was set up. He managed to feed one round into the rifle, then mustering all his remaining strength, he pulled himself slowly and agonizingly up the basement stairs. As quietly as he could, he made his way up the stairs to the second floor, and in the hallway, his eyes blurring, he took aim for his one shot at Nance...He squeezed the trigger. He hit Nance, knocking him backward. But then Nance got up and started coming for him. The shot hadn't been deadly enough. Nance kept coming for him toward the staircase. There was nowhere to go and Doug couldn't leave Kris alone there, so he did the only thing he could. He charged forward at Nance, using his empty rifle as a club. He kept hammering at the powerful Nance until Kris could get herself free and help him."[4]

As workplace stalkers go, Wayne Nance was an anomaly. Clearly, he was obsessed by Kris Welles and wanted to have a sexual relationship with her (as if forcible rape constitutes such a thing). But his relationship with her was strictly work-related and based on their employer-employee connection.

Unlike with other stalkers, there was no failed sexual or employment relationship; she had not ended a dating relationship with Nance nor fired him for some work performance problem. And like other love-obsessed stalkers, Nance kept his distance from Ms. Welles, worshipping her from afar, so to speak, with his collection of her photos, letters and other "souvenirs," as Special Agent Douglas put it.

What makes this case both eerie and disturbing is that there was little if any warning of Nance's later violent behavior. His case speaks to none of the usual intervention methods and techniques used by workplace stalkers, i.e. cards and flowers, threatening notes and phone calls, following, or other face-to-face confrontational behavior.

By keeping his feelings to himself and not drawing attention to his obsession, he managed to attack the Welles family without warning. So without a working crystal ball to identify possible warning signs or other verifiable threats, what could have been done to prevent this painful event from happening in the first place?

---

4. Douglas, John and Olshaker, Mark. MINDHUNTER: INSIDE THE FBI'S ELITE SERIAL CRIMINAL UNIT. New York: Scribners, 1995, p. 329-334.

DISCUSSION QUESTIONS

1. Discuss this case with regard to its prevention possibilities, both from an organizational and law enforcement perspective.

2. In hindsight, what might have Kris Welles done about her concerns regarding Wayne Nance's mood swings?

5

Acts of Workplace Violence: Moving Across The Spectrum

KEY POINTS TO THIS CHAPTER

- Incidents of violence
- Escalating use of violence
- Employee suicides
- Domestic violence in the workplace
- Management's duty to protect

Now that we're more aware of the perpetrators of workplace violence and their targets, it's time to focus on their acts of actual or threatened violence. We can learn from not only types of workplace violence, but why the perpetrators made certain choices, and what is the apparent symbolism behind specific acts of violence. Preventing these acts starts with understanding why they occur.

And any prevention strategies must be grounded in the philosophy that work behavioral problems that border on violence or include actual workplace violence interfere with performance and productivity of the victim-employees, co-worker/witnesses, and the perpetrators.

As we will discuss in Chapter 12, the use of progressive discipline and safe termination strategies is based on the answer to the question: "What is the impact of this behavior upon the organization, its employees, its customers, and the perpetrating employee?"

Moreover, management has a well-defined duty of care to intervene in cases where other employees are put at risk by the potentially violent behavior. Courts and labor law hearing administrators now expect to see due diligence—effort on the part of company managers or supervisors who take immediate, legal, and intelligent steps to correct or remove problem behaviors, especially those related to workplace violence prevention.

Acts of Workplace Violence

It may help to see the use of violence in our workplaces as part of a horizontal spectrum, with the less severe acts on the left side and more intense or injurious events increasing toward the right. As you review the following list, consider that the seriousness of each act increases.

The key to minimizing or avoiding the potentially horrific damage from these incidents is for either employees, managers, supervisors, or even customers or law enforcement officers to discover and intervene in these incidents before or immediately they occur. And this intervention must happen at the lowest levels of the occupational violence spectrum, before the problems exacerbate. This requires employee-to-employee communication, manager-to-employee communication, and a sense of the emotional well-being of the organization and its people.

Further, remember that these acts can be caused by employees against other employees, employees against their bosses, or less rarely, employees against customers. Outside influences include non-customer criminals who commit crimes of violence or disgruntled customers who use violence against the organization, its employees as a whole, or against a specific employee.

Threats or Intimidation

This is the most common form of occupational violence, since it serves as the gateway to actual physical violence. A well-noted 1993 study conducted by Northwestern National Life Insurance found that while over 2 million U.S. workers were in some way physically attacked at work, over 6 *million* employees reported being threatened at work.

What makes this form of violence so perplexing is that it comes in many forms, and it mean many different things to different people. Further, what constitutes a threat is as different in the dictionary—"a menacing statement, an expressed intention to injure"—as it is in real life on the job. The employee who says to a co-worker, "You'd better do my work for me while I go out and have a cigarette, or else..." can create the same actual uncomfortable feelings of dread as the one who says, "Forge the boss's signature on my overtime slip or I'll punch your face."

Therein lies the value of threats to the disturbed employee who uses them to get his way at work. Because they can be vaguely worded, misconstrued, or viewed in different ways, the manipulative employee can use them to his advantage.

And threats take on several sub-forms as well: veiled and covert versus open and overt; publicly voiced in front of co-worker witnesses versus privately discussed with the recipient; anonymous and on paper versus anonymous and on a company voice mail message or a home answering machine.

The use of intimidation, which is similar to threat behavior, is often more aggressive and "hands on." In order to intimidate another co-worker, the highly-aggressive employee will use physical size, body proximity, or inappropriate touching, pushing, or force; hence the use of the phrase "in your face."

Some threat assessment experts believe that while intimidation creates fear and is used to dominate other employees, threats tend to be more serious because of the language used. That is, threatening phrases are much more concrete, and sound like, "I'm going to kill you!" as opposed to intimidating language, which tends to be formed with conditional language. Examples of this include, "If you don't..., then I'll..." or "When these people fire me, I'm gonna..." While the differences lie in the interpretation and both types should be taken seriously, there is a prevailing belief in threat assessment circles that threatening behavior is more grave.

There may be more than one employee-victim of this kind of behavior and it usually serves as the stepping stone to much more aggressive behavior. This especially true if the threats or intimidating behavior fails—in actuality or in the minds of the users—to get the appropriate response from the intended targets. In other words, co-workers who will not abide by their threats or who report them immediately to superiors, may find themselves physically attacked. This represents an obvious escalation to higher acts of violence as per the rising violence spectrum.

Regardless of the form, the intent of most threats and intimidation is to get other victim-employees to do or not do something. Management sensitivity to these acts is critical, both to respond correctly and legally, and to send the right message to the victim-employee(s), co-workers who know of the circumstances, and obviously, the perpetrators.

Highly Aggressive or Excessively Emotional Behavior

Each of us has the occasional bad day at work where nothing goes right and everything we touch breaks, disappears later, or fails to function as planned. And we all have the occasional disagreement with one or more co-workers that cause either side to blow up and rant and rave about it.

These are normal and unavoidable parts of human and working life, within reason.

Organizations are living and breathing entities, in the respect that they are staffed by people, operated by people, and function to serve the needs of internal people (employees) and external people (customers). For everyone involved in the operation of a firm, there are different personalities, educational levels, goals, plans, hopes, and dreams. People respond differently to both the needs of the organization and the demands placed upon them by the workload, peer pressure from co-workers, and supervision from management as to work outputs, performance, productivity, and behavior.

All this means we can expect personality conflicts, petty or heated arguments, employees avoiding each other, i.e. "the silent treatment." In extreme cases, we can observe how the work culture divides itself into sets of employee cliques who seek to serve their own personal and professional interests at the expense of others in the organization.

If we agree that most of these communication problems and employee behavioral issues appear normal and part of the quality of worklife, there is a darker side, where certain employees cannot control their frustration and who may lash out in anger and even violence when pressed.

A corporate lawyer from a large multinational defense firm reports that one nervous manager came to him with reports that one of his employees began exhibiting bizarre behavior. The attorney, who has become quite aware of employee behavior issues and related workplace violence threats, listened to the manager explain that the employee would get extremely upset during discussions with either him or his co-workers. Retreating to his office, the highly-upset employee would close his office door and proceed to heave books and other heavy objects against his walls, for periods of 15 to 45 minutes.

Clearly, this highly inappropriate behavior made the man's co-workers nervous and his manager uncomfortable. And yet, both the employees and the boss asked each other and themselves, "Is this behavior threatening? Dangerous? Is it is sign of some other personal and workplace problems?"

While there are no easy answers to human behavior difficulties, it's hard not to agree that the book-thrower's behavior is inappropriate, unproductive, and anxiety-producing for those who witness it. As mentioned at the start of the chapter, the key to management intervention in this specific case, lies in the impact upon the work performance of the problem employee and his co-workers.

At a minimum, the book-tosser's manager needs to speak to him privately to raise the behavior as inappropriate, distracting, and subject to discipline. The manager should suggest the employee get counseling through the company's Employee Assistance Program (as happened in reality with the case) with an emphasis on anger management, stress control, and violence avoidance.

Arson, Vandalism, or Sabotage Directed at Personal or Company Property

Several years ago, a former lab worker for IBM in San Jose, California set fire first to his former supervisor's office and then to his home. The man had been terminated from the lab and held an obvious grudge against his boss. The two fires came as a culmination of *two years* of threatening phone calls and letters made and sent by this ex-employee to his supervisor.

In a December 1996 case in El Cajon, California, a disgruntled customer returned to a watch repair shop to complain that he couldn't set the time on his plastic sports watch after the store owner had replaced the battery. He poured a can of gasoline on the store owner and on parts of his shop. He lit the store on fire as the owner fled. While the store owner was not burned or seriously injured, his shop was nearly destroyed.

What these two cases have in common is first, the rarity of using fire as a weapon for workplace revenge, and second, that certain disturbed people want to send a message, which is, "Not only do I hate you and your company, I hate your personal property as well."

As any victim of any fire will attest, insurance can pay for a new building and furniture, but it does nothing for cherished mementos, like photographs, diplomas, or personal records. Aggressive people who use fire as a tool for vengeance do so with this knowledge either intuitively or obviously. Used in the workplace, the damage from fire is more than just physical to the victim-employee and the company; it's psychologically painful as well.

What makes the IBM case and the watch repair shop case so different is that the latter happened without warning and the former, took place over a long period. Unfortunately and not uncommonly, the people involved with the arsonist and his crimes failed to heed his constant and hardly ambiguous warnings until it was too late to intervene.

Damaging or destroying personal property is unique and separate from the use of violence in some respects and understandable and related in others. Anecdotal studies of burglars — either by on-scene police officers or investigators or by interested criminologists — reveal the startling use of scatalogical crime scene vandalism.

Certain psychologically disturbed, rage-filled, or vengeful burglars will urinate or defecate in the victim's house. Samples of these activities appear under bed pillows and couch cushions, in refrigerators, on kitchen floors, or on countertops or tables. While a few of these cases result from weak-bladdered novice burglars fears of apprehension, most stem from the desire to send a highly-personal and specific "I hate you" message to the home-owners in particular and society in general.

In the workplace, we see a similar pattern or progression of vandalism or sabotage behavior as with threats; much of it is covert and secretive and some of it is overt and full of defiance to both work and society rules.

The employee who secretly damages, vandalizes, or sabotages company property inside the office, facility, or more commonly, in employee congre-gational areas like breakrooms, restrooms, or locker or changing rooms, does so to express anger and rage at one or more co-workers, or the organization as a whole, or both. A sporadic or regular pattern of "smash it every time they fix or replace it" can continue for days, weeks, months, or years, until man-agement is willing to take the necessary identification and apprehension steps.

But even more effective and powerful than security cameras or two-way mirrors is the development of better management-employee com-munication processes, designed to use peer pressure and the desire for a safe and nurturing workplace as the best identifying method. This might include holding general staff meetings that publicly raise the issue, "Who is dam-aging, stealing, or destroying our equipment and why? What are we not doing as managers or as a company, to not just protect everyone from this problem, but to prevent it?"

Not surprisingly, companies with serious labor problems face more inci-dents of the destruction of company and personal property. In the heated environment of angry, fearful union employees and an entrenched man-agement group, the rise of employee vandalism cases foreshadows other relationship problems inside the organization. Because the company "suits" hold the power of the paycheck over the workers, for some, vandalism and sabotage become the only viable means to strike back at the organi-zation in a meaningful way.

Further, these damaging tools of intimidation are used on some indi-vidual union employees to pressure them into joining labor stoppages, wildcat strikes, or other work slowdowns. Incidents may include the destruction of an employee's metal lunchpail with a sledgehammer ("You're hurting our meal tickets, we'll hurt yours), stealing and bending his or her hardhat, to return it later with the unspoken but clear message, "This time your hat, next time your head," or vandalizing the employee's personal car in the employee lot with spray paint, a knife to the tires, a key across the paint finish, or a brick through the windshield.

Even more terrifying is the time-honored workplace violence tactics aimed at non-union employees who are either attacked for their hesitancy to join a union, or worse, violence, vandalism, and sabotage directed at strike replacement workers ("scabs" in the historical vernacular).

At this writing, some strikes continue, including one years-long at the Frontier Hotel in Las Vegas, Nevada. Other episodic strikes hit certain firms or industries over and over again, like at the Big Three automakers, in the aerospace manufacturing industries, at the commercial airlines, and at large plants owned by John Deere and Caterpillar.

During these and other regional or national strikes, eggs, bricks or bullets get fired at company buses carrying replacement workers, managers' vehicles, and even at union or non-union vendors who provide materials or resources to the strike-bound firm.

Sabotage, as a weapon of workplace harassment or as a sign of potential violence, serves a similar purpose as threats and intimidation for the perpetrators. Usually, this type of destructive behavior is aimed at the organization and not an employee. For the "entitled employee," who believes he is underpaid, underappreciated, and overworked, sabotage is a way to get back at everyone from demanding bosses and customers to co-workers who "work too hard and make me look bad."

Unlike most threat behaviors, it's more covert and secretive. As an example, if a manufacturing firm has a policy to send employees home with pay if the assembly line cannot be repaired within three hours, it only takes a few seconds for one or more disgruntled workers to break a gear box, jam a tool into a complex piece of machinery, or otherwise halt operations.

One security manager from the Midwest reports that during one period of labor unrest, some factory employees discovered that by calling in a bomb threat or pulling a fire alarm within a few hours of the end of shift, security officers and managers would have to initiate a complete factory evacuation and building search. This left the evacuated employees plenty of time in the parking lot to drink coffee, socialize with each other, and avoid work.

The company faced a dilemma: Do we take the precaution of evacuating our plant every time these work-sabotaging threats come to our attention or do we keep the employees at their work stations, search the premises, and assume the risk of facing an actual bomb or fire? In this case, the company's risk management and security managers created escalating response plans based upon the nature, type, and severity of the threats.

Once the employees discovered that not every bomb threat call or fire alarm pull initiated a complete evacuation (and once the labor disputes were settled), the number of bomb threats and fire alarms went from several per week to one or two per year. But in that interim, the company and its security people faced many difficult decisions, thereby proving the theory that even one or two disgruntled employees can cause tremendous losses of time, work productivity, or performance for an entire facility. This last realization is the saboteurs' stock in trade.

As with the destruction of company property, damage or destruction of an employee's personal property demands a swift and intense management response. The victim-employees may want satisfaction, and not just financial renumeration, but psychological satisfaction as well. In other words, they want to see the guilty party caught and punished, either with discipline or termination. But because the context of the destruction may be based upon threats of violence, they may be reluctant to come forward to management and voice their complaints.

In these cases, the perpetrator wins twice: once by damaging the victim's personal property and then again when the victim doesn't report the incident out of fear. And even if the victim-employee reports the problem, managers and supervisors must use discretion to see that the situation does not escalate into retaliatory violence.

As with other incidents of workplace violence, these "property crimes" may call for perpetrator sanctions, victim-employee transfers, or even the use or introduction of security guards or law enforcement officers into the facility.

Assaults, Batteries, or Attacks Involving Fists, Feet, or Non-firearm Weapons

As we will discuss in Chapter 12, which features a serious examination of the proper use of law enforcement inside an organization, there is a time to solve occupational violence incidents internally without outside help and a time to realize the scope of the problem demands police intervention.

As the violence spectrum escalates, the disturbed employee reaches a point where threatening talk is no longer the only alternative; violence is literally at hand.

Often at this point, the perpetrator lashes out, often impulsively, using his body or a nearby object to assault or batter the employee-victim. Cases like these may involve the perpetrator's use of an actual lethal weapon, i.e. knife, club, or a motor vehicle.

Obviously, these types of incidents differ from firearm assaults, not only in the seriousness of the injuries or potential for fatalities, but because there is often less premeditation.

In workplace attacks with firearms, the disturbed employee, non-employee trespasser (former spouse, stalker, etc.), or the robber, has made a conscious decision to arm himself prior to the confrontation with a boss, co-worker, or service employee. His arrival at the facility or site in an armed state demonstrates forethought and pre-planning—although this is not always stressed in court cases, where defense attorneys sometimes argue that the presence and use of a firearm in the workplace homicide was somehow a spontaneous act.

The male work culture is full of historical examples where fists are used to show machismo, dominance, power, and authority of others. Examples include the post-work barroom brawl, the fistfight in the parking lot, the pushing and shoving contest in the employee breakroom.

One employee of a Texas firm described to me what some people in his company call a "beat 'em up day," where one targeted employee was told to go to a loading dock by his angry co-workers and face a "punchout." When the employee reluctantly arrived, he was set upon by several of his co-workers who battered him repeatedly. Some of the reasons why this employee both showed up to fight and didn't report the threats to management are tied to the male culture of defending one's honor, fighting "fairly," protecting oneself in the face of danger, or not "ratting on" fellow employees, even in the face of serious injury.

Management intervention into non-firearm assaults should start long before fists fly. Supervisors should watch for potential disagreements or confrontations between employees; trouble brewing between employee work groups (examples include the disturbing presence of documented gang members from opposing factions in the workplace); or the presence of bullying behavior by one or more notorious employees who have used similar activities in the past.

Before and certainly after any fight, management needs to separate the participants, protect the employee-victim, provide medical services, document the incident on paper, and involve the police.

Physical Sexual Harassment or Sexual Assaults

While these incidents appear similar, the overt seriousness of the offenses should call for more than just in-house sanctions against the perpetrators.

We can define physical sexual harassment as unwanted, inappropriate, and actual or attempted sexual touching, either on or under the victim's clothing, where the perpetrator uses hands or other body portions to make contact with the victim's body. This description differs from non-physical, verbal, or visual sexual harassment, where the perpetrator may use suggestive or graphic remarks, gestures, objects, photos, body positioning, or similar inappropriate behaviors designed to make the victim feel uncomfortable, vulnerable, or fearful.

From a management perspective, the differences between these two types of acts are significant. While non-physical sexual harassment demands a management response, physical sexual harassment may necessitate police involvement, depending upon the severity. In other words, the victim may tell her boss enough about the incident for he or she to conclude correctly that a crime just occurred.

Imagine for a moment your response to the news from an important woman in your life (mother, sister, daughter, wife, etc.) that she had her breasts or buttocks groped by a male co-worker. The intensity of this action moves it up the scale from verbal sexual harassment to an actual case of sexual battery.

Statements from female employee-victims often contain the language found in serious rape cases, "I felt violated," "He assaulted me," or "When he was done I felt as if I had been raped."

In these cases, immediacy of action is critical to the mental health and emotional well-being of the victim-employee. Now is not the time for company officials to debate the state Penal Code or the circumstances of the incident with regard to intent. Coercive, aggressive sexual assaults of any type, especially with injuries, no matter how slight, should be reported to the security department (if one exists) and to the police for action, investigation, possible arrest, and follow-up.

Domestic Violence Starting at Home or Continuing at Work

One battered womens' shelter worker in Atlanta said, "If you have 20 women in an office, two of them are being abused by their partners."

What makes domestic violence such a pervasive workplace problem is that it ruins productivity and work performance for the victims. They get no peace from their tormentors, even at work. The suspect (usually male) can control the victim (usually female) even if she is on the job and away from her home.

The evidence of this psychological and physical interference takes the form of notes left under her car windshield wiper ("Come back to me or else!"); harassing, threatening, or just plain annoying phone calls (asking "Is Darlene there?" ten times per day and then hanging up when she picks up the line); unplanned, unannounced visits; or waiting in the parking lot for her to go home.

What makes all this even more disturbing is that some domestic violence suspects are not content merely to bother their victims; many of them are acting out their frustrations in public. Today we are seeing more examples of violence at home becoming violence at work. These two problems — that used to be mutually exclusive — now go hand in hand.

There is an alarming rise in the number of incidents where some men have decided that it's perfectly within their scope of marital control to take their home problems out in public and physically confront their partner at her workplace.

A 1994 case near Omaha, Nebraska illustrates this disturbing trend. A distraught man — estranged from his common-law wife — waited outside the computer assembly plant where she worked and shot her and her new boyfriend to death, before (as often happens) turning the gun on himself. This was the second similar incident in six years at this factory. This trend is not the fault of the factory operators; it points to the way some disturbed people solve their marital discords today.

The Omaha case is far from the only one. In 1993, a rental car agency in Dallas was the scene of a shooting when a terminated employee returned with a gun and shot and wounded his ex-girlfriend and her boss.

This problem is happening regularly. Where once there were a few random instances, there are now more cases of men ending their partners' lives within the confines of their workplaces.

What do you think happens to a woman's productivity and performance at work if her partner either threatens to attack her at the workplace or comes in and does it?

What message does a workplace homicide or other significant domestic violence event with injuries send to other women in the organization who have their own hidden relationship-abuse problems?

And what message does it send to all the employees, especially if top management knows about these problems and yet failed to take appropriate action?

In the old days, these kinds of problems might have been handled with no police involvement whatsoever. Companies and their leaders often took the position that said, "We'll handle this in-house," which is another way of saying, "God forbid that our customers, vendors, stockholders, the media, or our competitors found out about this."

This point of view is changing, thanks both to increased media attention and the real possibility that companies can be sued for failing to intervene with all available resources. In other words, if they knew about the problem and failed to offer some solutions, they can be held liable.

Just as law enforcement and the criminal justice system have intervened in these kinds of problems, businesses have to intervene as well. It's no longer possible to ignore these situations that start at home and get brought to the workplace.

Today, the employer and even the police have no choice but to intervene in some of the off-the-job problems some people bring to work. Besides providing help to the employee-victims, preventing injuries or deaths, and avoiding civil liability, in this age of work and home coming together, it's the right thing to do.

Stalking Behavior

Stalking, as a workplace and domestic crime, has always shared a difficult past with other behavioral crimes like rape, where the victim and the suspect often share a painful bond that is unwitnessed by others. In the past, police departments were reluctant to make arrests for this crime — mostly because the laws supporting it were vague at best and non-existent at worst. Further, prosecutors either didn't understand the elements of stalking or did not want to try cases where they could not point to significant injuries with the victim or a well-documented pattern of behavior on the part of the suspect. In other words, someone had to die before stalking laws changed.

California led the nation in the development of a hard-edged stalking law, partly because of the more progressive nature of its law enforcement officers, prosecutors, and legislators (who recognize that anti-stalking is quite voter-friendly) and because so many people were dying at the hands of stalkers. Every state now has a stalking law on the books.

As a result, the old way of handling these cases changed from "Call us if he injures you" to "We can arrest him for a felony crime merely for making you feel afraid over a period of time." California Penal Code section 646.9 states in essence:

> "Any person who willfully, maliciously, and repeatedly follows
> or harasses another person and who makes a credible threat

with the intent to place that person in reasonable fear for his or her safety, or the safety of his or her immediate family."

Note the addition of language "follows or harasses" and the absence of language that says "must assault or cause injury," which used to call for much more overt, physical aggression on the part of the suspect, including the use of violence or a firearm, to fulfil the elements of the statute.

Further, the language of the law avoids putting limits or boundaries on the nature of the relationship between the stalker and the victim. The gender of the suspect or victim is not an issue, e.g. females can stalk males just as easily as the reverse, and the relationship between the parties need not be on-going, sexual, or exist at all.

Incidents of stalking in the workplace usually take on two forms, one more common and one more rare. The most prevalent form of stalking comes from the common obsessional stalker, or the "simple" obsessional stalker, less common is the "love" obsessional stalker as they are known in the psychiatric and psychological literature.[1]

The common stalker appears in up to 70 per cent of all stalking cases and is also most noted for violent behavior. As such, this type of stalker is responsible for the majority of stalking-related homicides. In the cases where this stalker makes himself known (the suspect is almost always a male), he knows his stalking victim as a former spouse, lover, co-worker, or boss. In these cases, there is some form of social, sexual, or work relationship that gives the victim and the stalker some kind of common ground, hence the name.

This stalker usually begins a campaign of harassment after the love or work relationship fails or following his perception of "mistreatment" at the hands of the victim, i.e. a breakup, some form of victim-created humiliation, a discipline event at work or termination from the job all together, etc.

In terms of behavior, this type of stalker uses many well-known techniques of physical, psychological, and emotional harassment. This campaign may begin relatively innocuously enough, but it soon escalates. The stalker will often begin with incessant phone calls at home or work, which may start out as relatively cordial, move to irritating, and shift to threatening over a span of days, weeks, or months. Other acts include: placing letters or notes on the victim's car; leaving gifts or packages at home or work; or following the victim away from the workplace.

---

1. Zona, M.A., Sharma, K.K., and Lane, J. *"A Comparative Study of Erotomanic and Obsessional Subjects In a Forensic Sample."* Journal of Forensic Sciences, JFSCA, Vol. 38, No. 4, July 1993, pp. 894-903.

Like the common or simple obsessional stalker, the love obsessional stalker is also usually male. What makes him so potentially dangerous is that this person is the product of many failed social and sexual relationships, often up to a decade or more. As such, he is more likely to misconstrue innocent or routine contact with women, or misinterpret their disdain or negative feedback as a signal to press harder.

What makes the romantic obsessional stalker different from the common stalker is his lack of a formal or pre-established relationship with the victim. Unlike his previously-described counterpart, he is in most cases a stranger to the victim. There has been no previous real love or work relationship and it's his belief that it's now time to start one.

While we'd like to think this kind of stalker only goes after women he sees on MTV, in soap operas, or on the movie screen, the reality is that there are far more romantic obsessional stalking cases involving normal women who don't happen to be famous. Examples might include a bank teller stalked by a customer she sees regularly at her branch, a waitress who works at a restaurant the stalker frequents, an employee or member of a health club where he works out, or even someone she speaks to regularly on the phone as part of her job.

The pattern for action and reaction the love obsessional stalker usually exhibits in two stages, one, where he professes his brand of "love" for the victim and two, where this image of love is finally shattered, either by the victim or by circumstances beyond his control.

In the first part, the stalker may believe that the victim shares his desire to pursue a relationship, but that she's "shy," or "playing hard to get" or "not ready to make a commitment without seeing me prove myself to her." It's from here that the obsession begins and then the stalking soon follows.

For the man who sees a female bank teller or waitress everyday and becomes increasingly obsessed with having her by his side, the smallest of her gestures or movements can be construed as a come-on or encouragement for more aggressive "courting" behaviors. If she simply smiles at him or her hand touches his briefly while passing a piece of paper across a counter, he may perceive that act as a subtle but unmistakable signal that she wants him too. Clearly, since this is not usually the woman's intentions, this is where the problems begin for her, her co-workers, and the company officials who must begin to manage this threat with the police.

Employee Suicides

As mentioned in Chapter 3, in January 1992, former General Dynamics (GD) employee Robert Mack shot and killed a labor relations supervisor and shot and wounded his direct supervisor following a termination hearing at the now-closed San Diego, California plant. While the vast majority of his co-workers were outraged, saddened, and dismayed at his horrific crimes, there existed a small following of equally disgruntled GD employees who, while not actually condoning his actions, certainly sympathized with his plight.

In any union plant employing longtime workers, it's usually no secret that a rift between management and the employees may exist. The grapevine can serve as a powerful, informal, if notoriously unreliable, to send messages company-wide about employees and their concerns.

In Mack's case, he suggested that he intended to commit suicide during his termination hearing, as a way to express his rage with his bosses. Since he wrongly believed that his attendance problems were too mild to warrant termination, he could not justify their response to his failing work performance. As he put it,

> "if it meant so much to them for that one minute I was late, or if it meant so much to the company and it put them so far in the red for the late days I came in, and the work I did put them so far in the red, then I was willing to give my blood back to them. I was willing to give myself back to them in blood, for their red ink."[2]

And yet while Mack did not kill himself at the General Dynamics plant, someone else did after he was convicted for his crimes. While at the California Men's Colony at San Luis Obsipo where he is housed, Mack received a news article describing a GD employee who had killed himself in the employee parking of the same facility where Mack had went on his shooting rampage. The investigation into this case revealed that the employee felt he faced the same threat of termination as Mack and decided to end his life. Clearly, the message from this case was, "If I did not chose to kill myself, perhaps I would have killed someone inside the plant."

This case and others involving employee suicides that take place in or near the workplace offer an eerie symbolic message to the survivors. One human resources manager in San Diego, California reported that an employ-

---

2. Mantell, Michael and Albrecht, Steve. *Ticking Bombs: Defusing Violence In the Workplace.* Burr Ridge, Illinois: Irwin Professional Publishing, 1994, p. 108.

ee had killed himself inside the offices of their facility. Worse yet, he completed the act so near a main doorway that the employees had to step over or around his body to enter the office.

And while this employee had exhibited increasingly serious emotional problems over the months preceding his suicide, even with some sense of his unease, every employee was shocked by his death. The painful symbolism of this event and others like it is not lost on the surviving employees. Their feelings range from, "How could he have done this here?," "Why did he choose to do this here?" and "What is it about this place that made him kill himself here?"

Company officials were sensitive to the employees' feelings, giving all of them time off to grieve or deal with the issue, and most importantly, bringing in a psychologist to offer trauma counseling to all who needed it.

Mental health experts say the primary motivation for suicide is depression, which manifests itself in feelings of sadness, despair, and a sense the victim feels discouraged about the state or progress of his or her life. Former NYPD Lieutenant Commander Vernon J. Geberth suggests in his encyclopedic book on homicide investigations (Practical Homicide Investigation, CRC Press, 1996), other more common motivations for suicide include: drugs, alcohol, stress, frustration, fear, anger, hostility, guilt, terminal illness, illness in the family, marital or family crisis, severe emotional trauma, psychological problems, physical deterioration, loss of a loved one, the death of a child, financial situations, teenage problems, loss of employment, despair, and a general inability to cope with life.[3]

Interestingly, many of these same problems appeared in Chapter 3 as possible motivations for workplace violence.

Crimes of Fear, Violence, Injury, or Death Taking Place Near the Workplace — Street Crimes at Work, Non-relationship Stalking, Use of Terrorist Threats

In these incidents, either employees are injured or killed as they work outside the workplace (driving a delivery route, making a sales call), or in proximity to the workplace (killed in the employee parking lot, robbed and injured while working in a warehouse alone, etc.) or others are injured or killed as a part of their interaction with the organization.

---

3. Geberth, Vernon J. *Practical Homicide Investigation: Tactics, Procedures, and Forensic Techniques.* 3rd edition. Boca Raton, Florida: CRC Press, 1996, p. 371.

These examples include the route driver who is shot during an aborted carjacking attempted in the vicinity or on the company grounds, a salesperson who is mugged in the employee parking garage by a criminal, a customer injured or killed during a robbery on the premises, or a vendor whose own on or off-the-job problems spill over into his or her customers' workplaces. In these latter cases, the vendor may be the victim of domestic violence or stalking, so much so that the perpetrator doesn't care where he makes his attack. The point to this category is that companies, managers, and supervisors must pay more attention to security measures that protect anyone who does business with the firm, not just the employees. This includes customers and vendors, who may be subject to assault, attack, injury or death at the hands of an outsider who doesn't not care they happen to be standing in or near a business with no connection to the attacker.

One of the more difficult phrases attached to the subject of occupational violence prevention is "foreseeablility factors." Here, civil courts are in effect asking firms, their leaders, and security managers to predict the future. In essence, the concept of forseeability says that we must be able to gauge the current level security with regard to the possibility of crime, violence, or employee, customer, vendor injuries or deaths. If gaps exist in the security coverage and the leaders of the company are aware or should have known of them within reason, courts have held the firm responsible.

Further, the similar concept of premise liability signifies the need for companies to provide safe working, shopping, or interaction conditions for customers, patrons, visitors, and employees. But even knowing about a physical security concerns, an unsafe area, a hazardous condition, or a personnel or customer security problem and caring for it does not automatically relieve the company or the landlord. Posting a "Danger! Do Not Enter!" sign across an open elevator shaft will not suffice if a delivery person carrying several heavy packages doesn't see it and falls.

This issue of premises liability is becoming more prevalent:

> "According to premises liability case statistics compiled by Jury Verdict Research, U.S. courts have handed down 342 guilty verdicts awarding $1 million or more since 1962. Several times that number of million-dollar settlements have also occurred. Of the premises liability cases going to trial in 1990, the plaintiffs won 55 percent of the time, up from 52 percent in 1989."[4]

---

4. Kahn, James R. "The Premise Behind Premises Liability." *Security Management,* February 1994, pp. 61-63.

Firms can be held liable even if they have security guards on site, if they knew of crime problems and failed in some way to prevent them, i.e. a security guard who failed to act legally, properly, or in a timely manner:

> "One controversial aspect of premises law is the liability of property owners and contracted guard services for harm done to persons by criminals on their property. For a business to be held liable for a crime on its property, the victim must show to the jury's satisfaction that the business knew of the likelihood of the crime from past experience and that it failed to take reasonable measures to prevent the crime."[5]

One example of this occurred in a San Diego, California case which went to court:

> "On October 25, 1992, the 20-year-old female plaintiff, a part-time student and sales clerk, left the nightclub at the Naval Training Center at approximately 1:30 a.m. and drove to the AM/PM Mini-Market at the corner of Lytton and Rosecrans in San Diego. The market was owned by the defendant X, which previously hired defendant Y security firm to provide armed security guards for crowd and traffic control on weekend nights. While plaintiff was in her vehicle parked on Rosecrans, she was inadvertently struck in the right ankle by a 12-gauge shotgun slug fired by an unknown assailant near the AM/PM premises. The shotgun blast, which followed an argument between the assailant and other persons near the premises, caused defendant Z, an armed security guard, to return fire and exchange several more rounds with the assailant."[6]

At issue in this case was whether or not the security guard had a duty to shoot at the assailant when he first saw his shotgun. The plaintiff contended that because he was working as an *armed* security officer, he had a higher standard of care for the plaintiff's safety (and for anyone else in the vicinity of the store) when confronted by the assailant. The court agreed and awarded the woman $105,000.

5. Ibid.
6. "Premises Liability: Gunshot Wound To Ankle." *Trial Trends*, Spencer Busby & Associates, San Diego, CA. January 1995, p. 23.

Security guards and their firms are now facing more of the premises liability risk; the training and legal requirements for both security guard companies and the firms who hire them, has never been more necessary.

Workplace Homicides or Serious Injury Events Involving Firearms

Of the approximately 1,100 workplace-related murders per year, the majority—over 75%—are committed by perpetrators using firearms. As noted previously, the category of occupational violence that is by far the most visible involves the disgruntled current or former employee who returns to kill, and yet these are the least prevalent in terms of numbers. But no matter who does the shooting or who is killed, where, and under what circumstances, the fact remains people are dying on the job as a result of a complex interaction with people who somehow see a bullet as a solution.

These acts of violence offer descriptions of our most extreme human response. Some disturbed employees, customers, or street criminals may certainly possess the *desire* to take a gun out and shoot someone, either as part of a "payback" for a perceived slight, as a twisted subsection of the male code of honor, or the need to feel all-powerful over someone else.

Yet, thinking and doing are separated by a millennium of norms, mores, and social controls built into our actions and interactions as human beings. The actual act of shooting another person with a gun is both a part of our heritage and an absolute violation of what we know is right and wrong.

So for a deranged employee to go to his home or to the trunk of his car and retrieve a handgun, rifle, or assault weapon, represents a quantum leap from thinking to doing. But what disturbs so many psychologists, psychiatrists, sociologists, criminologists, law enforcement officials, and others who work in the fields of security and threat assessment is that the barriers appear to be crumbling between violent thoughts and violent actions or reactions.

We can include many of the most discussed reasons, like the prevalence of cheap, accessible handguns; the need to defend one's "honor" against a "bad" boss, an unwilling co-worker or a resisting victim; or the use of a gun as the "ultimate equalizer" in any confrontive situation. But the simple fact remains that people who use a firearm in the workplace are either not impressed by the consequences of this act, are too disturbed to care or understand the ramifications, or have simply given up on their lives.

These inabilities continue to provide the clarion call for even more security devices and procedures, management and employee awareness training, detailed management prevention steps, and law enforcement intervention.

REVIEW/SUMMARY

Problem people will act out their frustrations in various covert and overt ways. This chapter identified these behaviors and discussed how to recognize and deal with them. These include phone threats and letters, sexual harassment, sexual violence, sabotage, suspicious "accidents," vandalism, arson, extortion, assaults, domestic violence, stalking, and—the last resort of a disturbed employee—homicide. By engaging in one of more of these deviant behaviors, the problem employee can create an environment of fear that runs through the entire organization.

DISCUSSION QUESTIONS

1. Using the model of the workplace violence "spectrum," what types of acts start at the least-serious point? The most-serious point?
2. How might a manager and supervisor handle an employee with a serious anger problem?
3. Discuss how management's responsibilities for sexual harassment prevention and investigation parallel those for workplace violence.
4. Explain the concept of forseeability. How can organizations demonstrate this in court?
5. Explain the concept of premise liability.

6

The Manager's Paradox: Fighting the Battle Unarmed

KEY POINTS TO THIS CHAPTER

- Management's fear of conflict and confrontation
- Communication problems between management and employees
- The need for management and employee training
- Educating senior management
- The management punishment paradox

Now that we know more about the problem of occupational violence —who commits certain acts—the question remains as to what we do about it. Can we really fix a problem related to the intricacies of emotional behavior, human interaction, and organizational bureaucracies?

The answer lies in the differences between the definitions of prevention and elimination. While the latter is not possible, the former is reasonable, given our acceptance that violence is not only a workplace issue, but a societal one. While we will never be able to go back to the idea of the workplace as some kind of separate enclave protected from the violence of the rest of the world, that does not mean we should give up trying to make it as physically and psychologically safe as possible.

Management Fears: Conflict and Confrontation

If we agree that occupational violence begins usually at the lower ends of the spectrum of acts—overly aggressive or irrational behavior, threats, intimidation, or assaults—then the prevention and elimination of these events can serve as one of the best ways to protect the employees from harm.

And the prevention of violence in the workplace is a two-step phase: awareness, at either or both the management and employee level, and then intervention, by the firm's executives, managers and supervisors, and others who can set or enforce rules and policies.

Knowing this, why does clearly inappropriate employee, customer, vendor, or outside criminal behavior still exist or take place in or around the workplace? Why, even with prior warning or knowledge of the existence of these activities, do so many managers, supervisors, or employees wait until these problems get worse before they act? Why do they allow these acts to escalate along the violence spectrum until they are practically impossible to solve or until injuries or death may result?

Without castigating every boss in the nation for his or her inability to act, it's important to understand human behavior, especially in the workplace. The vast majority of us don't like conflict with others. In general, managers and supervisors dislike confrontation with their subordinates, especially with problem employees. And few things are more difficult for a boss than to confront and attempt to correct marginal, borderline, or ambiguous workplace behavior.

In cases where the employee's behavior is clearly violent—he strikes a co-worker during a fight at work—it's easier for his boss to point to the employee policy and procedure handbook and say, "You've violated work conduct rules, so you're fired." The rules violation—"No Fighting"—is in print (or it should be) and serves as a court-defensible, labor board-justification for an employee termination.

What is supremely more difficult and less concrete, are those cases of questionable employee behavior where no fists are thrown as yet or no guns are brought from home to the office or plant. What can make these situations worse is that the employee, who may use these pre-attack behaviors prior to a full-blown workplace violence incident, can be intelligent enough to manipulate the manager, the organization, and the "system" to his advantage.

Like street criminals who can talk their way out of encounters with rookie police officers, the problem employee may have more knowledge of union rules, grievance procedures, discipline rules, and termination criteria then his boss. Facing a verbal confrontation ranging from "Yes, but what about..." or "If you do that to me, I'll call, file, report...", it's not surprising that some new or untrained managers will back down and "wait for a better time" to confront the employee's behavior.

The uncomfortable manager may face pressure on two sides—from peers who say, "Don't make waves," (which may be a response to their own discomfort with their subordinates) or from the problem employee's co-workers, who tacitly or vocally support the employee (either as true advocates or out of fear of his retribution or retaliation).

Even veteran or less-worried managers or supervisors, who may have engaged in countless discipline sessions or termination events, and feel relatively comfortable and confident dealing with "normal" employees, may not have similar confidence when forced to confront "abnormal" employees. Human resources policies and procedures in some less forward-thinking firms may be archaic; in some small businesses with only a few employees, they may be non-existent, or poorly-written boiler-plates taken from other firms or books. As such, these rules may not fit, apply, or work for situations involving problem employees who exhibit behaviors that just aren't mentioned or covered adequately or legally.

Firms without well-trained, well-read human resource or personnel managers for other supervisors to use as resources, or without much training or experience in handling difficult employees, whose behavioral problems may be outside organizational norms, may seek an uncomfortable status quo. In these cases, it's not uncommon for anxious managers or supervisors to say or think statements about a problem employee like, "Maybe if I wait or ignore this situation, he'll just retire, quit, move, or transfer to another department and become someone else's problem."

It's always easier to take the path of least resistance, even when the proposed solutions fail to solve the problem and in some instances, make it worse. Not only do these kinds of quasi-solutions avoid the problem and may allow it to exacerbate, they do a disservice to those managers who want to correct employee behavioral problems and are willing to confront them. Collectively, we may find fault with the manager who says, "This is not *my* problem. It's for Personnel, Security, or the police department to fix." But placed in similar situations, most of us would agree that we would much rather avoid correcting serious behavior problems when we discover them in our friends, families, or colleagues.

No manager or supervisor should or will admit to enjoying the process of discipline or terminating any employee, even those with the kinds of behavioral problems that deserve and demand both. In the best cases, the employee agrees not only with the need for discipline and termination, "You're right, I have been doing that and I do need to stop...", but also the sanctions and changes that must follow. In the worst cases, these behaviorally-based problem-solving encounters deteriorate into shouting matches, threats, or retaliatory acts of violence.

We all have various comfort zones, which serve as a level of physical or psychological pain we are willing to tolerate, endure, or seek out. And since each person's comfort zone differs from another's, there is no sense in trying to force individual conformity. In organizations, the existence of comfort zones show us what one manager will or will not do in certain circumstances. This ranges from what projects they will tackle or avoid, what relationships they will seek out or ignore, and how they will solve or dodge various problems, using either contact or avoidance, aggressive action or apathy, or direct intervention or hasty referral.

Not surprisingly, the threat of violence in the workplace jars most managers out of their comfort zones by forcing them to confront people and behaviors they would just as soon not. And as the media reports of occupational violence suggests, their fears are not so out of place.

Managers and supervisors *are* often the targets of the perpetrators of workplace violence; during acts of homicide, they are often slain not only for who they are, but for what they represent—power and authority over the disturbed employee. Since managers and supervisors are in positions of control and influence and because they can set policy, enforce rules, or make the workload easy or heavy for employees, their power is more than symbolic; it's actual.

Stories abound of homicidal ex-employees chasing horrified employees around the company, bent not on harming them, but on finding and killing the boss. It's difficult to discern whether these victims were simply and tragically in the wrong place at the wrong time or were actually singled out for attack. In some cases, managers have been shot and killed simply because they responded to a disturbance or even the sound of gunfire, thinking it was their duty to solve problems for the employees and the company. Others were killed by the same people they had disciplined or terminated days, weeks, months, or even years before.

And with regard to Category 1-type acts of violence and their criminal perpetrators, it is often the store or bank manager who is injured or killed because he or she is thought to have more control of the cash. Robbers know that as supervising employees, they have the keys to drop boxes and cash drawers or the combination to the store safes.

With Category 2-type violence, the manager, administrator, physician, teacher, or customer service supervisor is attacked or killed because he or she responds to requests for help from their subordinates, who may not have been able to deal with a highly-disturbed customer, patient, student, parent, or passenger.

And in Category 3-type acts of violence, the manager can become a target of the ex-husband who stalks his former wife. In these cases, the perpetrator may believe his estranged partner is having an affair with her boss, or he may blame the manager for helping the victim-employee change work locations, get a restraining order against him, call the police upon his arrival in the workplace, or otherwise impede his connection with what he believes to be his "property."

The Need for Communication

In circumstances where workplace violence has made its way into an organization and the perpetrator has escalated his behavior along the spectrum from potential violence (threats, intimidation, vandalism, etc.) to actual violence, the boss is often the last to know. Some managers and supervisors are quite shocked to discover the existence of threats or overly-aggressive behavior, vandalism and sabotage, stolen or damaged personal property, or even the presence of weapons in their facilities.

Often, when news accounts portray a serious workplace violence incident like a shooting or a homicide, the on-scene reporters manage to get quotes from shaken witnesses or co-workers similar to, "When we heard the first shots we thought immediately about Crazy Larry from the Shipping Department. He was always acting strangely at work and none of us are surprised that it was him that did all this."

Sadly, it is often the employees who know this information well in advance of a perpetrator's violent outburst. They may have to work with the perpetrator on a daily basis, be forced to interact with him on a regular basis (if he is a customer or vendor of the business), or otherwise cross his path and see him in a depressed, manic, or abnormal state.

As an example, one employee in a 1992 case who had shot and killed one co-worker, wounded another, and murdered his mother at her home, had come into the facility wearing his underwear on his head. To say this person was psychologically disturbed understates his behavior. Yet, his supervisors took the usual human resources route—suspending him for his work performance problems and failing to see them as the root for something more serious. His co-workers didn't have to be trained in psychotherapy to see that he needed immediate mental health help; they knew of him and about him based upon his other bizarre behaviors. For all this, why didn't his superiors intervene sooner or with more aggressive steps to see that he got counseling?

One of the most distressing issues related to intervention into occupational violence problems starts with the failing or failed relationship between not just the perpetrator and his supervisor, which is often a causal factor, but that of the supervisor's subordinates.

In organizations where the employees are either afraid to come forward to report problems to their bosses, or have been told either directly or indirectly what is or is not an acceptable way to communicate personal concerns, we see evidence that the manager is indeed one of the last to discover an employee violence problem.

Imagine the reaction when a manager says to his or her employees, "Look, I'm busy here with all this work. I expect all of you to act like adults and handle your differences accordingly. Don't come to me with petty problems that you should be able to solve yourself."

Or consider the mixed messages sent when a supervisor says, "I have an 'open door' policy. There's always time if you need to come to me with a problem," and then is seemingly too busy to discuss anything.

Managers who tell their employees, either through words or actions, that it's not acceptable to "tattle" on their co-workers, come to them with off-the-job problems, or otherwise let co-worker relationship problems distract them, will reap the behavioral ground they have sown.

Many managers and supervisors attest to what management writers Tom Peters and Ken Blanchard called "M.B.W.A." — or "Management By Walking Around." This calls for them to be visible, aware, and communicative, not just down the chain of command but actually face-to-face; not "to" or "at" people, but with them, in a more collective, "We're all in this together" spirit.

Instead, they practice "M.W.D.C." — or "Management With the Door Closed." In this habitat, the manager or firstline supervisor is usually the *last* to hear about potentially disturbing employee problems. And too often, by that time, it's too late to intervene successfully when an employee's behavioral problem becomes unmanageable. This is often when we hear the plaintive wail, "If I had only known about this problem sooner! I would have done something...."

The relationships between supervisors and employees needs to be more than figurative or symbolic. The company leaders must impress upon their subordinates that nothing should stop them from confidentially reporting a safety or security problem, no matter how slight it seems. To hear employees say, following a serious incident, that "We thought you didn't want to be bothered," or "We thought you already knew about this" is to point out the communication gap between the two sides.

One manager found out that one of his employees had a gun in his locker on the premises, only after another of his employees went to the security manager. When the situation was resolved — gun recovered, employee terminated — the manager was shocked to know that nearly all his people knew about the weapon, yet none wanted to tell him about it.

His first post-incident meeting with his staff started with the questions, "What is it about our relationship that we can improve? And what is it about the way I communicate with you or encourage you to talk to me that we can improve right away?"

The Missing Link:
Formal Workplace Violence Training

The discussion of occupational violence as a subject in most corporations is distracted by the "It Won't Happen Here" rationalization. Many managers and supervisors believe that since "those kinds of problems happen at other companies," they have nothing to worry about. In statistical terms, this may be correct; their respective industry may not have much to fear in terms of employee violence.

Worse yet, the subject of workplace violence in television, radio, and news media accounts gets clouded by an overabundance of discussions on what the typical workplace killer looks like. People in the media like to point to the existence of various psychological "profiles" of perpetrators of workplace homicide. Worse yet, these profiles are incorrectly and even illegally bandied about by managers in firms as yet untouched by violence as some type of pre-screening device. Both uses are flawed.

There is much value to profile information, as long as it is taken within the proper context as an awareness tool and not as a prediction device. Many workplace violence or occupational homicide profiles are valid, thought-provoking, and based upon the examination of many cases by qualified psychologists and threat assessment professionals. Most offer similar descriptions of the perpetrators because each expert has had only a finite number of cases to make the predictions.

The problem with these pen and paper descriptions of a "typical" workplace killer is that words printed on paper are not as real as a human being and there is no such things as a "typical" perpetrator. Each incident and each suspect is unique, even if he has used similar weapons, committed similar acts, or struck in a similar place as others before him.

While well-drawn profiles may raise many red flags in terms of warning signs, behavioral problems, and intervention opportunities, they are not the Rosetta Stone. The problem with profile characteristics is in either overreliance or in haphazard application.

They may not and should not be used to screen out job applicants, i.e. "Oh no, he's a white male, over 30 years old, and a Vietnam combat veteran, let's not hire him." (Chapter 10 offers a detailed profile and some suggestions for applying it to more extreme employee behavioral problems.)

The workplace violence profile requires careful consideration as a precursor to future violence (and in the best case, help from a trained facilitator). Similarly, there are other conventional or unconventional employee behavior problem-solving tools. The problem is that most managers and supervisors have had neither formal training nor much experience in these usages with disturbed employees. Most of these behavior management or correction techniques require help from a qualified, professional consultant.

Experts in workplace violence assessment and prevention typically work in the fields of clinical, forensic, and behavioral psychology, security management, personnel and human resources management, employee assistance, threat assessment, crisis management, and may include former or retired members of specific federal, state, or local law enforcement agencies and divisions who handle threat crimes, personnel protection, and home or work violence. And while most consultants work for themselves or in related consortiums, some are employed in larger corporations in departments that highlight their special skills.

The primary benefit to the use of outside consultants is that they bring an intensive expertise to the organization and its managers. When brought in to tackle specific employee behavioral problems, they can bring an immediate sense of relief to a worried firm. Just talking about workplace violence as a potential problem, even if no evidence of it exists as yet, helps to make most managers and supervisors feel empowered and more comfortable about the subject.

Another benefit to the use of specialized outside or internal consultants is mainly because they help provide evidence of due diligence to other employees, plaintiff attorneys, potential perpetrators, or outside observers. And if other managers in the company may be struggling with difficult employees in their departments or teams, who may be in various positions along the violence spectrum, they can offer immediate assistance.

Training for occupational violence prevention, awareness, and intervention should start in subject areas related to human resources. Examples include:

- **anger management training**

These courses are often taught by organizational or clinical psychologists, psychotherapists, qualified mental health professionals, or counselors with a social work or behavioral modification background. Even using short sessions of less than one day or a half day, these trainers can teach managers and supervisors how to: understand acceptable, appropriate anger in the workplace versus unacceptable, inappropriate anger; recognize the early signs of anger, including the physical movements leading to outbursts or violence; defuse anger directed at themselves, or more significantly, mediate anger problems between employees; resolve problems so that they neither escalate or continue; and document anger control problems so that in extreme cases, the employee can be subjected to discipline or termination and the supervisor will be able to justify his or her intervention response.

- **conflict resolution**

People who are experts in conflict resolution recognize that it is a form of negotiation. When two parties have been locked for a long time in a pattern of hostile action and counter-action, they are desperately in need of a new way of looking at things. Much of this type of training involves the use of negotiation techniques, directed not at closing business deals, but at solving employee communication problems. Conflicts in the organizations can erupt between managers, between managers and employees, and between employees.

Often an outside third party can apply the same skills required to mediate anger between these parties. This person doesn't have to be an outside consultant; an internal manager who has good facilitation skills can resolve conflicts that interfere with performance, productivity, morale, or communication.

One technique for conflict resolution is called *Added Value Negotiating* and it asks the third-party mediator to help both sides change the context of their situation, understand the perspective of the other person as best as possible, and add value to the proceedings in a safe manner.

In situations where the use of threats or the possibility of violence is imminent, the mediator will work quickly to get the emotional temperature down between the two people.

- **stress management**

Often, the best place to start with this training inside an organization is with the managers. Depending upon the nature of the firm, the industry, and the level of built-in anxieties related to the work culture, many managers and supervisors may be feeling and exhibiting signs of tremendous distress.

In companies where downsizing is either imminent or on a large scale, many of the managers who must wield the axe show the effects of stress disorders. And in firms where there is much covert or overt animosity between employees or employees and management, stress can hover over the operations like a fog bank.

Stress programs help managers and supervisors see the stress in themselves first, and then in others. The more they can understand what it is, when it manifests itself, how the physical and psychological symptoms appear, and how to respond to it, the better they can apply this knowledge to help manage and minimize the stress in their subordinates.

While it's not sound to make too many sweeping generalizations about violence, anecdotal studies and discussions with surviving co-workers attests to the direct and undeniable connection between a high-stress work environment and assaultive, aggressive, angry, inappropriate employee behaviors.

• the use of crisis teams

Some consultants specialize in a highly-unique form of corporate firefighting known as crisis management. They gather their knowledge and information from security and physical plant surveys, employee quality-of-life surveys, through their observations of polices and procedures in action, and culminate these with intense discussions with senior management about the company's vulnerabilities to events such as workplace violence.

No matter the size of the company, someone in top management must take the responsibility for action, leadership, and direction during any out-of-the-ordinary event like the threat or an actual case of occupational violence. This person doesn't have to be the CEO or company owner, but the decision and subsequent order to create this position must come from that level.

A crisis team should be made up of as many executives, department heads, or managers as necessary to make the nuts and bolts decisions about how problems will be solved, what resources will be called upon, and who will take what roles, i.e. the who, what, when, where, why, and how of workplace violence intervention, organizational support, and crisis management. This can include the initial development of internal and external resources, supporting information, phone lists, callback sheets, violence-specific policies and procedures, etc.[1]

No Knowledge of Resources

In some firms the managers and supervisors may lack both formal training in workplace violence awareness and intervention techniques, and not be aware of the resources available to help them understand and solve

---

1. Albrecht, Steve. *Crisis Management For Corporate Self-Defense: How to Protect Your Organization In a Crisis.* New York: AMACOM, 1996, p. 103-104.

employee behavioral issues. This serves as a double handicap: the boss may not know what to do and may not know who to turn to for help.

Under periods of great stress, we tend to revert back to how we have been trained. And during emergencies, this imprinting is even more intense, causing people to make decisions within a narrow window of choices, largely because that is all they know.

In Chapter 11, we will examine the wide assortment of resources available to concerned managers and supervisors, either within the organization or externally, to help solve employee behavioral problems and threats or acts of violence. This answers the question, "Who do we turn to and when?" by demonstrating that team problem-solving offers the safest, synergistic approach to these difficult circumstances.

Top Management Apathy: Until Something Happens

The subject of occupational violence rarely receives a warm reception in most organizations. It tends to give most executives, managers, and supervisors feelings of anxiety and a desire to rationalize the existence of employee behavioral problems as episodic or as those that plague other firms.

These beliefs may resonate at the top management or executive level largely because these people are often far removed from the day-to-day interactions with the rank and file employees. They may be out of touch with issues related to discipline or behavior inside the firm and must look to the line managers and supervisors for updates and information.

All this can create a sense that as long as things are running smoothly, there is little need to change the status quo. This is especially true when the recommended changes from management cost money.

The task of developing response plans to employee behavioral problems and more specifically, to the threat of violence in the workplace often falls on the Human Resources, Personnel, and Security Departments. Managers and their subordinates in these divisions are often the first points of contact for other departments who need answers to these types of problems, either when they notice them in their people or they are brought to their attention by concerned employees.

As such, these first-response managers tend to self-educate themselves about issues of violence in the workplace. In the best cases, they will create new and updated policies and procedures, alter pre-employment screening practices, and improve security practices. This may be done with only minimal or tacit support from senior management, who feel distanced or too uncomfortable to discuss violence issues in an open forum with the line managers.

In the worst cases, senior executives will actively resist management's efforts to initiate changes, purchase equipment, or retain outside help. An example illustrates this: managers for one firm with a high degree of employee turnover and behavioral problems began to examine their hiring practices to make some retention and selection improvements. One of their first discoveries was that they did a poor job of pre-employment screening for the applicants.

Working as a task force with the human resources, legal, and the personnel administrators, they developed a new program proposal for hiring, starting with the retention of an outside background investigations firm, a drug testing policy and relationship with a local lab, more application review and interview training for the managers, and an orientation program for new employees that paired them with experienced workers until they had learned their position more fully.

Clearly, these sweeping changes to the personnel practices of the firm cost money. And that became the sticking point with senior management; the cost of the total package, to them, outweighed the perceived "bottom-line" benefits of the proposal. Instead of accepting it outright or with a few cost-saving changes, they rejected the proposal as too expensive. They did suggest the use of a few ideas, but the minimal impact did little to assuage the task force members, or more significantly, did little to correct the turnover problems.

The number of marginal employees hired by the firm stayed high, as did their poor work performance, and their turnover rates. The senior executives managed to damage morale on a variety of fronts; by showing little faith in the task force members, by not supporting the pre-employment screening changes needed to stem the turnover tide, and allowing marginal employees to continue to plague the firm with work or behavioral problems. Later in the year, as expected, some senior executives complained about employee difficulties to the managers, as if to say, "What are you doing to fix these problems?"

Even under the threat of workplace violence, senior executives will ignore or sabotage the best laid plans of security managers when they make recommendations for improving the safety and security of the firm and the employees.

When a worried security professional comes to his or her boss—often a vice president of operations or human resources—with a proposal to install an employee badge keycode security system at all entry and exit points, what is a typical response?

"How much will all this cost? Thirty thousand dollars! Have you seen the budget figures for this year? Have you seen our department costs, including yours? How can you possibly justify this expense, especially since nothing has happened to warrant the need for this kind of security?"

In a perfect world, the vice president will be proved correct and nothing bad will happen to any employee as a result of lax access control procedures. In the real world, access control is the central theme for all effective security measures. Locks exist to allow or keep the right people inside the facility and to prevent or bar the wrong people from entering.

To continue this illustration, let's suppose a former employee returns with a gun and shoots and kills his boss, or the ex-husband of a female employee enters the facility and assaults her as she sits at her desk, or a transient walks into the building and threatens a secretary. In the case of the workplace homicide, it's quite possible that the surviving family will sue the organization for his wrongful death. Facing a huge lawsuit and little defense in terms of access control policies, will the vice president say later to the security manager, "Thanks for saving us $30,000"?

A sad phenomenon that exists in some workplaces faced with the threat of workplace violence, is known as "The Chicken Little Syndrome." In this description, as with the children's story, certain managers and employees develop the reputation that the "sky is always falling."

Faced with growing employee behavioral problems, evidence of threats, intimidation, vandalism, or sabotage, these managers or employees will call for help in private or public forums, like individual meetings with their bosses, or during staff meetings with their peers.

Unfortunately, those with the "Chicken Little" brand may get shouted down by their superiors or their peers as being overly-cautious, conspiratorial, and even paranoid. Faced with long periods of this kind of scorn and derision, even the sturdiest manager or employee will learn to keep quiet.

What changes this perspective, however, is when something does indeed happen—a manager is assaulted, an employee is stalked, a customer is killed in a robbery attempt. Then executive hindsight becomes crystalline and the questions begin: "Why didn't you install better security devices? Why didn't you check that employee's background more thoroughly? Why did you allow that person to come in here in the first place?"

Notice both the tone of these questions and the use of pronouns. Following a security breach or an actual violence outburst, some executives and department heads shift from, "What can we do now to help this situation or later to avoid it in the future?" to more accusatory statements aimed at specific managers, supervisors, or employees.

This follows a well-traveled line that seeks to blame the victim for the actions of the perpetrators. Examples include the woman in a domestic violence-stalking relationship who is chastised for "not just leaving," or a manager for being "too hard" on an employee who assaults him, or for a supervisor who fires an employee who later returns with a gun, as being "inflexible," as if this provides any justification for the attack.

This diatribe (and the one that follows below) may sound harsh and unfair, but it offers a realistic description of the state of response to employee behavioral problems in some organizations large enough to know better. Nor is this to say that this is the norm in every company; some executives from more forward-thinking organizations have crafted well-planned responses to the threat of occupational violence that serve as models for others to follow.

Yet, it's difficult to be more hopeful, when one manager said, following a workplace violence training program, "I don't worry about that stuff here. Besides, that's why we have insurance."

The Inverse Reward System

Some organizations function by using a highly-structured, visible, or bureaucratic chain of command. Senior executives fill certain leadership positions, followed by department heads or division/unit managers, then first-line supervisors who have the most contact with the employees, and then the employees themselves.

As often happens in firms using this design, gaps emerge between the personnel levels. Falling back on the adage "Rank Hath Its Privileges," each group tends to stay within its own level and keep its own counsel. Communication tends to be vertical, up and down the chain of command, rather than horizontal, or across the divisions of personnel.

In terms of duties, work tasks, and responsibilities, senior management tends to focus its activities on leadership, strategy development, and direction-setting for the organization. Department heads and line managers serve as the problem-solvers and delegators, working with employees, customers, and distributors. The first-line supervisors engage in similar customer relations activities and maintain closeness with the employees, who perform most of the workday tasks.

This slotted order makes for a well-defined organization, at least on paper. Where much of this starts to crumble is when a manager or supervisor comes to senior management with reports of a problem employee. As it often happens, the inverse reward system rises up to punish the wrong people for the wrong things.

When faced with the news that an employee is engaging in the types of behaviors that make everyone uncomfortable—threats, intimidation, bullying, coercive behavior, extortion, creating fear in others, vandalism, sabotage or theft of personal or company property, possession of dangerous weapons or illegal drugs at work, assaults, batteries, or assaults with weapons—the response to the inquiring manager or supervisor is skewed.

In some firms, executives or senior managers fail to support and even reward their people for bringing potentially serious safety or security problems to light. What the anxious, concerned manager or supervisor would like to hear is words to this effect: "Thanks for coming to me or us with this issue as soon as you learned of it. Let's start a complete investigation into the problem and then work together to solve it."

Instead, they hear, not "What's wrong with that employee?", but "Why can't you handle this problem yourself? You're a manager, so go manage the problem. You're a supervisor, so go supervise the employee who's causing us all so much grief. After all, that's what we're paying you for."

If a manager runs a 10-person department or work team, the message from some executives or department heads is, "Why can't you handle this one bad employee and his problems like you handle those other nine?"

The real response should be, "You're doing a great job with the other nine employees in your group. Thanks for bringing this one employee problem to our attention at this early stage so we can work together to manage it safely and effectively," (and before it ends in injury, death, or in a courtroom).

Employees, customers, vendors, or other people who come into the workplace and engage in inappropriate, threatening, or distressing behaviors make everyone uncomfortable. During these times, people in leadership positions in the company must fight the urge to criticize people at the lower levels for some perceived or even real failure. The time for incident review can come later, after the problem person has been counseled, disciplined, or removed safely from the facility.

This inverse reward problem—punishing well-meaning managers and supervisors for reminding senior managers or executives that problem employees exist, even in their company—helps not only to destroy morale, but to cause many other problems in the future. Heard often enough, this "Don't come to us unless it's good news" or "Fix your own employee problems" response causes frustrated managers, to think or say, "Why should I bother? Every time I report what I think are significant problems, I just get ignored, humiliated, or told not to be so paranoid."

This "shoot the messenger" response creates serious detriments to the resolution of behavioral problems. Not only does it interfere with the process of problem solving, it can put all the employees at risk of further or future harm. And this position puts the organization at significant civil risk as well.

Recall the discussion of due diligence requirements in this text, especially regarding the need for immediate notification of potential violence problems, immediate investigation of any incident, no matter how minor, and the need for immediate corrective action for both the behavior and the perpetrator.

REVIEW/SUMMARY

Many managers don't feel too empowered about this subject. Most fear confrontation and conflict and fail to take action when the situation calls for intervention.

Lacking the initiative, training, or knowledge of or access to resources, many managers struggle with the correct, legal, or ethical response. This chapter also discussed the failure of top management to help managers and supervisors cope with disturbed or fearful employees.

DISCUSSION QUESTIONS

1. What are some ways managers and supervisors can overcome their natural tendency to avoid confronting inappropriate or potentially violent employee behaviors?

2. How can management improve communication processes with the employees? What strategies or tools could they use to encourage reporting potentially violent situations?

3. Who should receive formal training in workplace violence awareness and prevention? Discuss the pros and cons of bringing in outside consultants to conduct the training.

4. How can middle managers and supervisors best educate senior management and the executives as to the need for more emphasis on workplace violence awareness? What would convince them to approve more training or a policy review?

5. How might a manager or supervisor best discuss an employee behavioral problem with his or her boss?

7

Training Interventions: Management Improvement

The last chapter pointedly discussed the need for management training in the on-going identification, immediate intervention, and future prevention of violence in the workplace in its many forms.

Here's a basic question asked by college students in business classes or employees aspiring to higher positions within their organizations: "How do you get to be a manager or supervisor?" The answers are deceptively short: be good at your job, have more job skills and/or education than others around you, and have enough time on the job to qualify for the position.

Since there are few colleges, trade or vocational schools, or universities that offer certificated programs in "How To Be a Good Supervisor 101" or "People Management 102," most managers and supervisors pick up their people-handling skills along the way. Where else does the average new manager get his or her indoctrination into the finer points of employee relations, interviewing, performance appraisal, counseling, discipline, and goal-setting? If their current firms did not teach them these skills, they learned them through their observations and experiences while employed previously.

With the prevalence of one-day seminars, three-day courses, or even week-long training programs, new managers or supervisors who want to improve their personnel can learn the basics and keep up to date in the latest laws, practices, and motivational techniques.

The problem is that many of these same people who need this kind of training either won't take it because they are "too busy" to attend or worse, can't get the time off from their firms (who won't pay the course fees either). Those that choose not to get formal management and supervisory training freely admit that they have enough years on the job, time in grade, or savvy to self-educate themselves as to what will work for them.

Note that one of the listed criteria usually required to make the transition from a staff, hourly, non-exempt employee job to a line, salaried, exempt position is years on the job. This is especially true with civil service positions, where the best person is not always promoted to management, only the one who has been there the longest.

This technique of last-hired, first-promoted can lead to a number of conflicts between the employees and the new or even veteran manager, who may lack the requisite management skills to keep a work group happy and productive, or fails to bring new thinking to the position.

We see many examples of this in civil service positions, where employees who have a long government tenure rise to supervisory ranks over less experienced but perhaps better qualified employees. In the best cases, these new managers learn on the job and develop their skills through continuing education courses. In the worst ones, they drain the energy and enthusiasm of their work groups with either overly-apathetic or overly-harsh leadership practices.

Laurence J. Peter's well-used "Peter Principle" suggests — only somewhat tongue-in-cheek — that people will be promoted to their highest levels of incompetence.

An example of this is often found in technical fields, where engineers with superior job skills are later promoted to supervisory positions to manage the work outputs of other engineers. What many of these new leaders find is that not only do they miss the day-to-day technical designing and problem-solving work of engineering, they dislike the typical manager's functions of paperwork, meetings, and supervision. Worse yet, either they or their superiors soon discover that although they may be excellent engineers, they're lousy managers. It's not uncommon in these scenarios for some technical people to give up their new positions — title changes and pay raises included — to go back to their old jobs, which don't involve direct supervision.

Shakespeare's statement that some are born to greatness, some achieve it, and some have it thrust upon them applies here; not everyone is destined to be a manager or supervisor. The reality of leadership in business today is that there are some employees who want to be bosses and don't get the opportunity, some who don't want the job and get it, and some who shouldn't have it and get it anyway. It is this last category that creates the kinds of communication, discipline, and morale problems that can lead to improper, retributive, or potentially violent employee behavior.

In today's unstable business climate, with mergers, downsizing, limited resources, the need for management training has never been more necessary.

Theory X Revisited:
Why Don't They Just Do Their Work?

Douglas McGregor's landmark book from 1960, *The Human Side of Enterprise*, is best known for introducing Theory X and Theory Y to our business vernacular. These principles are based upon McGregor's idea that an organization's management practices and its structures are shaped largely by how the top and middle levels of management perceive their employees.

Back in the 1900's, when the scientific management approach was popular, mangers broke down each employee's work into simple, standardized tasks. Most organizations were rigid and autocratic, and relied heavily on clear lines of authority and responsibility, discipline, and order.

In McGregor's opinion, managers who espoused what he called Theory X saw their employees as basically lazy, undedicated, self-centered, unable to delay self-gratification, motivated by money, and in need of constant supervision and control.

McGregor suggested that managers who followed a more human relations-oriented approach to supervision were proponents of what he called Theory Y. They tended to see their employees as inherently responsible, basically good, hard-working (if gently motivated), not just concerned with money, and able to work more or less autonomously.

He further believed that as the organization changed to a more Theory Y approach to management—less bureaucratic, flatter, more concerned with employee empowerment rather than rigid job duties—so changed the employees. In effect, as the organization evolved to a more humanistic leadership and supervision style, the employees evolved themselves as well, becoming even more responsible and receptive to challenges.

There is more than just a little conflict between the perception of employees in Theory X and Theory Y. So what prompts the average manager or supervisor to take up a position that is more toward one side over the other? Is there a significant factor that tells them inside their heads, "This is how I see my employees and therefore, this is how I will treat them"?

Regardless of what the business textbooks or magazine articles say about "enlightened" managers who recognize that people are people and we all need to be sensitive to each other's way of working and getting along, the one thing that influences most managers and supervisors in terms of both their perception of their people and their subsequent treatment of them comes from their own experiences. And even this can be broken into two distinct parts—first, how they were treated by their former supervisors when they were subordinates and second, what their work experience has taught them about what it means to be a boss.

There is much to be said about so-called "learned behavior," that is, what we observed or experienced at various stages in our development as children, teenagers, and young adults. From a negative standpoint, learned behavior is what teaches some children that since daddy hits mommy when he gets mad, that's how you deal with anger, or if all your friends steal from the grocery store, it must by okay. From a positive standpoint, learned behavior teaches most of us how to follow rules, get along with our family, teachers, bosses, and friends, and not break the rules of society.

And so it is with our work experiences; if new managers' first supervisors were hard-hearted taskmasters who treated them like wretches and made their working lives unpleasant, this may be one way they see the role of the supervisor. And conversely, if their first supervisors were friendly but firm, empowering and teaching, then their perception of what it's like to be "the boss" was probably greatly influenced by this exposure.

In the second part, dealing with their first introduction to the world of management, how their employees initially responded to them helped to shape their future leadership style. And if they work or worked in certain service or manufacturing industries where turnover is high, the labor pool may be undereducated, and somewhat lacking in maturity, they may have had problems with their motivation, attrition, and responses to their orders. This can cloud their perceptions of the employees and help turn their thinking more toward a Theory X supervision style.

And if they were fortunate enough to begin their management careers with motivated, dedicated employees who responded well to their instructions and helped meet work goals, then they probably viewed their employees using more of a Theory Y perspective.

Since many people are expected to develop their supervision and management styles somewhere and somehow along the way in their careers, their initial exposure to good and bad bosses and good and bad employees may give them their only sense of leadership perspective.

What brings this learned behavior perspective full-circle is that their employees have had similar experiences, both in their relations with bosses and co-workers. As they moved from job to job, they have been exposed to good and bad supervisors, and must have responded accordingly to the treatment they received from each.

Since we know that learned behavior experiences continue into adulthood, employees who are mistreated as they go from job to job tend to perceive their bosses as "bad" and not surprisingly, themselves as "bad" employees as well. Workers who are told for years by their supervisors that they are unmotivated, lazy, and barely worthy of consideration for promotions, training classes, and opportunities for advancement, will start to believe it.

And the reverse is true as well; employees who are nurtured, rewarded, and given many chances to grow, promote, and develop will see themselves as valuable to their bosses and valuable to the organization. Their perception of their bosses tends to be more positive as well. From a workplace violence perspective, it's harder to hate, injure, or kill a supervisor who helps you do your job with more effectiveness, kindness, and skill.

This cycle of employee perceptions of their organizations and their supervisors creates a behavioral loop. Good treatment by the boss often leads to higher work performance; bad treatment often kills employees' morale and their desire to work productively. More of the same on either side produces more of the same.

During those times when the company and its employees face the threat of violence or related problems, various parts of the organization will go into motion. The managers and supervisors will need the help and support of their employees at nearly every level. In response to an actual serious event, they'll want and need everyone to come together and do their various parts to help keep the company running.

Since we recognize that in times of crisis the need for teamwork and rapid responses is at a premium, it stands to reason that people who respect each other will work better as a team. This is not the time you want to see various employees say or do things that suggest an "everyone for themselves" approach.

If a production manager who is widely despised by the employees as being hard-hearted and unethical comes to his people and says, "We're going to get tough on rule-breakers around here," he may receive negative responses that parallel his treatment of them. The unpopular manager who tells his employees not to speak to the press following a well-publicized incident of workplace violence can only watch in horror as some of his people tell the TV cameras, "We knew this kind of thing was happening. We tried to tell our boss, but he wouldn't listen."

If the employees don't support the managers, the company policies, and the organizational stance on various issues, in times of crisis, they may choose their opportunity to "get back" at the firm in some political, public, or damaging way. Some executives are puzzled by this last statement:

"Why would they cut their own throats too? Don't they realize that things that hurt the company can hurt them too?"

Perhaps, but not enough to make them hold their tongues or curb their retaliatory actions. Like the child who gets tagged out in baseball and then throws the ball in the sewer so no one else can play, troubled employees, those who believe they are being mistreated, or those who feel like their boss and the organization has let them down may be the ones who push the teetering company right off the edge of the cliff.

For even more clarification as to why some employees seem to follow a Theory X path and others tend toward Theory Y behaviors, we need to consider the culture and climate of the organization.

In many cases where employees have victimized the company and certain employees by using violence, created crisis events through their actions or decisions, or put the other human, physical, and psychological assets at risk, the root causes lie in their perception of their treatment while on the job.

Adrian Gozzard, group personnel director of Cadbury Schweppes, sums it up best in his statement that people are the most important asset a firm can manage:

> "In the company you have one resource; it's people and the management of those people...it is motivation [of those people] that makes the difference between mediocrity and excellence. It is the glue that holds together the objectives and strategies of the organization..."[1]

The overall corporate climate at the time of any violence outbreak will either aid your efforts or hinder them. How the employees respond to a request for help right now may go way back to management's treatment of them up to that point. Some firms and their managers go out of their way to improve the climate in the organization; others simply blame the employees for their mistakes and help to create a culture of destruction.

Just as there are toxic and nourishing managers and employees, there are toxic and nourishing companies. From a workplace violence standpoint, it may help to use the true definition of toxic as "poisonous" in the context of the sick organization.

---

1. Sherman, Arthur W. and Bohlander, George W. *Managing Human Resources.* Cincinnati, OH: South-Western Publishing, 9th edition, 192, p. 459.

Toxic Versus Nourishing Workplaces: The Need for Positive Supervision

In Tom Peters and Bob Waterman's landmark book *In Search of Excellence* (Harper & Row, 1982), one of the strongest messages they devised from their study of 62 "best practices" firms related to the connection between the culture of the organization and its success. In their view, the strongest, most effective companies were the ones who managed, literally, with the health and welfare of the corporate culture in mind.

And while it's hard to give a pinpoint definition for culture — it can mean different things to people, depending upon their role in the organization — we can look at some of the intangibles that make a good culture thrive: job security, the sense of well-being, safety, ethical considerations, the company's treatment of its people, assets, customers, vendors, and the "we're in this together," greater good message it sends out to all observers.

Terrence E. Deal and Allan A. Kennedy published their book, *Corporate Cultures The Rites and Rituals of Corporate Life* (Addison-Wesley, 1982) the same year as Peters and Waterman, and not surprisingly, the ideas of each group of business authors parallels each other.

Looking at the literature of 80 large American companies over a 30-year span, they identified five important elements that make up a strong corporate culture:

• **Business environment**

What the company "does" —sells, creates, invents, markets, invests in, produces, etc., makes up the largest influence on the shape of the culture. The employees, customers, and outside observers know exactly what it is that Southwest Airlines "does"; it offers many flights at super-discounted prices. People know what Microsoft "does"; it creates software products to make our business and personal computing experiences more effective. It sounds simplistic, but when the employees can clearly tell their peers, friends, and others, "This is what we do..." it gives them a stronger sense of purpose.

• **Values**

These are the core concepts and primary beliefs that the company and its leaders exhibit to the employees. These values tell the employees what is important, and more importantly, whether *they* are important to the company. In organizations where the workforce does not feel very significant to the leaders, i.e. "This would be a great company if only we did-n't have all these damn employee problems…" there is little sense of loy-alty, continuity, or work ethic.

• **Heroes**

Good companies and their leaders encourage a bit of hero-worship. Energy rises when the CEO strides out on to a lighted stage, faces a packed house of his workers, and announces the firms' newest product, latest sales success, and which employees were personally responsible for them. People want to see that they do have the chance to be noticed and rewarded for their efforts. They want to see strong role models, from all areas of the company, who give them hope and more reasons to persevere.

• **Rites and Rituals**

Whether it comes in the form of remembering birthdays and anniver-saries over the intercom system, Friday "casual dress" days, a company-sponsored co-ed softball team, or annual "spring break" barbecues, there is power and value to helping employees celebrate not just their accom-plishments or milestones, but their existence as people in a work group. Assigning the best parking space to the "Employee of the Month" is not life-changing, but it does send a message to lots of employees who are plugging along in their own special way. It's not just the activity or reward that's important, it's the *presence* of those things.

• **Cultural network**[2]

Better known as the "grapevine," the way messages are sent around the organization can have a big impact on the cultural health. In some firms, communication between divisions is not encouraged, nor is "frat-ernization" between the labor ranks and management. Formal or infor-mal policies and procedures that create a "closed society" do little to fos-ter team spirit, harmony, or any sense that we're all in this thing together. Companies who try to stifle the existence of social groups or otherwise hinder the way people naturally communicate can expect to see a culture develop that is based upon fear and secrecy.

Deal and Kennedy discovered that the best firms and their leaders had focused their efforts on the on-going development of a healthy culture. And a strong culture is a self-fulfilling animal; the more people feel protected, nurtured, and empowered, i.e. happier about what it is they do, who they

---

2. Ibid., p. 63.

do it with, who they do it for, and why they do it at all, the harder they will work. And the harder they work, the more the company rewards them for their efforts.

To continue this last point, when was the last time you heard about a company paying a performance bonus to a bunch of miserable employees?

Of course, all this talk of the need for a healthy culture conveniently ignores the opposite side of the scale—the toxic culture. Here, the employer is at odds with the employees. There is little sense of community, spirit, or teamwork in the organization. Loyalty and the concepts of working together, for the greater good of all, are out the window. Management eats in one cafeteria, the frontline people eat in another.

People in adjoining departments treat each other like competitors, haggling over chores, backstabbing each other with spurious information, and otherwise sabotaging internal service relationships.

Jobs are designed to create as much stress in the employees as possible; policies and procedures are written and thoroughly enforced to punish the employees for their errors rather than reward them for their successes; and the employees are spoken *at* and treated as if they are the root cause of what's wrong in the company. Issues like employee participation, mentoring, empowerment, and feedback are thought to be too "soft" by top management.

It's safe to say that this archetype of the "toxic company" doesn't exist in its purest form, largely because no firm could operate entirely at that level and still survive. But thanks to inept, ignorant, and insensitive management types, some firms offer up a pretty fair imitation of the perfectly toxic organization.

With no evidence of sensitivity toward the employees' needs or concerns, no visible leadership skills exhibited by top management, and no sense that the quality of worklife in the organization is critically important to its success, these toxic companies can roll along in turmoil for years.

Worse yet, leaders from these same firms—who struggle in their markets, lose money consistently, and fail to satisfy their shareholders—are fast to find fault with every other thing. For them, the employees—who don't work hard enough in the first place—are largely to blame for the company's rousing lack of success. Other culprits include the government, the economy, the competition, the R&D Department who failed to find the flaws in the product, or the Customer Service Department who just chased away the firm's most important client.

The fault in the toxic company lies not so much with its people but with its culture. The healthy, nourishing culture develops equal quantities of healthy, nourishing employees. This is not to say that every day has to be like a stay at Disneyland, just that top management sends a message down through the layers of the organization that says, "We care as much about our people as we do about making money. If we don't take care of them, they won't take care of us."

Culture has much to do with a firm's handling or mishandling of events surrounding actual or threats of violence. Culture is a thermometer in the organization; management's ability to take the company's temperature from time to time (using attitude surveys, feedback questionnaires, and conversations with the employees) can help them make the right kind of decisions under the stress of those moments.

As Tom Peters et al. have shown us, healthy companies have healthy cultures and vice versa. This doesn't happen by accident; improving the quality of worklife that makes for a nourishing culture requires an obsessive commitment to the employees and their needs.

From the perspectives of this textbook, the need for fair, ethical, and humane employee treatment exists today for many important reasons. Besides the fact that it's the right thing to do, the use of proper people management helps minimize the damaging effects of those toxic work environments that breed a violent response in those employees with poor coping skills. Better yet, it offers an antidote to the need by many observers—violence perpetrators, victim-employees, witnessess, or outsiders—to blame management for somehow "driving" the violence-using employee to lash out.

It's true that circumstances exist in organizational relationships where management cruelty has lead to employee outbursts of violence. Interviews with workplace murderers often fall upon this theme that somehow, the boss "drove them to kill." It's easy for them and others to put this kind of spin on acts of workplace violence as a simple answer to a difficult and complex organizational problem. Beyond the reality that we all need to take responsibility for our actions no matter the consequences, this claim unfairly minimizes the damaging effects of these incidents on the surviving families or co-workers.

What's more arduous for these actors to admit is that while no workplace is perfect and not every manager is nurturing, there can be no valid excuse for workplace homicide save for outright self-defense. It's time to stop falling back on the "Devil made me do it" excuse as a justification or rationalization for any act of occupational violence. Bad bosses should be fired and short of that, in highly difficult circumstances, good employees can respond positively by changing positions or leaving the firm to avoid further abuse.

There is little to be gained by decrying the fact that some bosses are terrible people who deserve to be fired instead of leading others. We need to refocus our attention on teaching good, bad, or indifferent managers and supervisors to be better, more humane leaders and on how to recognize this need as a prevention solution for problems related to workplace violence.

Filling the Management Training Gaps

The subject of occupational violence is complicated, multi-faceted, and requires further understanding and training of management tools and practical human resources. No matter if the training comes from offsite programs, outside facilitators, consultants, seminar trainers, or other experts in these fields, organizations need to focus more resources on management development.

Specific areas for management improvement will help reduce violence among employees, especially at the frontline, hourly levels in typically high-turnover industries. These include training to improve the selection of employees; awareness of the signs of behavioral problems, especially along the earliest lines of the workplace violence spectrum; management intervention into personnel issues regarding fairness, legality, and the good of all employees and the organization; and a greater knowledge of resources, both inside and outside the organization to help concerned managers and supervisors either solve problems or refer employees who need help.

Finally, for either new or existing employees of the company, training for work performance improvement starts with education for them as well.

Pre-Employment Screening

The hiring process has never been more fraught with legal peril than today. Much of this is due to restrictive legislative rules designed to protect all applicants from discrimination. While the spirit of most federal and state labor laws is sound — to offer equal hiring and advancement opportunities — companies who hire employees must exercise concentrated diligence to keep from violating them.

Because of these limitations and the problems that result from poor hiring practices, there are a number of practical, cost-effective solutions offered by internal or external consultants who specialize in human resource solutions.

This training should focus on interview skills, current legal advice, the ability for managers and supervisors to be flexible, and think, ask, and interview employees in creative ways outside the normal human resources without breaking the law.

The discussion on pre-employment screening gets more specific in the next chapter, to include the need for better background checks, application and resume reviews, and questions related not just to whether or not the candidate can do the job, but also how the applicant handles teamwork, stress, anger, ambiguous situations, or those where others get credit for the work of one employee. These types of inquiries may seem distracting or outside the scope of employment, but they matter, especially regarding future behavioral problems. In reality, they have much to do with the quality of worklife for more than just the applicant.

Learning how to select the right employee for the right job is an art as much as a methodology. Current training approaches use group discussions of the best techniques, the legal ramifications, and small group role plays designed to help managers and supervisors put best-practice hiring guidelines into real practice.

Management Awareness

Employee, customer, vendor, criminal, or trespasser-based occupational violence nearly always starts with warning signs — multiple clues, multiple episodes, violent acts, inappropriate behavior, contact, repetition, access, safety, or security breaches, or failure to learn from a problem employee's repeated trips to the Human Resources or Security office.

The myth of the employee who simply "snaps" is just that, a myth. There are few cases where employees work productively and with no interaction problems with either their bosses or their co-workers, and then erupts into violence without offering any warning. Just as snakes coil, pose, and hiss before they strike, most disturbed, overly-emotional, or irrational people offer signs of their distress.

The key to successful intervention is first to realize the existence of the potentially violent employee, understand how the warning signs manifest themselves, and then recognize similar problems when they arise.

This kind of training does not require managers and supervisors to be psychologists or behavioral specialists, only to be able to recognize the signs and know how and when to intervene, discipline, refer, or terminate the problem employee.

Specific seminars or training programs, which are best taught by external consultants who specialize in these fields, can focus on the behavioral issue warning signs, security issues for non-security personnel, anger and stress management, conflict resolution, safe discipline and termination strategies, and other subjects that come under the occupational violence umbrella.

Intervention Skills

Seeing behavioral problems is one thing, reacting correctly to them is another. Successful, practical, safe, and legal intervention into potential workplace violence incidents requires prior training. In terms of the proper path, the difference between the right choice and the almost-right choice is, to quote Mark Twain, "the difference between a lighting bug and a lighting bolt."

Management intervention requires a sense of what the future will hold, both for a disciplined or terminated employee, his possible reactions or responses to these behavioral modifications, and the needs of the organization and its leaders to respond in new ways to problems that aren't in the usual human resource manuals.

Here's one example, devised by the security manager of a large utility company. When faced with a longtime employee whose at-work behavior began to change for the worse and whose performance began to fail, even after repeated counseling, warnings, and discipline, the Personnel Department decided that he would have to be terminated. Prior to this move, the employee exhibited various at-risk behaviors, saying things like, "I won't leave this place alive, and before I go, I'm taking some people with me," and "They can't do this to me, not after all I've done for them."

These remarks were correctly reported to the Security Manager, who conducted an investigation, reviewed what he learned with other managers from the related departments, and then took a bold step. Working outside the organization, he hired a man to play a role best called "The Intervener." This person was well-skilled in personnel, human resources, and career issues; threat management; behavior modification; and industrial security.

Immediately after the employee was terminated, the intervener offered his services to him as a walking, talking outplacement service. Over a span of a few weeks, working with the fired employee, he managed to prepare the man's resume, help him look for another job in a different, less-demanding field, and saw that he went to his psychological counseling appointments (paid for out of the utility's employee assistance program budget).

Within months, the terminated employee learned how to deal with his anger and hostility toward his former employer (and his bosses), prepare himself for a new career, and get another job. The intervener's work was done.

Critics would argue that this use of an outside resource was too costly and too subservient to the terminated employee. While this intervention process was both unique and far from inexpensive, it worked. Though it's not possible to put a price on success, this technique worked well at the time when cost was less important than the safety of the company and its people.

These kinds of highly unique intervention methods require explanation, discussion, meetings, and training, to understand them fully.

Internal and External Support Resources

The single most significant complaint voiced by managers and supervisors concerned with workplace violence is that they feel alone when dealing with the problems. Since they believe, however rightly, that a problem employee is their sole responsibility, they tend to turn inward to themselves for self-help, rather than turning to the organization for support.

In seminars, I tell these people that the sheer size of the organization is their ally, not their impediment. In other words, they should not have to lay awake at night worrying about the behavior of the employee alone; other executives or managers should be drafted into service. There is power and safety in numbers, both within the ranks of management colleagues, and support from other departments inside the company, either at the headquarters or divisional levels.

Formal training in these areas help managers and supervisors see why they can and need to change the dynamics of correcting behavioral problems with certain disturbed employees. The number of support resources inside even small companies (where we may find co-workers with intensive management, legal, or personnel experience) can help to dwarf a seemingly impossible problem.

Most managers and supervisors know, at least intuitively, who and where the problem solver people and departments dwell in the organization. What they require is a more formal understanding and thorough explanation of the people and places who can help.

Employee Education: The Employer As Teacher

In our search for reasons why a certain segment of the employee population seems to have checked its ethics or respect for property or human life at the door, one theme comes to the surface — a lack of education.

Even though the general educational level of the workforce has improved over the last several decades, it is by no means complete. We would like to think that all of applicants enter an organization already armed with the basic educational coping skills — reading, writing, simple math, etc. The sad fact is that many frontline employees (and sadly, a few managerial candidates) still cannot perform these tasks at the levels we would like to see.

The number of high school dropouts (those who either leave before getting a diploma, fail to earn one for a variety of reasons, or who never return to get some sort of diploma-equivalent) is higher now than it has ever been before. Social scientists can manipulate their own statistics as they please, looking for the reasons for increasing crime rates, drug and alcohol abuse, and other societal ills, but a lack of education has to plague many of the unemployed, under-employed, sporadically-employed, and menially-employed.

According to a 1990 study by the U.S. Department of Education, functionally illiterate workers — those unable to read past a fifth-grade level — make up 30 percent of the unskilled, 29 per cent of the semiskilled, and a surprising 11 percent of managerial, professional, or technical employees.

Former Xerox CEO David Kearns comes right to the point when he says that businesses will have to bear the load of this lack of basic skills:

> "The American workforce is in grave jeopardy. We are running out of qualified people. If current demographic and economic trends continue. American business will have to hire a million new workers a year who can't read, write, or count."[3]

Other figures are even more alarming. It's estimated that *2.5 million* functionally illiterate adults enter the workforce every year. This doesn't include the workers who don't meet the strict definition of illiteracy, but rather, who function at a marginal level, with notable deficiencies in the way they read, write, and communicate, either orally or on paper.

David Kearns often says in his speeches, including one to the American Society of Training and Development, whose members aim much of their efforts at employee training and HR improvement, that it is now up to the

---

3. Ibid., p. 50.

employer to provide the *employee* with the basic educational skills he or she should already have learned in school.

This suggestion causes most employers and managers to grimace. "Why should we have to teach our people how to add a column of figures without a calculator, or to read warning labels, or to write simple sentences? We aren't a schoolhouse, we're a business!"

And yet, as Kearns and others have suggested, business firms have the new responsibility to increase or improve upon the skills, knowledge, and abilities of some of its undereducated workers. It's not a question of philanthropy or being good-hearted, it's a question of survival, for both the workers who need this basic "survival" training and for the companies, who need and expect employee competence.

An outsider hearing of an industrial accident, judgement error, or other expensive business loss may ask, "How or why does a company hire someone with literacy problems? Why would they put their business at risk by using people who don't have the basic survival skills?" These are tough questions with even tougher answers.

In some cases, it's not for lack of effort by the personnel and HRD people tasked with bringing the best workers into the company. As many HR professionals are quick to lament—especially in certain Rust Belt or Snow Belt states—there are not as many well-qualified candidates to pick for certain jobs. The applicants who are best qualified for some jobs don't take them because of the low pay (as the retail, clerical, and fastfood industries can attest). Other companies, faced with new and large government or customer contracts and production quotas, need bodies and they need them yesterday. What they get in rapidly-deployed personnel, they trade off with limited or sometimes nonexistent skills.

As one personnel manager puts it, "If I waited for the 'perfect employee' to fill my lower-paying unskilled or semi-skilled positions, I'd never get anybody. Sometimes I have to pick the best of the worst and roll the dice with them. We try to give them the on-the-job skills-training they need to survive along the way." Thanks to a decline in the quality of the total labor pool, these training deficiencies can become a reality.

Companies like AT&T, Ford Motor Company, Aetna Life & Casualty, and Domino's Pizza have already bit the bullet with training classes for their frontline employees. Sometimes, the best benefit a firm can give its employees—and the one that will counter this prevailing sense of "entitled disgruntlement"—is knowledge and information. The more companies help them help themselves, the better they can protect their firms from the problems of troubled employees.

REVIEW/SUMMARY

Courts are now holding that companies who fail to intervene or allow dangerous or hostile working conditions to continue are in jeopardy of civil punishment. This chapter discussed the correct workplace violence intervention steps that start with training senior executives, managers, supervisors, and then all employees in the policies and procedures that surround this issue.

DISCUSSION QUESTIONS

1. Discuss the impact of management and employee workplace violence training as a way to reduce the organization's liability.
2. Explain the differences between Theory X and Theory Y. Are there times when a Theory X management style is appropriate?
3. Discuss the differences between a toxic versus nourishing workplace.
4. Does the organization have an obligation to provide basic educational skills to its employees?

Chapter Appendix:
Sample Learning Objectives For
Management Training Courses

Managers and supervisors who participate in workplace violence prevention seminars should be able to:

1. Identify, address, and correct initial workplace problems (intimidation, harassment, threats, vandalism, etc.) before they escalate into more violent acts.
2. Understand the makeup of potential problem employees—and avoid hiring them.
3. Recognize the early warning signs of disturbed or potentially dangerous employees and defuse their violent inclinations with positive intervention.
4. Know how to use existing local, state, and federal laws, along with the organization's own policies and procedures to enforce safe workplace standards.
5. Safely and legally discipline problem employees.
6. Safely and legally terminate problem employees.
7. Work more effectively with government regulatory agencies and law enforcement officials to better document workplace violence incidents.
8. Make informed decisions when evaluating your security needs and selecting security firms.
9. Provide emotional and psychological support to employees after any small or large-scale incident of workplace violence.
10. Create a workplace violence after-action plan to care for the employees, protect the organization, and get back to work in a safe, effective, and humane manner.
11. Protect the company from the threat of civil suits that may result from not recognizing early warning signs, problem employees, security risks, or other areas that courts have required firms to have a "duty of care."

8

Pre-Employment Screening Strategies: Hiring the Best

Key Points to this Chapter

- Benefits of pre-employment screening
- Application and resume review processes
- Interview techniques
- Background investigations

Since occupational violence is a problem caused by people against other people, one of the few sweeping generalizations you can make about the issue is that the single best prevention step is a careful choice of the employees brought into the firm.

A paradox exists, however, to make this widely underutilized response difficult. Although selecting the right employee is a critical key to preventing future workplace violence, too few organizations use effective pre-employment screening techniques to prevent the wrong people from being hired. It's as if the destination is in sight, yet the traveler keeps taking forks in the road that prevent a successful arrival.

Perhaps the reasons pre-employment screening serves such an effective deterrent to future behavioral problems are too simplistic for consideration. With regard to human interaction at work, the simple fact remains: it is always better to hire the most qualified candidate, who also can get along with others, and whose work history demonstrates stability and a noticeable lack of behavioral problems at past employers. Conversely, it is always more difficult to deal with behavioral problems once the applicant is already on the job.

Two problems emerge that may help to clarify why these differences exist. In many instances where the wrong employee gets hired, it's largely because the employer either overlooked past behavioral problems in an effort to give the employee "a chance" or because the employer was in too much of a hurry to fill an existing position and rushed the hiring process. Separately, either problem can lead to the wrong applicant choice; done

113

in conjunction, as often happens, can be especially wrong or even dangerous for the hiring firm.

In the first example, where the managers or supervisor overlooks past red flags from other employers, it's largely due to human nature. We want to give people the benefit of the doubt, even when mounting evidence tells us it's wrong. Instincts, which serve us so well outside an organization and in our personal lives, tends to get ignored as inappropriate in a business setting. True, it's hard to justify "gut feelings" on paper or during a labor board hearing for an employee discrimination case. But instincts should not be ignored or rationalized, only investigated further and backed up with real evidence of past deficiencies in the employee's character or work history.

The manager's attempt to give the applicant a chance to make a fresh start, to overlook large gaps in the employment history, to overlook jobs the applicant may have held for only a few weeks, or to suggest that information revealed during a legal and through background check is somehow flawed, puts the organization at significant civil and financial risk. And we must admit that in our current era of violence as an organizational problem, ignoring the mounting presence of negative data about the applicant puts the firm and its people at risk for safety or security problems as well.

In the second example, where the manager or supervisor is under significant pressure to hire someone, anyone in order to fill a position, there is even more opportunity to overlook even glaring work history problems.

This failure is less prevalent when the firm has to hire only a few people for positions; it's typically a problem faced by large manufacturing or assembly companies, retail stores with a seasonal rush, or firms faced suddenly with a new contract that requires immediate staffing.

More than one harried personnel or human resources manager (who, by definition and experience in the field, should know better) has said, "Look, I need to hire hundreds of people for this contract. I don't have time to dig into every little detail of their work history before they get to me. If they're upright and breathing, we take them."

While it's easy to sympathize or criticize this "Mirror Under the Nose" test from a distance, the fact that it exists as a hiring standard should tell us that businesses still have a lot to learn about hiring the right people.

Most business people know, from a hiring standpoint, they may not discriminate against people based upon a number of factors, including their sex, age, race, creed, birthplace, religious beliefs, disabilities (visible or not), marital status, criminal record, military service, clubs or memberships, sexual preference, or medical history.

But no matter what the law says, you and your co-workers will have to work with anyone you choose, so the people you pick must be compatible with your company at all levels, from the mission and direction, with the policies and procedures, with the work goals, and with the people who seek to fulfill them.

With workplace violence on the rise, the not-so-simple solution to the problem of weeding out potentially bad employees is this: Hire the good ones and turn the bad ones away. Stop the problem of violence in the workplace, at least at your own company, before it ever begins, by being very selective about who you choose.[1]

Cathcart's Law

My colleague, Jim Cathcart, is an internationally-known motivational speaker and longtime business owner. He has significant experience running his own firm and knows how to make the types of decisions necessary to ensure continuing success. He reflected upon workplace violence and the connection between problem employees and their subsequent problem behaviors. Cathcart suggests that managers and supervisors waste a lot of their personal and professional energies dealing with these employees and their morale-draining tactics.

Worse yet, Cathcart says that most managers and supervisors bring these kinds of people and their accompanying problems upon themselves and their organizations by hiring them. Thus, the creation of:

Cathcart's Law
"I REFUSE TO EMPLOY PEOPLE WHO WILL MAKE ME MISERABLE."
— JIM CATHCART

And it's not just frontline employees who can bring their emotional baggage into the organization. Some firms have hired toxic managers or supervisors who went on to abuse their employees. These people can be difficult for senior executives or managers to deal with because they hold positions of power. From a workplace violence perspective, we must keep the possibility of manager or supervisor-driven physical, sexual, or psychological abuse of employees in mind. It exists and it often goes unreported for the usual reason that apprehensive, scared employees don't inform others —due to fear of firing or further retaliation by the perpetrator.

---

1. Mantell, Michael and Albrecht, Steve. *Ticking Bombs: Defusing Violence In the Workplace.* Burr Ridge, Illinois: Irwin Professional Publishing, 1994, p. 46.

So while Cathcart's Law advises business people to bar the door from those applicants who will later go on to create many sleepless nights for those who work with or for them, it needs an additional corollary. To wit, the creation of:

Albrecht's Addition to Cathcart's Law
"Figure out who these people are and don't hire them in the first place!"
—STEVE ALBRECHT

In other words, ask the problem-filled applicant to take his or her application or resume to some other business doorstep. This begs the questions: Isn't this easier said than done? Yes, it usually is difficult to keep marginal, borderline or problem-filled applicants from becoming employees, if we choose to ignore the warning signs that are either visible or just below the surface. Consider these two scenarios:

If you were in charge of granting pilots' licenses and had a choice, would you let a marginal commercial pilot fly your family in a 757 jet airliner?

If you were a property manager and had a choice, would you rent an apartment to a perspective tenant who you knew already from past reports from other landlords was going to cause you grief via missed rent payments, vandalism to the unit, and loud parties at all hours?

It's tempting to qualify both of these "No" answers with a "Yes, but...", because the obviousness of the solutions make less concrete decisions tougher to make. But to review the scenarios, the first example points to the applicant's lack of the requisite skills necessary to perform the job safely and effectively. The second example suggests that the applicant has not been able to follow rules of behavior in the past and probably won't be able to starting in the near future.

Would you suggest that the marginal jet pilot would somehow be able to learn on the job? Or that the questionable apartment applicant would change his or her typically anti-social behavior simply by entering into a lease agreement with you?

In the first case, it's too dangerous to hope that the unskilled pilot could "catch up" to perform the job safely. In the second, we are asking someone who has demonstrated in past relationships that they are not completely trustworthy to change.

From the safety of the textbook pages and not the real world, is it wise to take a risk with either applicant? No, just as it is neither smart nor safe to take similar risks with job applicants who lack not only the ability to do the work required for the position, but also may not be able to get along with superiors, co-workers, or customers.

This last requirement gives many managers and supervisors trouble; what we are looking for during the pre-employment screening process is not just evidence that the applicant's work history is sound — formal education through schooling, on-the-job training, outside training, seminars, or coursework. What should be required is evidence that the applicant can get along with others in a group or team and has the personal and social skills to function effectively in an adult working environment.

This does not mean we must look to hire angels; none exist. We must, however, legally, effectively, and unemotionally screen out those people who have failed to demonstrate they are right for the job on more than just the work skills level. Since we have to hire people and not robots, we must be willing to accept their limitations, but only within reason.

Managers and their organizations will have to live with the choices made to turn certain applicants into employees. They have to be able make educated, informed, rational, and legal choices. Careful pre-employment screening processes, policies, procedures, and techniques will give them every opportunity to make the right decisions.

Employee Screening Techniques

Every discussion of pre-employment screening must come with the following caveat attached: Every organization who hires employees, no matter how many or how few, must get qualified hiring and labor law advice from either personnel, human resources, or legal experts. This includes in-house company experts who work in those departments, skilled outside consultants, retained attorneys, or outside employment agencies. To proceed without sound advice from any of these constituencies is to risk a future lawsuit, or worse, the damage or destruction caused by making the wrong employee choice.

That being said, companies who currently use haphazard, inconsistent, or borderline illegal hiring practices must seek compliance by changing and improving the process of taking an applicant through the many stages of pre-employment to employment.

It may help to view the hiring process using a standard decision-making flowchart model. The value to the flowchart as a tool for understanding the complexities of hiring is that many yes/no decision points are reached and answered along the way. At any moment, the applicants can fall out of the process by failing certain tests, not providing information, or otherwise revealing data that should correctly eliminate them from consideration.

And it should be carefully understood that the hiring process is indeed a *process*, a series of actions that bring about a result. And that result should be that the right candidates are brought into the firm and should exclude those whose lack of skills, poor attitude, spotty education levels, or past history of significant performance problems.

A standard flowchart uses boxes or rectangles to show tasks or activities, e.g. review application, review resume, conduct background check, etc.; ovals to show materials or information to start a process, e.g. resume reviewed, or to show the results, e.g. medical/drug screening appointment scheduled; and the diamond shape shows yes/no decision points, e.g. applicant passes background check, yes/no, or applicant passes drug screen, yes/no.

While reviewing the applicant review process, keep this in mind: The purpose of the pre-employment screening process is to screen people *out*, not screen them in. In other words, it should serve as a finely-meshed filter, not a gate.

Another important yardstick in hiring, especially with regard to screening to prevent workplace violence, is the "total person" concept. This says that we should see the information about or provided by any applicant as the puzzle pieces or mosaic tiles that fill in a previously incomplete space. Every piece of information that serves to complete the total "picture" that is the employee, helps the hiring decision. And conversely, every piece of missing information, that fails to fill in the picture, hurts the hiring decision for the applicant, but helps the choice for the hiring manager. Too much missing, incomplete, questionable, or even inaccurate information paints a picture of a possible unworthy applicant. This makes it easier for the manager to choose another, more complete, candidate.

The Paper Trail

In most organizations, the initial contact between the applicant and the firm starts after the company posts for the job, either in the classifieds, through an employment agency, by word of mouth, at a hiring hall, job fair, or through a variety of other means that get the need out to the labor pool in the community.

Application/Resume Review

Depending upon the position, the candidate applies for the job using an application form, a resume, or both. Thus, the hiring manager or an assigned Personnel Department manager makes his or her first impression of the applicant on paper. Following a careful examination of the application or resume, the hiring manager can move the applicant to the next step, an in-person interview, or a rejection.

The interview process is critical, no matter the job, the time deadlines or project urgency that requires someone to fill the position, or any other factor that suggests a shortcut. While it's perfectly acceptable to use the telephone to get more information from the applicant, in no way should it serve as a substitute for the in-person interview. The face-to-face process provides much needed information for the interviewer that cannot possibly come forward on paper.

The perspective employee's job application may provide a wealth of behavioral clues. Remember that the reviewer should look for more than just evidence that the applicant can do the job in question. In terms of identifying the potential for behavioral problems, job applications serve two purposes: they reveal information about the applicant based upon what is there *and* they reveal information based upon what is *not* there.

The most critical keys to a job application are consistency, length of employment, types of employment, and the presence of any unexplainable information. Keep in mind that the presence of one or more glaring inconsistencies is not grounds for immediate dismissal from consideration, nor are they absolute evidence of some psychological disturbance in the applicant. They should, however, give the reviewer either more grounds to dig deeper using a structured interview and a careful background check, or verifiable data that suggests the applicant should be dropped from consideration.

Consistency refers to this concept of totality again. The reviewer should ask himself or herself, "What is my first overall impression of this document? Is it complete? Seemingly accurate and plausible? Neatly completed? Full of seemingly complete information, dates, places, and contact names and telephone numbers?"

Other considerations include the legibility of the application. Is it full of spelling errors, mistakes, or crossouts? (The presence of more than a few of these may indicate the applicant is not serious enough about the job to provide a readable copy.) Are the printed responses written in overly large letters or exceedingly small letters, both to a degree that catch the attention of the reviewer as inappropriate? (Either expressions in print may indicate the possibilities of some emotional problems in the applicant, i.e. too large may indicate hostility or ego problems, too small may indicate secretiveness or self-esteem problems.)

Does the applicant answer seemingly normal questions with "None of your business!", "Why do you want to know?", or "I don't know!"? The presence of these responses may indicate the applicant's feelings of hostility, inadequacy, or paranoia.

Date gaps are another warning area for the reviewer. The applicant should be able to explain successfully date gaps of longer than one month. For example, the applicant should be able to explain a three-month gap between release from military service and successfully getting a civilian job. Date gaps are often normal and easily explained, but in some cases, they indicate such disturbing behavioral problems as a short county jail stint, a drug or alcohol rehabilitation stay, or other between-job or off-the-job problems documented in Chapter 2.

While neither a jail term or a rehab session offer solid legal grounds to dismiss an applicant outright, they do suggest behavioral difficulties that demand further explanations.

Date gaps are often accompanied by the presence of several "phantom" jobs—where the applicant states that his or her previous company closed, moved, or otherwise went out of business, and therefore, they cannot verify employment or provide references. The presence of more than one of these should create more questions for the reviewer.

Requests for personal references is often another source of inconsistent or evasive behavior. Sometimes the applicant will include people who don't exist, who never return phone calls, or who give exceedingly glowing reports of the applicant's many work skills. Many personnel managers realize the limited value to these names. One useful practice with references is to ask them for other names who also can vouch for the applicant.

The purpose of these reactions to inconsistencies or inappropriate responses on the application is not to make the manager a psychologist or other behavioral expert (unless that is his or her profession), only to raise certain red flags that should demand further examination or outright rejection.

In terms of applicant resumes, there is a distressing trend toward what might be charitably called "stretching the truth." More recent surveys of human resources managers suggest that nearly three-fourths of resumes have exaggerated claims on them, ranging from overly-expanded job duties or titles, to outright lies about educational degrees, job experiences, or technical skills.

The best safety valve (and legal defense tool) for the organization is the presence of a carefully-worded statement that says in effect, "Falsifying any information on this application is grounds for immediate rejection from consideration and/or dismissal from the position after hiring."

Pen and Paper Test Results

One of the reasons why the hiring process is so difficult and legally challenging is from the incorrect or improper use of so-called "pen and paper" tests. While most tests are often psychologically-oriented, others test specific job skills. The psychological tests are typically used to gauge integrity, honesty, the presence of deception, or valid signs of mental illness in the applicant.

One of the most popular and widely-used tests is the Minnesota Multiphasic Inventory (MMPI)™, which uses a variety of yes/no questions designed to look for the applicant's response patterns. While the MMPI is certainly well-proven as a valid testing instrument, it's not infallible. For legal use as a hiring tool, the applicant's answer patterns must be reviewed by a qualified psychologist, not the hiring manager. Critics of the MMPI and other similar response tools argue that the questions may discriminate against certain people, or that the final answers are subject to too much discretion between reviewers, in that two separate reviewers can come up with completely different and polarized recommendations.

While many firms swear by these types of tests as accurate predictors of future theft or violence-prone behaviors, they demand careful use. As with other sources of on-paper information about the applicant, these results should only serve as additional pieces of the total puzzle or completely-filled mosaic. The caveats for these are four: use a validated, reliably-proven instrument; have qualified examiners review the results; give it to every applicant for the job (not selectively); and don't use the results as the sole decision not to hire the applicant.

The Physical Interview

Once the hiring manager or supervisor completes the application/resume process, and conducts an initial sort of "possible" and "not possible" candidates, it's time to begin the interviewing process.

Some managers and supervisors are more comfortable during the application review process because the written data speaks for itself and requires no interaction with the applicant. The reasons for this discomfort concerning the intervention are many.

Comments abound like, "Let someone else do it. It's too much of a hassle," or "He or she looks okay to me." Much of this is shorthand for "I'm uncomfortable with this process and I feel I don't do it well." Applicants interviews can take many managers and supervisors out of their comfort zones, by forcing them to ask questions in a typically uncomfortable environment. Just as few people relish the thought of a job interview, most people who have not chosen human resources as their professional field feel similarly.

And as suggested previously, it's simple human nature for most of us to want to see the best in people, to give them the benefit of the doubt, and to overlook their foibles, as we ask others to overlook our shortcomings.

Putting too much weight toward one of the applicant's personal likes, dislikes, habits, or professional associations is called the halo effect. The circular (and flawed) reasoning here starts when the interviewer says internally, "Oh, he likes baseball too. Therefore, he must be a good guy down deep and worthy of this job in every way," or "She went to high school with Pete Jones in Marketing, therefore, he'll probably vouch for her as okay."

During the two-sided pressure that makes up the interview process, the halo effect can give the interviewer a convenient subconscious "out," to not to have ask more probing questions or conduct a more thorough investigation into serious red flags. Since most of us believe we are excellent judges of character, our gut feelings or the sameness of our personalities with the applicant can guide us in the wrong direction.

Worse yet, the halo effect can cause the interviewer to apply even more weight to a job candidate if they share not only the same interests or opinions, but the same gender or ethnic background. Labor law attorneys who handle discriminatory hiring cases attest to incidents where similar genders or races hire each other, but the examples they most often use is white males hiring other white males, over other equally or more qualified members of the so-called protected classes (women, minorities, older workers, homosexuals or lesbians, disabled people).

In an example of the opposite of the halo effect, it's illegal and unethical to discriminate purposely against any qualified applicant, regardless of what they look like and whether or not we agree or disagree with their opinions or the way they've chosen to live their lives. And yet, it happens.

Other factors that make the interview process just as difficult for the hirer as the hiree, also include the desire not to ask too many seemingly "impertinent" questions; the rigors of staying in compliance with the Americans with Disabilities Act (ADA); diversity issues and accompanying fears of engaging in stereotyping behaviors; equal employment violation worries; or asking the wrong questions with regard to the sex, age, race, creed, birthplace, religious beliefs, disabilities (visible or not), marital status, criminal record, military service, clubs or memberships, sexual preference, or medical history of the applicant.

There are many good books and training programs on the types of interviews used in business; typically these include the highly structured or patterned interview; the applicant-driven nondirective interviewer; the life-experiences or depth interview; the panel, board, or committee interview; or the stress interview.

Since this is a textbook for workplace violence prevention, we need to redefine the context of the interview to include certain behaviorally-based questions for the applicant.

Simply put, executives, managers, and supervisors who conduct hiring interviews for all positions, even at the executive level, must be willing today to ask questions that may seem out of the ordinary, and even abnormal. The purpose is not to embarrass the applicant nor the interviewer; it is seek out—safely and legally—the kinds of inappropriate responses that may lead to the kinds of employee behavioral problems that spark future violence.

These questions cover highly-specific areas not found in most hiring handbooks: anger management, conspiracy-seeking, and what can best be described as "blame response" questions.

As with other parts of this textbook, caveats apply toward the use of the following questions. Human behavior is a highly inexact science and the prediction factors for future violence are equally insufficient to prevent injuries or save lives. Yet, the use of questions that seem abnormal in the context of an interview may help the manager asking them to uncover the potential for behavioral problems if the applicant gets hired.

Let's look at an example of a question that may help reveal how a job applicant handles anger:

Interviewer: "Tell me about the last time you really got angry at your last job...What made you really mad and what did you do about it?"

Applicant (normal response): "A customer lied and told my boss that I made a huge error that was actually his fault. It was quite a mess and I was furious for a couple of days. My boss finally got to the bottom of it and figured out that not only had I done nothing wrong, but the customer actually did lie. I felt better afterward."

Applicant (abnormal response): "A customer lied and told my boss that I made a huge error that was actually his fault. It was quite a mess and I was furious for weeks afterward, even after it got straighted out. It took my boss forever to get to the bottom of it and I got jerked around a lot. Even after they figured out that I hadn't done anything wrong, it took a long time before I got it out of my system."

Here is an example of a question that may help reveal how a job applicant uses the "everyone is out to get me" conspiracy mode of operation while at work:

Interviewer: "What would you do if you couldn't solve a serious problem at work? Let's say you needed to finish an important project and no one you worked with would lift a finger to help you get the information you needed."

Applicant (normal response): "Well, if I couldn't get anyone around me to help, first I'd go to my boss, and if that didn't work, I might start making some phone calls around the company to see who could help me."

Applicant (abnormal response): "Actually, this happens to me a lot. Whenever I'm trying to do something important, I feel like people like to see me fail or they get a kick out of putting big blocks in my way."

Here's one example of a question that may help reveal how a job applicant views the world in terms of credit, blame, ambiguous situations, and the use of rewards:

Interviewer: "Most people don't like it when someone else gets the credit for their hard work. Let's say you thought up a great solution to a problem and one of your co-workers got not only the credit for it, but a bonus too. What do you do if this happened to you?"

Applicant (normal response): "I know I wouldn't be happy about it, that's for sure. I'd want to talk to my boss first to see if he or she understood my contribution. That's a tough spot. I've never been in a situation like that and if it happened more than once, I'd have to think hard if I wanted to stay at a company where they allowed this to occur over and over again."

Applicant (abnormal response): "I think some people get a kick out of seeing other people get shafted like that. I know I wouldn't take that problem sitting down. Somebody . . . actually a lot of people would know that I was upset that I didn't get what was coming to me."

In the protected environment of the textbook page, it's easy to see the differences. Sitting in the interview room, it may not be so apparent, mostly because the applicants may carefully couch their responses to tell the interviewers what they think they want to hear.

Readers of these scenarios may be surprised or even startled to learn that applicants reveal these statements during their interviews. In truth, many applicants disclose volumes of information about themselves during every phase of the hiring process. Any responses to these three types of questions that seem unusually hostile, evasive, or that appear to trigger the applicant's "hot buttons," should cause the interviewer to dig a bit deeper into the total picture that is the person seeking the job.

Faced with a series of normal, within-range responses to these kinds of questions or several abnormal, out of character answers, the interviewer must be willing to admit the applicant may have the kinds of anger management problems that may lead to future behavior problems or even acts of violence.

Background Checks

There is a general feeling of "wrong if you do, wrong if you don't" attached to the subject or use of background checks as a pre-employment screening tool. In truth, it offers a plethora of valuable information that can help the interviewer ask and answer this question: "Is evidence of past behavioral problems a good indication of future ones?"

At this stage of the text, you should know the answer is a solid yes. The majority of threat assessment professionals and mental health experts who deal with violence-prone people will attest that those who demonstrate an affinity for the use of violence in the past are more likely to use it in the future than those who don't ever consider it as an option.

Cases of domestic violence offer the most validity to this statement. Having handled over 1,000 cases as a police investigator, I know the statistical and anecdotal realities: perpetrators who have beaten their partners on one or more occasions are more prone to batter them or a future partner again.

In the case of a man who hits his wife once in their marriage, and either gets it reported to the police, gets arrested, is sent to counseling, or is prosecuted, he may never choose to do that again. But a similar perpetrator who already has more than one prior police contact for domestic violence is most likely to be a repeat batterer, with this partner or another later on. And added to this to make it worse, this perpetrator is also more likely to escalate the seriousness of the violence as well.

The use of background check information is subject to the same stringent laws as with other pre-employment screening tools. It can't be used to discriminate against certain groups, it can't be made public to other applicants or other employees who are not in a "need to know" personnel or human resources position, and it can't be gathered illegally or unethically.

Most firms who have a fulltime security manager on the premises will ask for assistance in doing background checks, usually following a pre-scribed set of guidelines as to what kind of information they need. Firms with no security contingent or who screen many candidates during hiring periods will outsource the background information search to highly-specialized data collection firms. Many of the larger, well-known security firms offer this service, and can create reports for large numbers of applicants in a relatively short period of time.

While background checks sound like the wave of the future, especially in this time of negligent hiring and negligent referral civil suits, more firms don't use them regularly than those that do. The primary reasons against them, in the eyes of most personnel or hiring managers, is due to the time and cost. Even basic personnel information reports could take one week to ten days to complete, at a cost ranging anywhere from $25 to $150 or more.

As suggested at the start of this chapter, many managers and supervisors are in too much of a hurry to wait for this information, or pay for it, especially if they think they can divine the same data from the applicant's application or during the interview.

The firms who currently use formal background checks do it because they want to make balanced, careful hiring decisions. The critical sources of information include the applicant's work history (dates, supervisors, job duties, wages), driving record (any accidents, citations, license suspensions or revocations, traffic-related convictions), educational records (presence of a high school diploma, college credits or degrees), military history (if applicable), criminal history (adult misdemeanor and felony *convictions*, not arrests), and credit history (bankruptcies, excessive number of late payments, tax or court liens, foreclosures, or repossessions).

The reason for these choices are largely based on completing this total picture of the applicant—how he or she has worked in the past and for how long; how they handle a motor vehicle; where or if they went to school or college; their military service record, also known as a DD-214 report; whether they have been convicted of any crimes; and how they handle their personal finances.

The rule of thumb for using the data provided by most background checks is that the specific information asked for and gathered must be job-related. Thus, it's acceptable for an airport passenger shuttle service to ask applicants to bring copies of their state driving records or for a check cashing store chain to require applicants to submit to a credit check.

However, most firms and personnel managers who believe in the power of background checks think all the information is valid because it completes the puzzle or mosaic that is the applicant. Therefore, the key to staying out of legal hot water regarding the use of this data starts by getting the applicant to sign permission waivers as part of the hiring process. Some firms use a blanket waiver form that allows for the collection of the above-mentioned data, others use individual waiver forms for each of the subjects.

As with the information gathered during the application/resume review process and the interview session, the data revealed following a careful and legal background check should serve as either a green light (hire), a yellow light (check further), or a red light (don't hire).

Drug Screening

As Chapter 3 discussed, people with significant off-the-job problems sometimes have accompanying illegal drug or alcohol abuse problems as well. And it's widely held by law enforcement officials and behavioral experts that perpetrators of violence use drugs and alcohol as a way to steel themselves for their acts. As such, testing for drugs and alcohol protects the organization and the employees from people who may be more than just impaired, but in fact dangerous.

Companies who use drug screening as part of the hiring process usually ask applicants to take the tests only after passing through the other pre-employment steps. Most firms use the successful completion of a drug scan as the last hurdle for employment. Hiring managers typically make a *conditional* and written offer of employment, based upon the passage of a medical exam, which usually involves a drug screen. In other words, pass and you get the job at our firm, fail and you don't.

Some people who have not had to provide a urine sample as part of their hiring or on-going employment seem to think that the drug screening process is somehow either flawed or plagued with errors. In reality, the majority of professional laboratories conducting these tests are both highly-skilled, and well-versed in the required collection, testing, and reporting processes.

Still, since errors are possible, some firms who believe in drug testing have hired labs who use a new hair testing method. This process is less invasive, usually only involves the collection of 60 or so strands of head or even body hair. The hair is liquified and tested like blood or urine would be. Proponents say hair samples offer a much more precise picture of not just recent drug use, but months of drug use history.

Is it possible for concerned hiring managers to do all the right things in terms of careful selection practices: read the application or resume with an eye for discrepancies; ask all the right questions, including behavioral types, during the interview; conduct a thorough background check, including a drug screen; and still hire an employee who will one day be capable of an act of workplace violence, including homicide? The bad news is the answer is yes. The good news is that with all the above-described checks and balances in place, the likelihood diminishes tremendously. Because knowledge is power, the more the current members of an organization know about a potential member, the better decisions they can make whether to hire that person or not.

REVIEW/SUMMARY

Using thoughtful questioning, fact-finding interviews, background checks, psychological screenings if appropriate, the review of carefully-designed job applications, and strict (and legal) guidelines, a business person can hire new employees with a higher degree of safety and assurance.

This chapter discussed how careful pre-employment screening reduces the risk of employee violence.

DISCUSSION QUESTIONS

1. Discuss the benefits of careful applicant screening from a violence prevention standpoint.
2. What types of behavioral clues can be found on a completed job application?
3. Do you think pen and paper tests are ethical? Valid? Useful as a pre-screening tool?
4. Is it appropriate to ask anger management questions during an interview? Why or why not?
5. Would you hire an applicant to fill a cash-handling position if he or she had severe credit problems, e.g. bankruptcy, many late payments, etc. Why or why not?
6. Discuss the relationship between drug or alcohol abuse and the potential for workplace violence.

9

Zero-Tolerance Policies and Procedures: No More Paper Tigers

KEY POINTS TO THIS CHAPTER

- The need for written workplace violence awareness and prevention policies
- Sample policies
- Zero-tolerance
- Enforcement strategies
- Policy review
- New and current employee orientation

Nothing is harder to enforce than an unwritten policy, and yet, some company leaders attempt to create a safe working environment using nothing but informal rules. Some marginal employees believe the old saying: "If it's not written down, it doesn't apply to me."

The problem with unwritten policies and procedures (P&P's) starts with the fact that they are difficult to enforce, especially when used retroactively, or after an incident surfaces that calls for their use.

Personnel or human resources managers of smaller or newly established firms may rely on "boilerplate" or pre-written policies and procedures, often taking them from firms who sell these types of off-the-shelf products. The value to these already-created work rules is that someone has already done most of the hard work, writing the policies using defensible legal language and accounting for most contingencies. The disadvantage to them is that they may be too generic, or lack specific behavioral policies.

Using these pre-written P&P's saves time and effort, which translates to dollar savings as well. But since every company is different, even in the same industry, the key personnel and operations managers will need to customize the P&P manual prior to putting them out to the employees.

And this customization process must include the creation and insertion of specific policies that discuss violence in the workplace. Companies and the people who lead and work in them are no longer in a position to avoid or ignore this subject, especially in light of the mounting number of cases of employee-based threats, assaults, or the use or possession of weapons at work.

And it is because workplace violence is such a difficult subject to discuss in an open forum, that so many managers and supervisors feel out of their comfort zones when asked to help create policies. A survey by the American Management Association (AMA) tells this tale: According to an April 1994 written survey conducted at the AMA national conference, titled "Workplace Violence: Policies, Procedures, & Incidents," the numbers of firms who had specific workplace violence prevention policies in place was not high. Answering the question, "Does your organization have policies and procedures in place instructing employees what to do in the event of a potential or actual incident of workplace violence?" Only 35% of the respondents said yes and 65% said no. The follow-up question is as equally revealing, "Does your organization provide formal training in dealing with workplace violence?" Only 8.4% said yes for all employees, while 22.2% said yes, for some employees, and sadly, 69.4% said no, that it did not provide any training for any of its employees.[1]

While these numbers have certainly improved in the three years since this survey, they do give the impression that the threat of workplace violence is not taken seriously in many firms. This reluctance to deal with this subject will improve as more off-the-job problems come into the workplace, as domestic violence issues continue to plague our workplaces, and as the number of people who choose violence as a solution to their work continues to increase.

Sample Workplace Violence Awareness and Prevention Policies

The following examples offer a starting point for concerned managers and supervisors who need to provide input into workplace violence policies. Notice that the language in these examples is both broad and specific, identifying both inappropriate employee behaviors, unacceptable actions, sanctions for violations, and intervention opportunities for managers and supervisors and the organization.

---

1. National conference survey, "Workplace Violence: Policies, Procedures, & Incidents." American Management Association. New York, April 1994.

The first example was created by the security managers for a large financial organization:

"This company will not tolerate threats of violence, bodily harm or physical intimidation by employees. Such actions may be grounds for immediate termination. In instances where an employee exhibits any of these types of behavior, the company reserves the right to request an evaluation by a mental health professional to determine fitness for duty.

Likewise, this company will not tolerate threats or intimidation of employees in the workplace by individuals outside the company.

If you receive or perceive a threat, notify your representative personnel officer and the Security Department. You also may call our Employee Assistance Program manager if you want to discuss your concerns in confidence.

This company defines workplace violence warning signs as: intimidating or threatening behaviors or actions; written or oral threats to injure, hurt, or kill someone; harassment or hazing behavior; someone who is easily enraged, provoked, or who becomes overly-emotional or explosive; someone who discusses or has exhibited past assaultive behavior; someone who has engaged in spouse or partner abuse; stalking or other inappropriate romantically-driven or following behaviors; exhibition of paranoid behavior; alcohol or drug abuse; serious off-the-job problems that cause workplace stress; and recent escalation of any of these behaviors over time."

Notice how this sample policy manages to pack a great deal of information in one page. It specifically mentions unacceptable behaviors, which also may serve as warning signs for the employee and their supervisors. It outlines the sanctions for violation of the policy, up to and including forced mental health counseling as a condition for further employment, or immediate termination. The policy states that the firm will not allow its employees to be threatened or attacked by outsiders like customers, vendors, or trespassers. And it offers three separate yet related internal resources for concerned employees: the designated personnel manager, a security manager, or the employee assistance manager.

The next policy sample comes from an aerospace firm, which employees executives, managers, supervisors, clerical, and assembly line employees.

"This company and our subsidiaries are committed to providing a safe working environment for all employees and visitors. We will not tolerate any acts or threatened acts of violence from anyone. Any employee engaging in such acts will be subject to employment sanctions, up to and including immediate termination. Any person threatening or committing an act of violence also may be personally subject to civil or criminal liability.

Under this policy, we define violent behavior as: the actual or implied threat of harm to any individual(s), group, or relatives of individuals; the possession of any unauthorized weapons on company property; the brandishing at others of any object which could be construed as a weapon; loud, angry, or disruptive behavior that creates fear or anxiety in the workplace, including threatening, intimidating, or violence-inducing words; intentional disregard for the physical or psychological safety of others; intentional destruction of company or someone's personal property; committing any misdemeanor or felony crime on company grounds, during company-sponsored activities, or while on official company business; and any conduct or behaviors which a reasonable person would view as threatening or potentially violent.

Any employee who is subjected to, participates in, witnesses, or has knowledge of events, behaviors, or actions that could be perceived as violent, or believes these actions may occur, is required by this policy to report it promptly to a company supervisor, security manager, or human resources representative. All employees should know they can raise concerns or make reports in confidence without fear of reprisal."

Notice the careful use of language to encompass more than just employees, but visitors, customers, vendors, or family members of any of these constituencies. The policy mentions also weapons issues, crimes on company property, vandalism or sabotage, and "blanket" statements about violent threats or acts both on or near company grounds, and while acting in an official capacity for the company. And like the previous policy, it makes it clear that termination may result from any violation.

The next policy example comes from a community college district. It includes policies, definitions, and the roles and responsibilities of specific district employees.

"It shall be the policy of this district to immediately investigate all allegations of workplace violence and take appropriate corrective action to remedy any situation where a district employee is threatened or assaulted. To this end, the district has adopted a 'zero-tolerance' policy which will not tolerate personal threats or violent behavior from another person.

Workplace violence is defined as personal, verbal, or written threats, violent behavior, or physical conduct which interferes or threatens an employee's safety in the workplace.

The Chancellor shall: appoint a district officer to be responsible to the Board of Trustees and ensure compliance with the rules of this policy; establish procedures for implementing a workplace violence response plan, and develop strategies designed to prevent incidents and educate employees about the potential for violence throughout the district; provide all employees with information and training to increase their ability to recognize the early warning signs of a potentially violent person or situation, to show them how to record and report potential violent problems, and to encourage them how to report suspicious incidents through the existing chain of command."

Because of the size of this educational organization, the policy defines the need for management responsibility, employee training, and the proper personnel responses.

This final workplace violence prevention policy comes from a city municipality.

"Violence in the workplace and in our communities has motivated this city to be proactive and implement a consistent, city-wide, zero-tolerance violence and threat management policy. The city workforce reflects the community at large and has experienced its own increase in the number of reported threats over the past few years. This policy was developed as a prevention measure to reduce the potential for violence and applies to all city employees, including managers and supervisors.

A threat is defined as a direct or implied expression of intent to inflict physical or psychological harm or actions that reasonable persons would see as a threat to their physical safety or personal or city property.

The increased concern over violence in the workplace has resulted in all threats being taken seriously. Employees making threats will be suspended without pay for the reminder of the day and up to 30 days pending completion of an investigation.

Threats are not an acceptable way of interacting with others in the workplace. They are not acceptable even in a joking manner. All threats will be taken seriously. If city employees become aware of a threat to themselves or to others, they shall notify their supervisor or management immediately. They may also discuss or report threats to the city employee assistance program as well."

The "Airport" Model

The above-mentioned policies and others like them often make reference to the phrase "zero-tolerance," a phrase that found its origins in the fight against drugs in the United States.

In essence, it states that once a policy is in place preventing various inappropriate behaviors, e.g. smoking near flammable liquids, possessing or using drugs, possessing or brandishing a weapon, etc., any violation, no matter how small, seemingly insignificant, or even based on ignorance or error, is subject to the same sanctions.

Zero-tolerance is a difficult concept to enforce because it means different things to different people, from the managers and supervisors who must enforce it to the marginal employees who try to exploit it, and to the employees in the organization who must understand it with regard to their own conduct and that of their co-workers.

The most common problems with zero-tolerance enforcement practices for workplace violence prevention comes from either overactivity, underactivity, or worse, a sliding scale from one to the other.

With overactivity, or more succinctly, "over-proactivity," managers and supervisors become hypervigilant, looking at every out of the ordinary encounter in the workplace as having the potential to erupt into violence. This can lead to the kind of overreaction to common co-worker interactions that makes people suspicious of each other, resentful of so-called "micromanagement," and soon convinced that problems exist where none have before.

In parallel with this is an overreaction toward the protection mindset in and for the organization. As an example, the phrase "possession of any weapon" appears in many workplace violence policies. This is meant to prohibit firearms such as handguns, shotguns, rifles, or assault weapons in the workplace. And most people understand it to prohibit the display or use of large knives or similar weapons related to cutting, stabbing, or piercing.

But under true zero-tolerance, a Swiss Army knife qualifies as a weapon, as does the ownership by a female secretary of chemical sprays like Mace or pepper gas. Most employees understand that the Swiss Army knife is not usually a threatening weapon and that the spray is used usually for defensive self-protection and not an offensive attack.

Yet, in the hypervigilant workplace where managers and supervisors passionately enforce zero-tolerance, possession of these kinds of items can lead to possible punishments and sure controversy.

Under zero-tolerance outside the organization, we have seen already high school students expelled for bringing penknives in their backpacks. And under drug possession zero-tolerance rules, we have seen now female junior high school students suspended from bringing aspirins in their purses.

All this over-enforcement of zero-tolerance rules is both self-defeating and excessive. We must understand that the spirit of the law is just as important as the letter of the law. Balance and the application of rational thought is the key to success in organizations (and other formal institutions where it applies).

Underenforcement, conversely, begins when managers and supervisors neither understand the zero-tolerance guidelines, nor wish to get that involved in the affairs of their employees. Speaking again of comfort zones, it's always easier to turn a blind eye and a deaf ear to issues, incidents, or actions that either come to the borderline of zero-tolerance violations, or step across it.

One example occurs during autumn in companies, factories, and plants in the South and Midwest. In many parts of these regions, fall signals the start of hunting season. As such, many hunting enthusiast-employees bring their personal cars and trucks into parking lots on company grounds with these weapons fully loaded and close at hand. As one plant manager in Georgia attests, "During deer and elk season, it's quite common to see row after row of pickup trucks in the employee parking lots with shotguns and rifles hanging in the gun racks. It's a cultural thing down here."

Faced with this historical obstacle, most managers simply concede that this is "acceptable" behavior, within limits, and they allow this and similar practices to continue.

Yet, for other firms who have chosen not to enforce zero-tolerance workplace violence policies, the reasons are less visible. Much of the failures of these types of policies occurs when managers and supervisors lack the motivation to intervene in lower level violations like the use of threats or vandalism between employees. Some of them fall back on time-honored excuses for failing to get involved as, "Boys will be boys," or "That's just how the guys on the loading dock are. You can't really do anything about it."

These rationalizations do nothing to protect the victim-employee and they certainly won't fare well in a civil court. The mere existence of formal, written zero-tolerance policies should put management on notice that it must investigate all reports or discoveries of violence threats, and then respond with appropriate measures, sanctions, or terminations. The only thing worse than having no P&P's addressing workplace violence concerns and then not responding to behavioral problems is having them and still not taking immediate action.

Lastly, the sliding scale response indicates that the organization, its leadership, and the employee relationships may be spinning out of control. In these instances, potentially violent behavior is allowed to escalate so that what was simply intolerable (and a clear violation of company zero-tolerance policies) before, is somehow more acceptable now. This occurs when pressure from employee groups, unions, or even society suggests that the company is "overreacting" and that the employees have the right to work or act however they want.

This laissez-faire attitude also grows following a significant intervention in to some form of inappropriate employee behavior that has ended in either failure, or a perceived "victory" for the perpetrator-employee. One example is where a company security officer conducts an illegal search into an employee's property and discovers a handgun. After the weapon is seized, the employee is summarily terminated, under the auspices of the zero tolerance policy. However, using a labor law attorney, it's possible and even likely the gun-toting employee can get his gun and his job back, with lost pay, because of the illegal search and seizure.

These kinds of harrowing episodes can create the kinds of "it's not my job" feelings in once-burned managers, setting the stage for future violations down the road.

There are many constituencies in an organization, and under the specter of workplace violence, there are groups who congregate together by action and definition. There are victim-employees, who may have been or are currently subject to harassment, intimidation, threats, or actual violence from their co-workers. There are the perpetrator-employees who engage in the kinds of behaviors the zero-tolerance policies were established to prevent. There are the witness-co-workers, who may have seen or heard about the behavior inflicted upon the victim-employee by the perpetrator-employee. These people may be associates of both parties, or they may sympathize with one person over the other, e.g. "He gets what he deserves" or "That guy should be fired for making us feel afraid of him."

Finally, there are what I call "fence-sitter" victims and "fence-sitter" perpetrators, who are the workplace violence targets or actors of the future. They may be involved in a violent situation at home or work that is largely subterranean. Or they may be victims or perpetrators in workplace events yet to come. Their position in this collection is one of observation.

Since they represent that special strata of future participants in the workplace violence arena, they watch the current proceedings very carefully. They want to see how management responds to threats of violence or an actual event because it may soon pertain to them. Perpetrators want to see if management truly enforces its zero-tolerance policies and to what degree. Does an employee who punches his boss get suspended for one day without pay or fired? Does an employee who brings a gun to show off in the employee breakroom get a written warning or a pink slip? And for more nefarious activities, does an employee who gets caught vandalizing company or personal property have to make restitution?

Fence-sitter victims ask similar questions to themselves, although their motives are usually the reverse of their perpetrator counterparts. They ask if the employee who slashed their tires will be fired and made to pay for the damages. They want to know if an employee or a disturbed customer beats up an employee, will the police be called? And if the police come, do they just take a report or will they make an arrest? And they want to see how management responds to the emotional, personal, and psychological needs of someone who has been injured at the hands of another while at work. Does the victim get medical attention, help with insurance bills, legal advice, time off, disability pay, or counseling sessions?

All this should illustrate why managers and supervisors need to intervene and enforce zero-tolerance violations. The threat of violence in the workplace creates many different subsets of people within an organization. Most everyone is looking to see if their own needs get met first, even if they have not been directly involved in the problem.

Perhaps the best way to enforce zero-tolerance policies is to take a logical, balanced, and reasonable approach on one hand and a tough, no-nonsense approach on the other. This is possible, as our national and international airports demonstrate every day.

When you approach an airport security station, replete with its metal detectors and security staff, a large sign should catch your eye. In essence, it states:

> "Don't bring guns, bombs, or other dangerous weapons or items into this area or aboard any aircraft. And just as importantly, don't make any jokes about guns, bombs, or other dangerous weapons or items. We take any violation of these two policies very seriously."

And they do, as well they should. Cases exist where passengers making passing or joking references to airplane bombs have been unceremoniously arrested by airport police officers and then turned over to agents from the Federal Bureau of Investigation for full prosecution.

But conversely, the airport security people realize that their zero-tolerance policies can be as flexible as they are stringent. This is why you can bring a Swiss Army knife on board a commercial aircraft, but not an 8" butcher knife; a cigarette lighter but not a jug of kerosene; or a baseball bat, hockey stick, or golf club, but not a billy club or a pair of nunchakus.

We all know words can be dangerous, used in an improper context. Just as we don't allow people to shout "Fire!" in crowded movie theaters, we cannot tolerate the use of the kind of language that makes people feel afraid for their safety at work.

Some experts in the fields of workplace violence prevention, threat management, and behavioral psychology have suggested that some workplace violence events, especially occupational homicides, breed support from other disturbed people who have seen or heard about them. This "copycat" factor is both puzzling and hard to predict. That certain disgruntled employees seem to identify with the homicidal actions of another is challenging enough; knowing how to prevent them from following suit is even more difficult.

As we will examine in the next chapter, overly-excessive interest in other acts of workplace violence, especially homicides, should serve as a warning sign. The employee who suddenly posts news clippings from recent events with notes of support or words of agreement should set off many behavioral warning bells for a passing supervisor.

Freedom of speech only goes so far. This carries over to the need to make it clear that a true zero-tolerance policy does exactly that: tolerates no discussions about workplace violence cases which carry the phrase, "Those people got what they deserved," or "If I'd have been there I'd have done the same thing," etc.

Correctly enforcing a zero-tolerance workplace violence policy is about balance, context, and the "reasonable person" test, as in "how would a reasonable person respond, given this situation?" It's neither possible nor safe to take one extreme position or the other, i.e. overenforcing the rules or underenforcing them. Successful use of the concept must allow for the kinds of situational, selective flexibility that serves the goal of protecting all employees.

Current Policy Review

Most executives or managers who aren't directly involved in the on-going use or modification of a company's policies and procedures don't relish reviewing them to update the language. Many notebook-size operational, procedural, security, or "open only in case of emergency" manuals gather dust on the shelves of executives, department heads, and managers' offices. While some company leaders like to tell their subordinates or each other that their various procedure manuals are "living" documents, i.e. used and refined regularly. In reality, most of these voluminous manuals simply sit on the shelf waiting for the time (usually a significant emergency or serious risk management problem) when they can indeed come to life.

And when many of these manuals are relegated to the dark recesses of the organization the policies lose touch with the employees and the employees obviously lose connection with the policies.

While certain less serious issues, e.g. the employee parking policy, don't demand immediate attention, constant finetuning, or frequent updates, others do, especially those related to behavioral issues or safety and security.

As mentioned at the start of this chapter, oral, informal, or "grapevine" workplace policies aren't worth the paper they're not printed upon. They are not defensible in court. They will not demonstrate a viable sense of due diligence to plaintiffs' attorneys, a labor law judge, or outside observers who will look hard at a firm should an act of violence occur.

The best way to prepare workplace violence-specific P&P's that will help protect both the organization and its employees is to create a policy review team. This group should be made up of members—usually at the manager or senior employee level—from the Human Resources, Personnel, Employee Assistance, Training, Legal, Risk Management, and Security Departments. In smaller organizations or companies without the luxury of so many employee-based departments, some committee members will have to wear more than one hat. In start-up firms, one or two people may make up each of these specialty areas and have to create, write, and modify policies to fit the needs of each of these departments, even if they don't yet formally exist. For example, one manager with the appropriate background may be tasked with designing the policies to organize the personnel, human resources, employee assistance, and training *functions* rather than actual, physical departments.

Where smaller firms may choose to use boilerplate P&P's as a starting point, policy committee members from larger organizations can modify existing policies to fit the new demands of the changing, and more violent workplace.

Any new policy, and especially those that deal with behavioral issues, discipline or termination procedures, hiring or interview processes, or sanctions for policy violations, must go through a careful review by the firm's in-house or retained legal counsel.

The committee process should not be an agonizing one for the members. Working together, the team can create organizational-specific P&P's for workplace violence awareness and prevention, within several sessions of discussion, review, writing, and—following expert legal advice—rewriting to a final form and inclusion in a revised and quarterly or half-yearly updated P&P manual.

The Need For Employee Orientation and Follow-Up

The best workplace violence prevention policies ever created won't do any good if they aren't available to the employees or other people who will need to read them, follow them, or enforce them. This goes back to the possibility that most employee P&P manuals may get read only once—at the time of initial hiring. If the manual is too thick and cumbersome, the majority of rank-and-file employees hardly bother to pick up updated pages, incorporate them into the manual to keep it current, or remove older pages that no longer apply.

An example explains the need to lead the new or on-going policy manual owner to the source of information. The administrators, department heads, and professors of a large community college district met to discuss why they had all seen such a marked increase in the number of classroom behavioral problems caused by angry, enraged, or simply disrespectful students.

The behaviors included threats to the professor or other students, confrontive or discourteous responses to requests by the instructors to follow class rules, fighting between students while in class, cigarette smoking, and even drug and alcohol use in class.

"Why is it," asked the group to themselves and collectively, "that so many students have forgotten the rules of behavior in our classrooms?" And in the statement was the answer. In years past, the actual rules of student conduct, either in class or while on campus, were posted inside each copy of the new student orientation materials. While the students were under no obligation to read these rules of appropriate classroom behavior, the location and presence in the orientation package helped at least to make them aware of them.

Over time, however, the people who assembled the orientation packages noticed that the packet was getting rather thick with pages. So they took it upon themselves to do some selective editing and removed the behavioral rules from the package. Instead, the rules of classroom conduct were left in the counseling center for the students to pick up if they so chose.

In a perfect example of cause and effect, the administrators realized so few students knew the rules of conduct because they were at first missing, and then not accessible unless they wanted to trek across campus and specifically ask for a copy from the counseling center staff.

Realizing that few but the most dedicated students would spend this time, the group ordered the rules to be replaced back into the new student orientation packages. Within months of this action, coupled with the additional help the professors gave this move by reviewing the rules in class by way of reintroducing them, class behavioral problems went down.

What this example illustrates is that we cannot rely upon the particular constituency group in an organization to self-educate itself as to the formal rules of behavior. Management must be ready and willing to take the initiative and discuss specific behavioral policies, like those attached to the subject of workplace violence prevention, attendance, work performance and productivity, and other work behavior rules, with all newly-hired employees and every current employee.

Some firms insist that all employees read and initial routing copies of new policies and put the originals into their manuals to keep them up to date. While this may seem tedious for managers and employees alike, it does help to set the standard for new P&P dissemination. If faced with a workplace violence incident and a subsequent civil court case, the firm's leaders can prove by date and number of recipients when they issued a specific policy to all employees.

REVIEW/SUMMARY

It's not enough to have unwritten, informal, oral, or word-of-mouth policies in place. These legal times call for a careful review of the P&P manual with an eye toward correcting deficiencies, adding new "zero-tolerance" language, and strengthening the company's legal position about the inappropriate behavior of its employees, customers, or vendors.

This chapter offered existing workplace violence prevention policy samples along with boilerplates to help readers create their own.

DISCUSSION QUESTIONS

1. Discuss the legal ramifications of missing, incomplete, or poorly-written policies and procedures addressing employee behavior.

2. What key words or phrases do the sample policies in this chapter share? Why?

3. Is it possible to install effective zero-tolerance workplace violence prevention policies in an organization? Why or why not?

4. Which discipline methods are used by managers or supervisors to enforce workplace violence policy violations?

5. Who should conduct the final review step prior to distributing any new policies to the employees? Why?

6. What are some ways management can make sure all new and current employees read and understand new workplace violence prevention policies?

10

Management Awareness & Recognition: Perpetrator-Employee Violence Characteristics

KEY POINTS TO THIS CHAPTER

- Violence profile characteristics
- Overreliance or misreading the characteristics
- Signs of psychological distress
- Intervention alternatives

Now that we understand the types of perpetrators of workplace violence, the acts they commit in or near the organization, and the company policies that must be in place to help combat these problems, it's time to refocus our attention on the behaviors of the workplace perpetrator.

Instead of examining specific acts or problems created by the disturbed employee, we will now review the behaviors that lead to these incidents. Some observers on the periphery of the subject of occupational violence tend to cluster their understanding of it around the many existing perpetrator profiles. Most of these have been created by well-established experts in their fields; some are neither valuable nor make a contribution to better understanding of perpetrator dynamics.

The primary problem with any behavioral profile is that it is not an absolute document. As much as we would like to be able to grasp on to the information provided by a profile as unfailingly accurate, it's not possible. If human behavior is always in flux, then violent human behavior borders on chaos theory. Seemingly mild-mannered people have killed their entire families while others with utterly contemptible behavior never raise a hand to anyone throughout their entire lives. People who we believe quite capable of extremely violent or even lethal behavior never cross that line, while others who would seem the least likely candidates can kill one or more people in an instant.

Profile Reliance Dangers

The reason most workplace violence profiles exist is to document, retroactively of course, the behavior of a group of perpetrator-employees who have injured or killed their co-workers in the past. At best, this information should raise our awareness to high warning levels so that we may intervene, help others in the organization to intervene, or call in mental health or law enforcement professionals for more immediate assistance.

However, no profile in existence offers a clear window into the soul of a potential workplace killer. Neither does it tell us exactly when this person may strike. Unfortunately, too many people in business, who have learned about workplace violence employee profiles in books or the media, want to see them as a cure-all for the subject. The use of any profile for information purposes should not be the only warning device used by the leaders of the organization. It is one tool, not the only tool. And like other large tools, it can be dangerous if it's used incorrectly.

Critics of workplace violence perpetrator profiles like to suggest that in the right light, most of the adult male population fits in or has engaged in these behaviors at one time or another. This is both distracting and deceiving. Profiles are not filters. If you put a person's behaviors or characteristics in at one end and shake vigorously, a workplace killer will not come out the other end.

People miss the point when they say, derisively, "I own guns. I was in the military. I'm a white male in his 40's. I've had several jobs. Does that make me a murderer who is going to come into my company and kill people?" This oversimplifies what we have already decided is a complex behavioral issue.

Consider that the United States Secret Service is known throughout the world as the best and most sophisticated personnel protection agency. Their protection details are staffed with extremely skilled and dedicated field agents whose sole function is to recognize and investigate threats on governmental officials and provide wall-to-wall, around-the-clock bodyguard services to prevent attacks on some of the most important people in the world.

And yet, with all their best agents using their behavioral expertise, computer software profiles of suspected attackers, information on crowd psychology, and threat assessment and management capabilities, presidents of the United States get shot. Since President Kennedy's assassination in 1963, we have seen highly disturbed people shoot at President Ford, shoot and wound President Reagan, and shoot at President Clinton's White House home.

Does this mean the Secret Service should abandon its behavioral profiling and protection efforts because of these incidents? Of course not; these acts of violence happened, despite the best precautions, because we live in a violent, unpredictable world. But what should give us hope is that the number of attack incidents against our presidents is as small as it is. This is because of profiling and prevention efforts, not despite them.

And keep in mind how difficult it is to prove a negative. Because the Secret Service drives the President to various functions in a bullet and bomb-resistant vehicle, perhaps many disturbed people have thought it impossible to injure or kill him and have kept writing hate letters instead.

In the workplace, it's not possible to predict the actual success rate of a well-designed security system or a well-crafted workplace violence prevention policy. But does that mean we can eliminate them as protection methods because they have yet to be visibly tested by a perpetrator? Of course not.

So as you consider the following information-valuable profile, remember that its purposes are to raise awareness, identify warning signs that demand intervention, and give managers, supervisors, and employees a better sense of the kinds of past or current behaviors that may signal the onset of violence in disturbed people.

A Workplace Violence Perpetrator Profile: Using the Past to Help Predict the Future

This information comes from a workplace violence profile created by Dr. Michael Mantell, a nationally-known clinical psychologist with long experience in crisis counseling, much of it on the scene of several horrific workplace tragedies. Dr. Mantell was instrumental in handling the aftermath of the July 1984 McDonald's massacre in San Ysidro, California, where James Huberty shot 21 people to death and wounded 19 others. He also served as a consultant for the U.S. Postal Service following the 1986 Edmond, Oklahoma shootings by Patrick Sherrill, which left 14 dead.

This information—gathered from many workplace violence cases— does paint a picture of the violent or potentially dangerous employee. Any combination of these "red flags," coupled with other irrational or threatening behaviors, should serve as a warning to the organization.

It's not legal or ethical to "cherry pick" from these criteria to hire, discipline, or terminate any employee, based solely on one or two factors. This profile is designed to initiate further investigations, discussions, and interventions for victim-employees and their perpetrators.

Many of these behavioral problems came from current or ex-employees who committed one or more homicides at work. The phrases used to describe each category can serve as warning signs for other than homicidal actions as well.

Common Characteristics of Workplace Violence Perpetrators

1. Disgruntled regarding perceived "injustice" at work.
2. Socially isolated, may be a "loner."
3. Very poor self-esteem.
4. "Cries" for help of some kind.
5. Obsessive fascination with the military.
6. Collector of large numbers of guns or other deadly weapons.
7. Temper-control difficulties may have been observed.
8. Threats may have been made.
9. Few, if any, healthy outlets for rage.
10. Excessive interest in media reports of workplace violence.
11. Unstable family life.
12. Other employees are "concerned."
13. Chronic labor-management disputes.
14. Numerous unresolved physical or emotional injury claims.
15. Problems with working conditions.
16. Complaints of heightened stress at work.
17. Majority of cases come from males between 30 and 40 years old.
18. Migratory job history.
19. Drug and alcohol use and/or abuse.
20. Psychiatrically impaired.[1]

1. Disgruntled regarding perceived "injustice" at work.

This is found in the employee who feels that certain people in particular and the organization in general is "out to get me." Other feelings include, rightly or wrongly, an inability to get fair treatment, being passed over for a promotion or a pay raise, being unfairly "punished" for rule violations, or the perception that the employee has been unfairly singled out for specific management attention.

---

1. Mantell, Michael and Albrecht, Steve. *Ticking Bombs: Defusing Violence In the Workplace.* Burr Ridge, IL: Irwin Professional Publishing, 1994, p. 79-88.

Notice in these descriptions of words and concepts like "fair," "fairness," and "treatment." These concepts, or the lack of them in the employee's life, are keys to understanding why he may react with violence once he reaches a perceived "point of no return" in his relationship with the organization or co-workers.

The warning signs for this employee behavior is usually recognizable by complaints. Managers, supervisors, or other employees may hear statements expressing concerns about how others keep the employee in a one-down position, "Everyone is getting ahead at my expense. No one respects me or what I do. I can't get a fair shake here and I never will. No one listens to me, least of all my boss. One of these days, I'm gonna let these people know I'm important, and then they'll be sorry."

The antidote to these statements starts with recognizing the disturbed employee's need to vent and his often overwhelming desire to have someone in a position of authority or importance to validate his concerns. Management must be wary of the disgruntled employee's concerns. not only from a violence-avoidance standpoint, but because of his toxic impact upon co-workers, customers, or others whom he encounters.

Improved communications and informal counseling encounters offer a good first step. More structured interventions may even involve a referral to an outside mental health professional who can help the employee vent in an environment away from work and redirect negative thoughts, feelings, and concerns in a constructive way.

2. Socially isolated, may be a "loner."

While this characteristic may sound like a stereotype, it's often valid, especially in cases of extremely destructive or excessively violent behavior. The definition of the employee "loner" exceeds the person who is just quiet or enjoys his own company over that of others; this person is abnormally alone, with no evidence of significant, conventional, or usual family, social, or sexual relationships.

The employee's inability to start or maintain normal social relationships may create a vicious circle of low self-esteem and a feeling that no one in the world cares about him. Faced with no friends or loved ones away from work or no collegial relationships with co-workers, the employee may become depressed and consider that the world "hates" him.

Loner-type employees typically can't or won't develop social relationships at work, and may have difficulty working or functioning in groups, even always eating lunch alone, with his back to colleagues in the employee breakroom.

Again, this characteristic is not describing the employee who is just quiet and wants to be left alone from time to time; it defines the employee whose marked inability to function or interact normally with other people and may suggest the potential for existing psychological disturbances. It's no secret or surprise that may of this nation's most notorious serial killers have exhibited loner qualities to an extreme degree. Their time, spent brooding or mischaracterizing the world and its people as bad or out to get them, leads some to scenes of incredible violence.

From a workplace violence perspective, the loner employee may entertain certain sociopathic or psychopathic feelings—lack of guilt, the ability to use and rationalize violence against others, and an inability to work, interact, or function within reasonable behavioral parameters.

In extremes, the loner employee may require professional mental health counseling to determine if he has a depression, substance abuse, or other psychological problem. Management must stay aware of signs of abnormal loner behavior in certain employees, especially if this is part of other significant problem areas related to work performance or with other factors in this profile.

3. Very poor self-esteem.

Many psychologists and psychiatrists see critically low self-esteem as a common indicator in people who use lethal violence as a coping skill. This may appear in thoughts and words like, "When I feel bad, I want others to feel that way too," or "Since the world makes me miserable, the only way I can feel better is to make others feel worse, or to hurt them so they know what I am going through."

The most dangerous person in the organization may be the found with the disgruntled employee who mixes chronically low self-esteem with a marked lack of respect for human life. Here, this person feels no sense of importance and worse yet, doesn't value the existence of others. Cases involving workplace violence homicides followed by the suicide of the perpetrator (either by his own hand or as a result of confronting arriving law enforcement) often feature this combination of self-esteem problems and little if any concern for the lives of others.

Employees with critically low self-esteem may reveal this in one of two ways, overcompensating in one direction or another with either classic "blowhard" or "mouse" behaviors. In the former, the employee uses excessive bragging, self-derived ego strokes, or putdowns of others as a way to feel superior. In the latter, the employee exhibits similar qualities of loner behavior and may not reveal much about himself due to depression, chronic fatigue, or other signs and symptoms of psychological difficulties.

Both tendencies may lead to dangerous behavior. The loud, aggressive, bullying employee may overcompensate for his lack of self-esteem by terrorizing others in order to feel superior. The loner may choose violence as a way to "show" people who he is, e.g. "No one seems to know who I am or care about me. Well then, I'm gonna do something that will make them remember me."

As with other behavioral problems, low self-esteem issues may not be completely apparent in the problem-plagued or violence-prone employee. Management needs to watch for signs where one employee seeks to degrade or injure others as a way to feel better, and then intervene with a request for counseling.

4. "Cries" for help of some kind.

As mentioned in this textbook previously, the myth of the seemingly-normal employee who comes to work one day, suddenly "snaps," and then pulls out a gun and starts shooting is exactly that: a myth. In the vast majority of workplace violence cases where an employee caused death or serious injuries, the perpetrator made his feelings of despair, disillusionment, or outrage known to many people surrounding him.

Whether it involves a real or perceived medical, psychological, work relationship, supervisor, or co-worker problem, if it is serious enough for the disturbed employee to complain about at length to all who will listen, then it should be serious enough to get the attention of the employee's boss.

Similar "cries" for help may involve talk or threats of suicide; pains, voices, or irrational thoughts going through the head of the disturbed employee; talk of retaliation, retribution, revenge from the employee, using violence or firearms; or other verbal or non-verbal signs that the employee is calling for attention, assistance, or additional support.

When reviewing an employee's complaints of mistreatment, personal problems, or health concerns, we must look at the totality of the person. Is this a rarity or has the employee developed a reputation for this kind of behavior? Are the complaints addressed to or about one person, boss, or co-worker? Does the employee use final-sounding language to suggest violence if his problems are not resolved to his satisfaction?

Managers and supervisors should take care to listen to cries for organizational or personal help as the warning signs that they represent.

5. Obsessive fascination with the military.

Two cases come to mind (previously mentioned in Chapter 3) when reviewing the obsessive behavior of some workplace violence perpetrators. One involved a Portland, Oregon delivery driver who returned to an office building containing some of his route customers and began shooting. When arrested, he was wearing military camouflage fatigues, a black military beret, and a sheath-knife strapped to his leg. The other case occurred at a Ford Motor Company plant in Michigan. The suspect was the spurned lover of a Ford employee. When taken into custody, he too, was dressed in camouflage BDU's (Battle Dress Uniforms).

In these workplace violence cases and others where the perpetrator was dressed partially or completely in military uniforms, it was as if they were trying to complete some type of "warrior" fantasy. Since these articles of clothing are not everyday wear items for most non-military employees, their use in acts of violence surely is meant to take on certain symbolic meanings.

Some employees with behavioral problems and who have the most interest in the military came from government or military service previously. In some cases, they may have had or are still going through a difficult psychological transition period between military life to civilian life. They may perceive the trappings of service life (honor, saluting, rank, status, privileges, uniforms, the use of weapons, etc.) as somehow necessary for the civilian world, especially in an organization.

If they work with or for people who did not share their sense of loyalty to the military, or with or for those who discount it or put it down, their inability to cope may increase tenfold.

Keep in mind that the use of this factor (and the one following it) as a warning sign indicator should be gauged with regard to reasonableness. A plastic model of an aircraft carrier on an employee's desk is certainly acceptable in most workplaces; a shrine built to an AK-47 assault weapon is not.

Most concerned employees will make the obvious association between the purpose of the military (war and defense) and those disgruntled employees who choose to focus obsessively about military equipment, regalia, or weapons, as part of their desire to make others uncomfortable or fearful.

6. Collector of large numbers of guns or other deadly weapons.

This profile factor often brings howls of complaints from gun enthusiasts and collectors who protest that they're unfairly assembled with homicidal workplace maniacs. Like the disgruntled employee obsessed with the military, an obsession with firearms occurs when the employee makes other people uncomfortable with constant conversation or visual references to guns and firepower. It's easy to see how the employee who nearly always wears military-style clothing to work and speaks unendingly about guns and which ones work best for "blowing people away" can have a highly negative impact upon his co-workers.

One characteristic proven after observing the aftermath of several workplace violence homicides is that the suspect often chose to "overarm" himself with more firearms than even a gun collector would admit is reasonable to own. Larry Hansel, a former employee of the Elgar Corporation in San Diego, California, shot and killed two people during a June 1991 attack. Following his arrest, police found a trunkload of guns, shotguns, bombmaking materials, and working bombs in his car. Homicidal attacks on other firms have lead to post-incident searches of a suspect's home and car with similar results; the presence of guns, guns, and more guns.

It's easy and convenient for people to say that guns don't kill people, people kill people. But access to guns, especially those semi-automatic, automatic, or assault-type weapons that are designed to fire multiple rounds, only provide the perpetrator more opportunity to do significant damage. In any organization (not related to firearms as an industry), the possession of weapons or uncomfortable conversations about them (especially when warned to stop) should raise the attention of management, the security department, and even local law enforcement if the situation escalates.

7. Temper-control difficulties may have been observed.

Again, we're attempting to describe irrational, abnormal behavior, not the employee who has the occasional bad day. Most managers and supervisors and their employees know the difference between a co-worker who is blowing off steam and one who has crossed the line to dangerous or potentially violent outbursts. This includes throwing personal or company property at walls or people; smashing or breaking things like furniture; punching walls; or violating someone's personal space with red-faced finger-pointing, chest-poking, or loud yelling that continues unabated for more than a very short period of time.

People who have a hard time controlling their temper make other people uncomfortable and afraid, and for good reason. If you were to speak to the majority of female domestic violence victims, they would admit that their abuse followed a period of intense anger, rage, or frustration on the part of their partner.

It's hard to deny the connection between temper control problems and the actual or threatened use of violence. People who have battered or killed others, even their loved ones or children, report being so "caught up in the moment" that they had no memory of what they did.

Mature, rational people know how and why to control their anger, even in the worst situations. Immature, irrational people may strike first and express their regrets later. Temper problems in employees may be a sign of off-the-job problems, drug or alcohol use or withdrawal problems, or the tip of the iceberg for a future workplace violence problem. Like the use of threats, the constant, excessive, or fear-causing displays of anger should be cause for management concern and a recommendation for immediate psychological counseling.

8. Threats may have been made.

As reported in Chapter 9, the use of threats to scare, intimidate, or assault other employees are valid and definite warning signs. The zero-tolerance policies discussed in the previous chapter adamantly state that threat behavior, especially as a precursor to violence, cannot and should not be tolerated in the organization.

Management has a duty to demonstrate due diligence (initiating an immediate investigation, counseling or correcting the perpetrator-employee, and monitoring the situation for future reoccurrences) in cases where an employee, customer, vendor, or outsider threatens a member of the organization.

9. Few, if any, healthy outlets for rage.

We titled my previous workplace violence business book *Ticking Bombs* to capture the sense of rage exhibited by some disturbed employees. The potentially violent worker who cannot vent his rage may show all the signs of a walking, talking ticking time bomb.

Normal people vent their frustrations in mostly healthy ways, using exercise; by taking time off from the job; through relationships with family, friends, or loved ones to vent their concerns; or even counseling sessions with qualified mental health professionals.

Those who cannot find similar outlets, or choose not to look for them may soon find that they feel out of control, full of stress and brimming with an overwhelming sense of anger. Like the disturbed employee with temper control problems, the enraged employee may frighten co-workers with his irrational behavior. If these outbursts occur enough to constitute what any employee considers a "hostile" or "dangerous" workplace, the company could face a civil suit if its managers fail to take action and remedy the situation.

10. Excessive interest in media reports of workplace violence.

Like the military or firearm-obsessed person who brings talk or examples of his "hobbies" everywhere he goes, an over-fascination with workplace violence incidents (especially homicides) is neither healthy for the employee or his organization. If you recall how the previous chapter discussed zero-tolerance "no joking" policies, similarly, we must restrict every employee from engaging in the kind of talk about specific workplace violence incidents or the subject in general if it's meant to frighten or intimidate others. (Even during company training sessions, I take care to avoid too many discussions of past workplace homicides because the imagery can be so distressing for employees who have had crime or violence somehow touch their lives.)

Obsessive and inappropriate interest in workplace violence and related homicides manifests itself for the employee who mounts newspaper clippings on the walls of his workspace, speaks in seemingly glowing language about the "success" of the perpetrator, and otherwise suggests that the actions and results of the suspect was somehow worthy of merit. Statements like, "I guess they found out the hard way how you can't push some people all the time," or "This place could use a guy like that to straighten some people out" should not be passed off as harmless.

Remember that the disturbed yet manipulative employee knows he doesn't have to lay a hand on his co-workers to get the desired effect of fear in the workplace. Management has an obligation to intervene when an employee decides to support the actions of a workplace killer as some twisted solution to his problems.

While a closed-door meeting with the employee may be enough to make him realize the damage he causes, those who fail to heed this first warning should find themselves subject to a more stringent application of the company's zero-tolerance workplace violence policy.

11. Unstable family life.

This characteristic may be highly subjective, discretionary, or have little historical, current, or future relevance. What this factor means is that the employee who has significant off-the-job problems may have family difficulties as well. And since we know off-the-job problems can have a negative effect on an employee's work attendance or productivity, an unstable family life may be more of an indication of a performance problem rather than a violence problem.

Yet, on the other hand, we also should recognize the reality of family problems as an instigator for workplace violence, especially as it's related to domestic violence continuing at work or stalking behavior on company property. There are examples in this book and others of employees who have shot and killed their wives and then returned to the workplace to kill co-workers and/or themselves.

In August 1989, Escondido, California postal worker John Taylor shot and killed his wife as she lay in their bed. He then went to work at the same station where he had worked for over twenty years. After having his usual morning coffee with two of his best friends at the plant, he stood up, shot them dead, wounded another employee, and then turned the gun on himself. Taylor had a long history of alcohol abuse and domestic violence, both in his family history and in his personal life.

It's not necessary for a supervisor to quiz his or her employees about their family lives or histories, only to make sure that family problems don't spill over into the workplace. The man who loses his family (divorce, separation, death, etc.) may feel he has nothing to lose at work if he feels threatened or confronted about his failing work performance.

When family problems become work problems, the employee should be referred quickly, quietly, and in confidence to an in-house Employee Assistance Program or an outside counseling service for care.

12. Other employees are "concerned."

In nearly every heavily-covered workplace violence homicide event, the television media manages to get frightened and shocked co-workers of both the perpetrator and his victims on camera. Once there, they either admit that they had "concerns" about the perpetrator's violent or irrational behavior prior to the incident, that they had told management about some of his more odd or worrisome outbursts or behaviors, or that once the shooting started, they had an accurate idea who was pulling the trigger and why.

These co-workers are neither clairvoyant nor behavioral experts; they simply know inappropriate, disturbing, frightening, aggressive, or violent behavior when they see it. Sadly, the perpetrator's co-workers often noticed his outbursts long before his supervisor. In these cases, more because of comfort zone-avoidance, a manager may reluctantly intervene and yet fail to head off a significant problem in time.

The employee grapevine being both powerful and persistent; news of problem employees and their bizarre behavior resonates throughout the organization before managers can take action to solve problems while they're still at potentially lower violence possibilities.

13. Chronic labor-management disputes.

This characteristic is more part of a personal, on-going dispute between the employee and his supervisor, where the worker tries to use union rules and grievance steps as part of a campaign of harassment or similar complaining behaviors. While union member dislike or even outright hatred of management is far from rare and is not necessarily related to violence, cases exist where one employee takes it upon himself to use union membership as a weapon against one or more managers or supervisors.

To recall again the case of convicted General Dynamics workplace murderer Robert Mack, he felt as though his relationship with his boss had deteriorated to a point where he needed union support from his shop steward. Due to some misunderstandings on his part and several miscommunications, even help from his union could not save his suspension for attendance nor his subsequent termination. At the termination hearing, when he was not allowed to voice his complaints (it was thought to be too late in the proceedings to affect the impact) and after his union representative could not help him win his job back, he opened fire on two managers, killing one and severely injuring the other.

Collectively, the potential for union member violence rises exponentially as contracts expire, negotiations fail, and the organization makes subtle or visible threats to hire replacement workers. Long before any possibilities of work stoppages, slowdowns, or strikes, management must have a security and employee protection plan designed and ready to put into action.

14. Numerous unresolved physical or emotional injury claims.

Some past cases of workplace violence have featured employees who have had real physical or psychological afflictions that made it difficult or impossible for them to work at their jobs. Instead of accepting this change in their lives, they took it out on people in their former organizations.

A California steelworker who had severely injured his foot on the job was recommended for a medical retirement by the company's doctor. Company officials met with the employee to decide if he should take a light duty position in the firm or medically retire. They agreed with the physician's recommendation and told the man he should retire. He disagreed and later went to the doctor's office with a shotgun, where he shot and killed him.[2]

In April 1996, a former employee of Hughes Electronics in El Segundo, California returned to the plant, shot and wounded three people, and held them hostage briefly before he was arrested. The suspect had resigned from Hughes in 1993 for health reasons related to an on-the-job neck injury. He had stated that he was angry because he wanted his job back and Hughes management had refused.

In these two cases, the person was unhappy with his health status and took it out on someone who he thought had something or everything to do with the pain. The employee with the foot injury and the one with the neck injury blamed the organization for their sudden change in employment.

What these incidents illustrate is the fragile nature of employee disability cases that—in the minds of the workers—are left unresolved. If it seems surprising that they would become upset at offers of medical retirement, remember that for many men, their work is their life. To be told that they are no longer welcome to come in and work, is too much for them to take, especially when coupled with the physical pain that forced them off the job in the first place.

As attorneys and administrators who handle workers' compensation, disability, and retirement cases will attest, it's easy for one employee's claims

2. De Becker, Gavin. "Managing the Violent Employee." *Security Management.* September 1988, p. 71.

case to look like every other one that comes into their offices. The disgruntled employee certainly does not feel that way, however.

15. Problems with working conditions.

In this era of the Americans with Disabilities Act (ADA), Chronic Fatigue Syndrome, carpal tunnel damage, ergonomic injuries, and the presence of various toxics, poisons, or other hazards in the workplace, some people have difficult times while on the job.

Certain disgruntled employees may choose certain new policies, buildings, procedures, or other operations as the focal point of their complaints. Taken to an extreme, these people can ruin the morale of other co-workers while causing management significant time or behavioral problems.

Sadly, there have been workplace violence homicides and shootings with injuries where the perpetrator-employee complained about the noise or song selections from a co-worker's radio.

16. Complaints of heightened stress at work.

Stress appears in different ways with different people. As noted previously, what might bother one employee to the point of near hysteria may not affect a co-worker at all. But like other warning signs found in this profile, numerous complaints of stress are often valid indicators of other physical or psychological health problems attacking the employee.

The disturbed employee may feel he cannot get his supervisor or co-workers to listen to his concerns about real or perceived job or life stressors, e.g. "I'm too stressed out. I feel like I'm going to explode" or "They can't expect me to work at this pace. No matter what I say to them, they keep giving me too much work. No one listens to me. No one answers my grievances and complaints. Something's got to change or I won't be held responsible for what I do."

While most disgruntled employees are vocal in their stress-related complaints, it also may be present in the loner-type employee who internalizes his feelings of stress, rage, or violence. Stress appears in physical forms in distraught employees as well, e.g. significant weight changes, sleep problems, increased alcohol use, complaints of pain, nervous tics, rapid hair loss, gastrointestinal complaints, etc.

Managers and supervisors need to keep their collective fingers on the pulse of the employee population, intervening as necessary with offers of counseling, time off, a new shift, or job rotation.

17. Majority of cases come from males between 30 and 40 years old.

Statistically, employee-on-employee workplace violence homicides (not committed during crimes like robbery, etc.) are most often committed by younger white males against older white males. This makes sense demographically because some victims are in positions of responsibility over the perpetrator-employee, as either executives, department heads, managers, or supervisors.

There is little to be changed by this fact, either in terms of race or age ranges. Though it exists, it's neither legal nor ethical to use it as some sort of pre-employment or current-employee screening device.

What it does suggest is that the perpetrators may have reached a point in their working lives where sudden changes on the job or an uncertain employment future are more difficult to cope with economically, psychologically, or emotionally.

18. Migratory job history.

This characteristic is not addressed to the computer software specialist who consults at 10 different companies over a two-year period, but at the problem-laced employee who has demonstrated throughout his adult life that he changes jobs, cities, trades, or types of jobs very frequently. While it may mean nothing but a string of jobs, more realistically it may indicate the presence of constant behavioral problems between the employee and his bosses or co-workers.

The presence of a seemingly high number of jobs in different fields, with accompanying date gaps or missing reference information, over a short period of time, should warrant further questioning during the pre-employment screening process (along with a thorough background check).

19. Drug and alcohol use and/or abuse.

As discussed in Chapter 2, some employees who have behavioral problems on and off the job choose drugs or alcohol to self-medicate themselves. But what's more frightening is their use of these substances as a preparatory, courage-building, mind-numbing tool for committing acts of violence in the workplace.

The employee with a performance-damaging drug or alcohol problem is usually in great fear of both management detection or termination. This may cause the person to act irrationally or violent in the false hopes of somehow "saving" his job.

Because the ADA legislation is so complicated, it helps to consult with a qualified attorney or personnel expert with regard to the organization's rehabilitation treatment obligations.

20. Psychiatrically impaired.

Making this determination about a seemingly disturbed employee definitely requires the skills of a violence-trained psychologist, psychiatrist, or other mental health professional. Since we shouldn't make assumptions when dealing with the intricacies of the human brain (especially if it is damaged in some way), now is not the time to make wild guesses about an employee's potential psychological problems.

Organizations and their leaders who hire and fire people must be willing to establish a relationship with a mental health professional. This can occur under the auspices of an internal Employee Assistance Program, through a retainer relationship with an outside therapist or therapy practice, or using the city or county mental health resources in the vicinity.

Through all of this profile discussion, keep in mind there is no finite or "right" number of complaints that should trigger further intervention by management. The presence of even two or three behavioral (psychographic traits as opposed to demographic ones) of these 20 factors could be enough to start the disturbed employee on a downward slide toward violence.

As an example, suppose we were near a dog's yard, and we saw it growling, snarling, and barking at us, with its tail down and fur up, and its teeth bared. And if we approached the dog's position, we saw it come toward us, puff its shoulders and chest forward, lay its ears back against its head and hood its eyes. How many people would not think this dog is ready to bite?

Most of us would agree that in the example of the dog, there is no "right" number of these characteristics that would cause us to reach the conclusion that a dog bite was in our immediate future. Some people might become very afraid if the dog merely growled aggressively, others might have to see several more indications that the dog was serious about having its space invaded. In either case, erring on the side of caution tells us that we don't need to go through the entire gamut of canine attack postures to realize we would either avoid the dog or take steps to protect ourselves from it.

In the workplace, there is no mandated requirement that a disturbed employee meet some profile criteria. In many cases involving employees with behavioral problems that make us believe in the possibility of future violence, intuition tells us in advance that we need to treat this person with more care and concern than on average. But while it's hard to pinpoint intuitive or "gut level" feelings, the existence of several of these characteristics can help to clarify or define the specific employee behavioral problems that need solving.

In other words, it makes more legal sense to suggest to the personnel manager that the employee in question has made threats, displayed a firearm at work, has shown a serious temper problem, and may have a substance abuse problem, rather than just saying, "He makes me nervous with his erratic behavior." The first set of descriptors can be put to paper as part of a discipline or termination process; the second judgement is subjective to each person looking at the employee and his behaviors.

A police officer with only a few months on the job can look at many people on the street or many cars on the road and make an amazingly accurate guess that one certain person, or one certain driver of a specific car is up to no good and involved in crime. While the phrase "I had a gut feeling about the guy and that's why I arrested him for possession of narcotics" will never make it into any police report, the intuition involved helped the officer use the other reportable factors (the person's activities, associations with others, knowledge of prior drug history, displaying objective symptoms of drug influences, etc.) to make the arrest.

Sometimes in organizations, we choose to ignore our gut feelings because they are not concrete. Instinctive feelings exist to help protect us, regardless of whether or not we can articulate them fully. So to put it into concrete terms: Inappropriate employee behaviors (related to the 20 profile characteristics or not) that make managers and supervisors and their employees uncomfortable, apprehensive, afraid, or concerned for their safety demand the organization's immediate attention and investigation.

REVIEW/SUMMARY

Since most managers dislike conflict and confrontation, they can let inappropriate, threatening, or violent behavior continue unabated while they decide what to do.

Violence in the workplace tends to be a hidden issue, especially if there is already a strong degree of physical or psychological separation between management and the employees. Executives, managers, and supervisors need to keep a finger on the pulse of the company and encourage and model the correct behaviors related to two-way communication about work issues, so managers can feel better about their relationships with all employees.

DISCUSSION QUESTIONS

1. Discuss the pros and cons of workplace violence perpetrator profiles. What is or is not effective about their development or use?

2. Is the profile discussed in this chapter a "proactive" or "reactive" tool for managers to use?

3. Explain the connection between an employee's low self-esteem and his use of violence in the workplace.

11

Problem-Solving Resources: Internal and External Help and Advice

KEY POINTS TO THIS CHAPTER
- Facility and personnel security needs
- Responding to critics of security practices
- Internal and external support resources
- Use of restraining and workplace protection orders

The New Need for Security

If real estate success is about location, location, location, then success with organizational security is all about access control, access control, and more access control.

This key to creating and maintaining a safe working environment sounds simple, but it's actually quite complex. The organization protects itself through carefully-written policies, the constant use of physical security devices and security procedures, and by helping to create and nurture the kind of employee-work culture that helps people communicate and watch out for each other.

One of the primary enemies of any security procedure, device, or professional manager, or even guard, is laxity. Some people in organizations find the need for security as inconvenient, excessive, or too much like a "police state" in their workplace.

These beliefs lead to a tradeoff between convenience and good security sense. Employees who don't put much stock in security are those who: don't wear their employee badges, offer big sighs when asked to present their employee identification cards, block open security exit or entrance doors, gates, or fences that need to be kept closed and locked, or who bypass front office or front desk security procedures by bringing or allowing unauthorized, unsupervised, or inappropriate people into the organization.

Some people only realize the new requirements for security after a workplace crime or tragedy—from a trespasser who steals five purses or a laptop computer, to a domestic violence stalker who attacks his former partner at her desk, to a recently terminated employee who walks back in and threatens his former boss with a gun.

Today, the realities of "crime in the streets becoming crime in the suites" requires more attention, at the employee and management levels, to security needs in the workplace. Regardless of the inconvenience factor or the idea that locked doors somehow transfer the organization into a more severe environment, security measures work, but only when used properly and routinely.

The problem we have yet to solve, from a security standpoint, is how to protect our public and customer-interaction business safely and effectively. This includes fastfood restaurants, retail shops and stores, convenience stores, gas stations, hospitals, and colleges.

The December 1996 shooting of three female teenage employees in a Vallejo, California McDonald's by a former male employee illustrates the problem we face: how do we protect a facility where we want customers to come and go without hassle or interference?

The former employee walked through the main customer door, saw the females working behind the counter and opened fire. He shot and killed one girl, and left two seriously wounded.

How do we respond to this from a security standpoint? A professional security consultant might advise the restaurant to install panic alarms or closed-circuit video cameras, but short of placing bulletproof glass between the customers and the food handlers, what stops an angry employee or customer from returning to an open-by-design facility with a gun?

Perpetrators and criminals bent on workplace violence can be diverted with better security devices and procedures, but will McDonald's or any similar facility want to put their customer-friendly people behind impenetrable walls? No.

But this difficulty doesn't mean we should give up and let anyone come into any of our workplaces just because they are not completely defensible. Good security balances the latest technologies, with knowledge of customers' service-driven wants and needs, and a continuing education and adjustment process that strives to protect employees and property using cost-effective yet thorough means.

Here's another example of the conflict between the need for security and the need not to intimidate or overwhelm the paying, non-threatening customers.

A large bank on the west coast has several hundred branches, some of which are prime robbery targets due to their location in high-crime neighborhoods, proximity to freeway ramps, or because they are out of sight from main roads patrolled by police. At several of these multiple-robbery branches, the bank's security managers had "mancatcher" doors installed. These consist of two sets of bullet-resistant double-doors that lead into the bank. The internal set of doors features an airport-style magnetometer calibrated to detect the presence of highly metallic objects, i.e. guns.

In practice, when a potential bank robber tries to enter the facility intent on committing an armed robbery, he opens the first set of doors closest to the parking lot and steps into a glass cubicle. When he tries to open the second set of doors and enter the bank, the scanner detects the presence of what is probably a hidden gun and automatically locks the door. When the would-be robber realizes he can't get inside, chances are excellent he'll flee.

Since the door glass is bullet-resistant, he can't shoot his way into the branch. In its best use, it's possible to double-lock the "man-trap" doors on both sides once the crook enters the first set and triggers the gun detector. This makes it rather easy for the responding police to take him into custody for bringing a firearm into a federally-protected facility.

The positive side of this system, besides its obvious use as a bank robbery prevention device, is that it's unobtrusive and looks like any other set of glass double-doors. It also helps to give nervous tellers (some of whom are veteran victims of many attempted or successful bank robberies) more peace of mind with regard to their at-work safety and security. The downside is that it is quite expensive to install and maintain.

The security industry and its professionals are constantly seeking to find the appropriate equipment and procedures to best protect employees and property from the threat of employee workplace violence or related crimes caused by outsiders. It's far from an easy task, largely because it's impossible to provide perfect security and still operate in a normal fashion.

Most people wouldn't patronize a convenience store or fastfood establishment where the employees worked always behind thick glass panels and spoke only through metallic intercoms. It's not normal to do business in this manner, even though it might offer maximum safety for the employees from outsiders or returning angry ex-employees.

Worse yet, this sterile situation only serves to remind people that we live in a violent society where the threat of violent crime is constant. To equip every store, restaurant, hospital, or public office building in this manner would signify that we have lost control of this country, the ability to function at work, and all semblance of a normal life.

The best security deterrent is the one that's invisible: people deciding not to come into a workplace and not steal from, harm, rob, or shoot the employees. Imagine how safely and successfully we could live if everyone adhered to the behavioral norms and rules of society. Since this day is far from here (if it ever arrives), we need to strike the best balance between too much security and not enough. And since security is an afterthought in most small to midsized-firms, we have much room for improvement, especially in the critical area of access control.

More leaders of firms need to start or continue to make the always-difficult investment in security improvements for their organizations. And this for the simple reason that every step they take to reduce the possibility of workplace violence or employee injuries benefits everyone involved.

Many security management professionals working inside organizations correctly see themselves as an underutilized or underappreciated resource. Their knowledge of protecting people and property often extends into this emerging area of workplace violence prevention. Many bring significant law enforcement or private security experience to their firms, and have had to deal with serious threats of violence or crimes on many levels. It's time for more companies to let these people start helping to fill in the corporate security gaps.

Stop Trying To Prove "Negatives"

One of my colleagues is both the vice president of security for a multinational defense contractor and a Certified Protection Professional (CPP), a professional designation from the American Society for Industrial Security (ASIS), which is the trade group for the corporate security industry. He is also a veteran of many meetings where his security improvement proposals and those drafted by his people receive either scant consideration or many variations on the "it's too expensive" theme.

He suggests now to other security professionals that they stop trying to convince non-security executives, managers, or employees that because nothing happened—the robbery suspect failed to appear, the employee-victim being stalked was not ever harmed, etc.—there was no need for security guards, policies, devices, or practices.

Some less than enlightened people in the organization say, "Why did we exhibit so much concern? Nothing happened, so everyone got all worked up for nothing."

This kind of thinking—"Stop scaring the employees," or "Why do we have to follow so many security procedures?"—can deter or prevent security people from doing their jobs correctly. Security people at all levels who begin to buy into this reasoning may pay a disservice to other employees who both want, need, and appreciate the presence of security in deed and presence.

And hesitant security personnel and the skeptical people who succeed in filling their heads with doubts both make one critical mistake: they don't realize the past, where nothing bad happened at work, is no indicator or the future, where something bad may still happen at work.

Recall that during the pre-employment screening process, it's possible and correct to use the applicant's past use of threats or violence at other jobs as a warning that he may behave the same way if hired here. Here, we look to the past to predict the future, since people who tended to use violence to solve other problems in their lives are more likely to use it again over those who have no history of personal violence.

But it's *not* possible nor correct to suggest that the absence of past workplace behavioral or security problems means the future looks equally as bright. Making an assessment during the hiring process of potential violence problems as exhibited by an applicant is acceptable as a threat reduction process because we don't have to predict the future; the past tells us much of what we want to know it. We don't have the same luxury of clairvoyance for the future. Therefore, when someone retorts, during any discussion of employee behavioral problems related to workplace violence, "Why worry? Nothing like that has ever happened ever here," the best reply should be, "Good. Let's work hard to keep it that way."

Internal and External Support Resources: Bringing In the Bigger Hammers

From an organizational perspective, there is safety in numbers and safety in size. Most companies and their leader have a number of resources, departments, divisions, and experts in many fields at their disposal, both on the inside and the outside. By putting these people and service groups to work, it may be possible to solve the problems created by workplace threats or employee-related domestic violence.

There are several functions and purposes to this list of support resources. One is to offer immediate help to the victim-employees of workplace violence incidents caused by other employees. The other is to provide similar help to employees, customers, or vendors who have become victims of workplace crimes caused by outsiders. Either problem may result in injuries or even deaths to these victims; management's responsibility to these parties is different in some cases, which will become clearer during the review of these resources.

Many of the following support resources exist to intervene and help solve the types of employee or outsider behavioral problems that may lead to or cause incidents of violence in the workplace. Some of them have a clear and well-established link to the problem; others may have a connection that, while less clear, is often more useful upon further examination.

Personnel or Human Resources Department

This is the department in many organizations that is tasked most with solving employee problems of all types, from counseling and grievance resolution to discipline and termination procedures. The value to this department and its members is that they are both the "keepers" of the employee records, but also of the latest knowledge of the legal side of company human resources management.

There are many personnel and human resources professionals who carry the designations "Senior Professional in Human Resources" (SPHR) or "Professional in Human Resources" (PHR). These titles, granted by the Society for Human Resources Management (SHRM), certify that the holder has passed one of two rigorous national tests on human resources management, laws, and procedures.

In many organizations, managers from the Personnel or H.R. departments serve as both sounding boards for managers or supervisors with employee behavioral problems and as the formal, procedural arm of the firm. They provide advice and either explain how to correctly, legally, and ethically administer a formal counseling, discipline, or termination proceeding, or they take over these processes once a manager and supervisor comes to them with an employee problem.

Further, these departments often serve as a liaison to other related departments, like Security, Payroll, or Employee Assistance. In some organizational chain of command charts, the Personnel or H.R. Departments are staffed by a vice presidential-level executive with direct access the Chief Executive and/ or Chief Operating Officer's office. This line connection can bring even more powerful people into the problem-solving process.

Security Department

Some firms use a formal security department, run by a security executive, department head, or security manager, and operated by a job-specific or technically-oriented staffers; a Chief of the Guards; and a uniformed security guard force.

The ranking members of this department often have a significant law enforcement background, often at the federal or state levels. Others may have much experience in recognizing and intervening in employee behavioral problems, especially those involving threat management issues, domestic violence incidents, or other risk management scenarios.

Like the Personnel or H.R. Departments, the Security Department staff keeps many records regarding past incidents (daily guard logs, vehicle accidents, injuries, theft reports, etc.). They also maintain separate policy and procedure manuals besides the standard employee P&P's that cover operational responses to security-related incidents.

As Appendix B illustrates at the close of this book, the members of the Security Department may have significant work to do if confronted with workplace violence or domestic violence problems that they discover or that are brought to them by concerned employees or their managers or supervisors.

In this regard, the Security Department should function as the primary problem-solver/intervener during any work-related criminal act or workplace violence incident, regardless of its size or seriousness. This response will include the security managers and members of the guard force, who will react to the situation by calling for medical aid or the police if necessary; separating the perpetrator(s) from the victim(s) and witness(es); preserving the scene if necessary, for later a police investigation; interviewing the parties involved; and preparing incident reports (and later executive briefing reports), the details of which should match the severity of the incident.

Employee Assistance Program

In the past, most Employee Assistance Programs (EAP's) existed outside the organization, usually via a retainer relationship. Now more EAP's are housed inside organizations as the demand for these types of services has grown.

Some external EAP's may be part of a large chain of psychological, medical, rehabilitation "group practice" services. They may establish a monthly or yearly retainer relationship, offering a 24-hour toll-free telephone to their client organizations. This number can be posted on company bulletin boards, hallway posters, and as part of new employee orientation materials.

The main advantage to this external relationship is that it saves money, since it's used on an as-needed basis and doesn't involve establishing offices and EAP employees inside the organization. The primary disadvantage is that this arm's length relationship lacks closeness to the employees of the organization. Using one of the larger national EAP programs may mean that the client-organization and the EAP provider are on opposite sides of the country. This makes it difficult for the EAP providers, i.e. psychologists, therapists, and counselors, to establish a truly personal working relationship with their employee-clients.

Some larger organizations are countering this outside approach by establishing an EAP department, specifically to deal with employee-related issues, concerns, or problems. Run by an administrator and staffed by various personnel or human resources specialists, these departments also may employ clinical and/or industrial psychologists who are on-staff, on-site, and ready at a moment's notice to intervene with many types of counseling. This may include crisis counseling, e.g. for an employee threatening suicide, following a workplace accident that kills a worker, for a victim-employee of domestic violence at home or work, and for our discussion purposes, to respond to a workplace violence incident involving injury or death.

Regardless of whether the EAP function is external or internal, every manager and supervisor in the organization *must* know the referral procedures and the related processes to get a victim-employee or a perpetrator-employee into the counseling environment. These referral steps should be written down in a readable, convenient, and non-threatening format, so that managers and supervisors can feel comfortable when referring an employee to the department.

Further, the subject of total confidentiality *must* be addressed and confirmed in all employee and management literature about the EAP department and process. Nothing will destroy the EAP function faster than threats to what should be a guarantee of confidentiality.

As an example, every branch of our military services offers some form of EAP, through a personnel or counseling department. Some of these programs address alcohol and drug problems, family or domestic violence, financial problems, or other on or off-the-job problems that may be exacerbated by military service. While these programs have been effective for service members, there are concerns and complaints around confidentiality issues. Many military personnel worry that their use of this form of EAP to combat their personal problems will be subject to review by their superiors or part of negative information that may affect their annual or bi-annual "fitness reports" or promotional evaluations. True or not, this perception exists in the military and can seriously harm the employee-services provider relationship.

In the private sector, managers and supervisors must feel confident in the EAP providers or they will not refer their employees to the program, regardless of the situation. It only takes a few negative encounters with the EAP program for its administrators to develop a reputation that will preclude people from coming in for help.

To use a workplace violence incident as an EAP service example, let's suppose that after a long series of disagreements, one employee threatens to batter another employee, and even grabs him before other co-workers intervene. The manager of both people will initiate an investigation by departmental members of the Personnel or Human Resources, Security, and Employee Assistance.

In this case, the EAP will serve different purposes for the two sides. For the victim-employee, they can offer counseling services to deal with feelings of fear or anger. For the perpetrator, they can insist on anger, stress, or behavioral management classes or formal counseling sessions as a requirement to return to work. Depending upon the language used in the organization's workplace violence prevention policy, the EAP can work with Personnel/Human Resources to enforce behavioral changes in the perpetrator-employee as a condition of continued employment.

Remember that the employee-victim may not necessarily require EAP services for a workplace violence threat or incident. You can't force a victim of home or workplace crime or violence to accept counseling; you can only offer it as an option, both to protect the rights and feelings of the employee and to protect the organization from future claims of insensitivity.

Psychological Services

Many firms retain or employ psychologists, either as part of the EAP department, in place of it, or as a resource for future employee behavioral problems.

And while the most common use of these services relates to an employee's personal problems, from a crime or violence perspective, they can be equally as useful. As the EAP description above suggests, victim-employees of real or threatened workplace violence incidents may want (albeit reluctantly at first) to talk to a mental health counselor to deal with their feelings of fear, anxiety, or death. And the perpetrator-employee may have no choice but to attend behavioral counseling, if he wishes to stay employed. More and more psychologists and psychotherapists who work in and around organizations are now very sensitive to the possibilities of violence in the workplace, especially at the more severe and dangerous ends of the violence spectrum.

And perhaps it is during the most difficult periods following a workplace violence tragedy that psychological services prove valuable. In the hours and days after a workplace violence homicide, suicide, or serious injury, on-scene psychologists can offer immediate crisis counseling to any employee who desires it.

And some firms who have had to face a workplace violence homicide witnessed by customers, vendors, or other non-employees have taken the rare and commendable step to offer free therapy sessions to them as well. One notable case involved a fastfood restaurant chain based in the southeast part of the country which had a serious shooting incident at one of its locations. Following the shooting, which injured several people during a robbery attempt, the parent company offered free crisis counseling to every employee who asked for it and for every customer in the restaurant at the time who needed it as well.

Unknowing critics would argue that offering counseling to non-employees is prohibitively expensive. In reality, the cost for the sessions (usually three to five meetings will help the people regain their emotional equilibrium) is far outweighed by the benefits to the organization. While paying for counseling for all who need it pays dividends in positive public relations, it exemplifies the need and desire for organization leaders to become socially responsible in their communities.

Family or Close Friends

Since we realize workplace violence threats and acts are driven or based on the behaviors of certain disturbed employees, perhaps the influence of people close to those employees will help divert their desire to injure others.

In this respect, as part of a complete intervention process initiated by members of Personnel/Human Resources, Security, or Employee Assistance, it may help to bring the power of either proximity to the employee or peer pressure into the process.

Obviously, bringing others into the realm of potential workplace violence requires much sensitivity to both perceptions by all parties and by the dangers it may create.

As an example, a man who had worked as a supervisor at an east coast defense plant for 15 years was told by his manager that within six months, his position would be discontinued for budget reasons. He was offered a transfer to a lesser-paying job in another department, severance pay, outplacement help, and career counseling as part of this wind-down period.

As the six-month mark approached, the man became increasingly depressed and began to make statements like, "If I can't work I have nothing to live for. If I have nothing to live for, there are some people around this place who should come with me." He also made some frightening references to a recent workplace violence homicide incident in a nearby city.

At this point, the security manager, who knew the man's wife from having met her throughout the years at company social functions, took the bold step to call her and express his concerns. She verified that the employee had made similar disturbing statements to her and that she was also quite concerned. Working together, she and the security manager developed an intervention plan where she helped to get her husband into a company-sponsored psychological counseling program. This helped the man alter his feelings and accept his career change. Using the company's offer of outplacement services, he was able to get another job when his ended.

Employee Leaders

Another example of this type of outside support or internal peer pressure may happen more informally. In cases where an employee is bullying others or making harassing phone calls to other employees, a more veteran employee, who is not necessarily a manager or supervisor, may intervene on the company's or the victims' behalf. The employee leader might say, "Look, what you're doing is hurting a lot of other people around here. It's bad for business and it makes you look bad. You've got to quit this stuff before you lose your job."

This may be enough to stop these behaviors or it may indicate that a more serious intervention is now necessary. Keep in mind that the informal employee leader doesn't threaten the problem employee, only tries to help him see the error of his ways. Sometimes, with certain people in certain jobs or industries, hearing "It's time to stop" from a respected employee can be more powerful than hearing it from a manager or supervisor.

Labor/Industrial Relations Department

In organizations with a union presence, controlling or preventing employee behavioral problems will require help from members of the Labor or Industrial Relations Departments. These managers have special and specific knowledge of union policies, contractual requirements, and grievance or discipline processes that other managers and supervisors may lack.

Any intervention into a union employee's problems with threats or the use of violence at work should cause an immediate response by the Labor or IR departments. They should know how to enforce company workplace violence zero-tolerance policies and still respect the rights of the employee as negotiated by the union contract.

This expertise is especially necessary in organizations that employ members of several different unions on site, not just one.

Union Representatives/Shop Stewards

Designated union representatives and on-site shop stewards will want to become involved in employee-member behavioral issues. This may happen at a macro level—offering input into the creation of workplace violence prevention policies (since they realize their members may be either victims or perpetrators) and discussions with management as to how to fairly and legally answer grievances, administer discipline, or initiate terminations. Or it may happen at a micro level, involving a specific employee who has violated workplace violence policies and may require advice from his union representative.

In either event, managers and supervisors should see the presence of union management or shop stewards as members of the organization's workplace violence intervention team.

It's no secret that union-management relationships have ranged historically from toxic and difficult to helpful and positive. During any investigation of workplace violence threats or acts, both sides need to respect the positions of the other, keep their actions and statements focused on solving behavioral problems, and keep both union employees and management safe from harm.

Senior Management

Executive members of the organization can best contribute to the prevention of workplace violence in three areas: help in the discussions and design of zero-tolerance prevention policies; support lower-level managers and supervisors in their efforts to enforce these policies; and "walk the talk" by being open, visible, and in communication with employees at every level in the organization.

One factor we know appears during some workplace violence incidents in large organizations is the perpetrator-employee's desire to strike back at senior management, i.e. the CEO or president's office by injuring a manager or supervisor. This hatred often rises out of the disturbed employee's feeling that the "suits upstairs" neither know nor care about the needs of the rank and file employees.

The visibility of senior executives, the president, or the CEO doesn't have to be a huge ordeal or a complicated process; people just want to know the company's key leaders are real people who care about their concerns.

Bill Marriott, whose hotel chain bears his family name, makes it a point to shake the hand of every single employee on the premises when he visits one of his hotel properties. Bill Gates leads his Microsoft employees in near-revival meetings to announce new products or new strategic directions for the firm. Executive visibility and verified and valid commitment pays hidden dividends in the employee culture. Frankly, it's also cheap workplace violence prevention insurance.

Corporate Counsel

Like the presence of company psychologists, corporate attorneys may work as actual employees of the organization or as part of a retainer relationship.

Part of any good business attorney relationship must include the presence of some lawyers who have skills and knowledge in labor law, hiring practices, discipline and termination procedures, and the legal response to employee behavioral issues.

Today, more and more corporate attorneys have familiarized themselves with the changing and complicated issues surrounding workplace violence and its prevention. Some of these attorneys help draft, review, and implement the firm's zero-tolerance workplace violence policies and procedures and then teach this information to company managers and supervisors in formal or informal training classes.

And while company attorneys help to create policies, they can assist others as they enforce them as well. Perhaps no other example is as clear as their ability to draft temporary or permanent restraining or harassment orders to protect individual employees and the organization in total.

We have seen more attention and awareness paid to the subject of domestic violence. We know from recent events that domestic violence and related stalking behaviors appear in the workplace more than ever. To combat the problem of domestic violence in the home, many cities and counties have increased the number of protection and restraining orders granted to victims of this type of abuse.

But while the use of personal temporary restraining orders (TRO's) has increased, the impetus to get these civil orders and have them served typically falls upon the victim. In a perfect world, the (usually female) victim of domestic violence gets time off from work, goes to a family court in the county, completes the paperwork, and then waits for a judge to review the causes, and either grant or reject the TRO request.

Then the marshals, constables, or other local law enforcers serve the perpetrator and file the order so any violation is now an illegal act.

And again in a perfect world, the perpetrator respects the order and leaves the victim alone, both at home or at work. (In actuality, TRO's are successful about 50% of the time; the number goes higher if both parties are served.)

Since we live in an imperfect world, what often happens is that the victim-employee of domestic violence (targeted at either home or work or, not surprisingly, at both) is chastised by her supervisor for the distractions caused by a domestic violence problem, is not allowed time off to get the TRO, and suddenly develops fears of both losing her job *and* being harassed, stalked, or attacked by the suspect.

Even after going through all of these steps alone, the victim-employee may face reluctance on the part of the organization to help her enforce and report TRO violations by the perpetrator. This may include trying to dissuade her from calling the police from work, or allowing the police to arrest the suspect on company premises (made even more difficult and complex if the perpetrator works for the same company).

In short, the domestic violence victim gets victimized by the perpetrator, the criminal justice/family court system that makes it often difficult to get a TRO, and by her employer, who may fail to see that a domestic violence problem at home may affect the performance or safety of others at the workplace.

In this spirit, some states and most notably, California, have created a specific restraining order that denotes the company and the victim-employee as dual victims in any threat of violence that suggests a protection order.

As of July 1995, the California Code of Civil Procedure section 527.8 allows for an organization to call itself a victim or co-victim and restrain a perpetrator from coming on or close to the premises with the intent to harass, stalk, or injure the victim-employee, or by proxy, any other employee of the firm.

This new protection order does not supersede or eliminate the need for a personal TRO; depending upon the state or circumstances, the employee may still need to get a TRO. The "Workplace Harassment Order," as it is sometimes called, broadens the protection umbrella from the specific employee, to *every* employee. This means that the organization can demonstrate due diligence as to the safety and security problems threatened by domestic violence.

And this new order is not just for threats of domestic violence. It could be used to protect the organization and an individual manager being stalked by a former and now disgruntled ex-employee.

While this order exists in California, company attorneys in other states may be able to use it as a template model to draft a similar order in their state.

Municipal, State, and Federal Law Enforcement

Some people in organizations still think of themselves and their problems as either immune from the hands of crime or violence or not deserving of the services provided by law enforcement. In reality, city police and county sheriff agencies can offer significant education, prevention, and intervention help to any type of size of organization.

Federal law enforcement tends to have highly specific duties that also can be applied to specific workplace violence problems, e.g. the Bureau of Alcohol, Tobacco, and Firearms (BATF) investigates bombing incidents at a factory during a strike or as part of a violence outburst; the Federal Bureau of Investigation (FBI) may respond to incidents involving federal crime violations or crime or violence incidents involving employees with security clearances.

There are two critical keys to working with law enforcement agencies: call them in early and help them do their job by providing access and information; and ask for more than a cursory response to a valid workplace violence incident, including a follow-up.

Some organizations violate the first concern when they wait too long to contact them following a workplace event where an employee is injured. (If a customer assaulted an employee or was assaulted by an employee, it's more likely that this time lapse would not happen.) The reasons for this hesitancy center around management's desire not to make a "mountain out of a molehill" following a "minor" incident between employees;

not to upset customers, alert the news media or competitors about the problem; or because they believe, perhaps correctly, that they are either "bothering" the police or that the police will not respond or give the incident due seriousness.

In reality, law enforcement has a duty to respond to all calls for service, even inside a company, and especially if it involves a workplace violence incident with injuries.

Cases that call for a police response should involve: the stalking of an employee by a known or unknown person; any incident where any employee, customer, or vendor is injured by another employee; any on-site employee suicide; where any employee, customer, or vendor is injured by an outsider/criminal; following robberies, burglaries, or serious cases of theft, vandalism, or sabotage of employee or company property or grounds; or stolen or sabotaged computer equipment or intentional data destruction.

The organization in general and anxious managers and supervisors in particular should see law enforcement as an ally rather than an outsider. The firm's responsibility is to assist the police as best as possible, but also to insist upon a complete investigation and a follow-up report that gives the organization options for prosecution, civil protection, or restitution.

Police officers and detectives who respond to unusual workplace violence events (assaults, batteries, over more recognizable criminal-driven acts like robberies) may exhibit tacit or real reluctance to initiate much action, not because they want to ignore crimes at work, but because they have been hampered by other organizations during similar cases in the past. It can be demotivating for an officer or investigator to conduct a full case investigation only to hear leaders of the organization say, "Thanks for coming out, but we've decided to just drop this matter or handle it in-house."

Just as the organization's leaders shouldn't take no for an answer when working with law enforcement or the criminal justice system, they shouldn't say no to their attempts to enforce criminal law violations in the workplace.

City, County, State, Federal Legislative Bodies

Finally, many government agencies have taken the lead when it comes to the subject of occupational violence, the protection of employees from the threat of injury or death, and specifically, the safety of women and other potential domestic violence or stalking victims in the workplace. In years past, few states had anti-stalking laws with any teeth to them. Now,

almost every state in the U.S. has a penal code stalking section that addresses the problem in terms where it's no longer necessary for the victim to be
injured before police or the organization can respond.

The existence of the workplace harassment order in California and its
growing use in other states demonstrates also that many legislators and
lawmakers are concerned about the safety of their constituents at home
and at work.

Since there are no perfect solutions to the threats or acts of workplace
violence, we can only attempt to apply the most practical and powerful
resources our organization or our communities can bring to bear. Some
or all of these aforementioned resource groups may work as a safe, legal
and reliable intervention solution to a workplace violence threat or incident;
others may work alone or only in conjunction with several groups, resources,
or steps.

Some potential workplace violence problems may never leave the confines of the organization; other more serious problems may require a massive intervention effort on the part of many people or departments inside
the firm, and many social service or law enforcement agencies outside it.

The value to this list is that it should help nervous managers and supervisors sleep more soundly at night, knowing they do not and should not
have to face a workplace violence issue alone. Regardless of the size of the
firm, or whether or not it contains these listed departments, groups, or
resources, there is always more help available than might first meet the eye.

REVIEW/SUMMARY

Knowing how and why to protect all of the company's assets — physical, intangible, psychological, and human — is one of the cornerstones of
providing a safe working environment.

There are dozens of available resources company leaders can use to solve
this problem from a position of power and strength. This chapter offered
guidelines about what types of people and groups, both inside and outside
the organization, can assist managers and supervisors with employee behavioral problems.

Once we know what behaviors to look for and what kinds of incidents constitute workplace violence or the threat of it, we must know how to safely
and effectively deal with problem employees. We must create viable and con-
flict-minimizing policies while still maintaining an atmosphere of compliance. When these steps fail, it's time to call in security or law enforcement help.

DISCUSSION QUESTIONS

1. What are some ways people take security shortcuts, either at home or work? What is their reasoning?

2. Do you think customers feel comfortable doing business with a gas station, store, bank, or moneyhandling establishment if high-security glass separates them from the employees? Why or why not?

3. Compare the differences between an internal EAP department and an external EAP service. What are the advantages or disadvantages of each?

4. If TRO's are only successful half the time in stopping stalking or harassing behavior, why should victims or the organization get them?

5. How could company management improve the way it works with law enforcement following a serious workplace violence incident?

12

Workplace Violence Prevention Strategies: Pre- and Post-Incident Responses and Plans For the Future

KEY POINTS TO THIS CHAPTER
- Safe discipline and termination strategies
- Pre-attack behaviors
- The need for better interaction with police
- The impact of workplace violence on victims
- Evacuation and post-response plans

Safe Discipline and Termination Event Strategies

The use of the word "event" to describe employee discipline or termination is no accident. It is and should be a major event for the manager or supervisor, just as we need to realize it is for the employee about to be counseled, corrected, or let go.

In this era of rising workplace violence, it's not surprising the subjects of employee discipline and termination now make more managers and supervisors uncomfortable. They read the newspapers and hear the media reports that describe cases where recently-disciplined or terminated employees have returned with fire in their eyes and firearms in their hands.

What makes these situations even more difficult is that because they exist, some managers and supervisors may be hesitant to use proper discipline or actual terminations for borderline, disturbed, or just plain ineffective employees. This reluctance may be under the surface of their thinking, and while they would never admit it publicly or to their peers, it exists enough to influence their actions.

Going back to the theme raised in Chapter 1 of fear of in the workplace, disturbed, disgruntled employees may recognize the power of fear to help control their own situations. Some people who have behavioral problems can become highly manipulative. This may lead to an uncomfortable mix: the manager's reluctance to intervene because of thoughts of future retribution, and an employee who successfully controls the situation with implied threats, rationalizations, or coercive negotiating techniques, e.g. "If you fire me, I'll sue."

At this point it's time to recognize that the vast majority of employees who are counseled, disciplined, or terminated, deal with the ramifications of these events in mostly normal ways. They may be unhappy, they may not like the fact that their behavior at work has come into question, and they may become upset at the prospects of having to go out and find a new job. But they will not choose to strike back at the organization or the people responsible for their unhappiness because no matter how mad they get, they realize on many conscious or subconscious levels that responding with violence is the wrong thing to do. For these people, their response to discipline or termination is conventional and while their anger may be fleeting and even intense, it does not jeopardize other people in the organization.

To go back to the old 80-20 rule, if this group, who responds in a reasonable manner to counseling, discipline, or termination, represents 80 percent of the adult employee population, then it is the remaining 20 percent who react unreasonably, inappropriately, or in ways that may make their current or former managers and supervisors uncomfortable.

And to continue this use of the 80-20 rule one step further, if 80 percent of the unreasonable group is obnoxious, argumentative, or hostile, but non-violent and non-threatening, then it is the remaining 20 percent who pose the most serious and likely threat of violence. In other words, the 20 percent of the 20 percent will demand the most management attention, in terms of careful handling, more legal documentation, the use of additional security measures, and stepped up awareness throughout key departments in the organization.

Experts constantly debate the reasons why some employees respond with violence following termination. Many suggest it starts with the economic shock of a sudden job loss (Even if the problem employee was well-aware of the possibility), where the employee realizes he might be out of money in a matter of days, weeks, or months.

Others speculate that some disciplined or terminated employees take these events as a personal affront to their ego, social status, or gender position. Some men see discipline, suspension, or termination as a blow to their iconic status as a male, job-holding, bread-winning, productive member of society. Any organizational intervention into this ego-fragile self-perception is seen as threatening and for some, must receive an equally threatening response in return.

Then there is the belief that people who respond with violence following discipline, suspension, or termination have reached their "dynamic moment." At this point in their lives, their personal problems, drug or alcohol abuses, and off-the-job difficulties hit an apex point of utter failure where the employee sees no reason not to respond back with violence. In other words, a suspension or a termination is seen as the final straw that breaks the camel's back, and that animal was already standing precariously near a cliff.

And finally, there are those who see the use of violence as the hallmark of an employee with serious emotional, personality, and psychological problems. These are people who are flawed or become flawed and make flawed choices, deciding that violence is both acceptable, and (in their minds) a logical solution.

The managers and supervisors who must initiate discipline or termination events need not be well-schooled in every behavioral problem possibility; they just have to know that the 20 percent of the 20 percent exists and will demand different handling. (For further intervention, they can get practical advice from the firm's EAP department or psychological services, or bring in a qualified threat assessment professional.)

Today, most managers and supervisors are familiar with the concept of "progressive discipline," where the organization takes the time to go through a number of progressively more serious interventions with problem employees to get them to change their work behaviors. This concept is best described in Dick Grote's well-crafted book, *Discipline Without Punishment* (AMACOM, 1995.)

Using progressive discipline, employees go through a structured process, starting with informal counseling, formal counseling, a note added to their personnel file, (referral to EAP for psychological or rehabilitation services, if necessary), an unpaid suspension, a paid suspension, and finally, termination.

Along this well-guided path, the motivation to change and keep their jobs is taken off the shoulders of the managers or supervisors and placed firmly on to those of the employees. This avoids much blaming, finger-pointing, whining, and rationalizing.

Notice the presence of the "paid day off" step, just prior to the employee's termination. Using this unique application of progressive discipline, the manager says, "We have decided to send you home to take a fully-paid day-off. We will pay your full salary for the day to stay at home and decide if you really want to continue to work here. If, after you come back the next day, you've decided you can no longer work here, we'll understand and help you wrap things up here. But if you decide you do want to stay employed here, you have to be willing to come in and tell me how you plan to change to keep your job."

The value to this approach is that it gives the employee a clear choice: make a decision to leave or make a decision to change and stay, without the sanction of missed money in the process. Because we now know that many disgruntled employees responded with violence because of their economic fears, this offers a bit of a pleasant surprise for them—a paid day-off.

While it may cost the firm some money from the payroll, it lessens the impact of the suspension and places the onus of the decision to stay and change or leave right back where it belongs—with the employee. This small investment in money demonstrates a strong sense of ethical employee treatment as well. If the employee decides to leave, the money spent for that one day is inconsequential; if the employee stays, it's with the understanding that one more violation is subject to immediate, non-negotiable termination.

This idea of special treatment grates many long-time managers and supervisors as excessive, unnecessary, wasteful, and unfair to other employees. "Why should we have to bend over backward because some guy doesn't like the way he was treated and starts making threats? Why can't we just send him packing and get back to business?"

This sentiment is understandable, but wrong. The fact is that some employees will demand special attention or treatment by management; wishing it were not true won't help much. There is little consolation to be found by saying, "We should have done this..." or "We should have recognized the problem and taken these steps..." following a workplace violence injury or death.

Further, most managers and supervisors who understand the potential realities of violence in the workplace know that they must respond with additional resources or practices when handling discipline and termination, or they will risk civil suits by either the disturbed employee or his frightened co-workers.

What every manager and supervisor needs to understand is that when dealing with the problem employee who suggests or threatens violence, it's time to change from the usual procedures to more specific, "unusual" ones.

The "usual" method for conducting a discipline or termination session is to put the manager and the employee, i.e. the "discipliner" and the "disciplinee" or the "terminator" and the "terminatee," in a room alone, with the door shut.

While this method may work well for the 80 percent of those employees who will accept, even grudgingly, the process, it makes little sense for the 20 percent group. If you knew prior to the session, or even during it, that the employee was already highly disgruntled, threatening, or even had used violence at work as the reason for the discipline or termination, would you want to be locked in a room alone with this person?

And yet, some managers, even those with significant personnel and human resources experiences, still put themselves into this potentially hostile or dangerous situation. It's time to change those dynamics and realize there is safety in numbers.

In this scenario, where the manager or supervisor must discipline or terminate a highly-disturbed or previously-violent employee for violations of company policies, including the zero-tolerance workplace violence policies, it's time to bring in more help.

Some people faced with this situation would jump to the conclusion that this meeting scenario requires the presence of two beefy and armed security guards. While this sounds plausible, it's hard to imagine how it would not make the situation inexorably worse by their mere attendance. Facing security officers during the meeting may, in reality, urge the employee to start more threatening or violent behavior.

More realistically, those attending this "unusual" meeting should include some or all of the following people: the manager or supervisor, his or her boss, a manager from Personnel or Human Resources, a manager from the EAP Department, or a psychologist or mental health counselor.

Now all of these people could not only crowd the room, but intimidate the employee in ways similar to the presence of the security guards. Each situation is different and will require careful thought before responding. This points to the need for managers to train and actually practice for high-stress discipline and termination events.

Here's how one firm does it: The employee is brought into a conference room that features a large table and a split-wall glass partition on one side of the room. The manager and his or her direct boss may start the meeting together, while some of the other participants wait outside the room and watch (somewhat discreetly) through the glass. Also with them on the outside of the glass is the security manager or a security officer who has close access to both an outside telephone line and an inside communication device back to the security office.

If the proceedings go along without incident, the employee will leave the premises and receive a "loose escort" to his desk or work area, and then another "loose escort" to the HR office (to sign exit papers and arrange for severance, etc.), the security desk (to turn in ID cards and security badges), or to the front door closest to the employee parking area. (Courts have sided with embarrassed employees who have argued that a security escort outside the building or blatantly in full view of co-workers is humiliating and subject to civil damages.)

If the proceedings turn tense, one or both managers can quietly signal to individual or collective members of the outside observation group to come in and assist. At this point, the security manager or officer continues to monitor the safety of the meeting from outside the conference room, ready to call in more security support if necessary.

If the situation deteriorates into shouts or threats, the most qualified person to abate the problem is now the company psychologist or mental health counselor. He or she can clear the room (sending the management participants back to their same outside observation positions) and offer immediate crisis counseling to the distraught employee. This portion of the session serves to offer the employee solutions, outplacement help, psychological counseling, and other options that defuse his anger away from the organization and specific people.

If the psychologist cannot defuse the employee or the threats continue, he or she can signal the security manager or officer to notify the police and additional security assistance.

This approach is not without its faults. It demands preparation, practice, and training. It uses also the time and use of many highly-paid organizational professionals. And it suggests the creation of a discipline or termination room setting that may be different then the usual locked manager's door.

But it offers more than a few pluses as well. It takes the manager and employee out of a potentially-dangerous one-on-one situation; it provides other observers who can serve as accurate witnesses to the events should the employee try to make later civil claims; it offers better security protection without being intrusive about it; and it suggests to the employee that his behavior now and in the future, is a serious management concern.

It works well to help defuse typical behavioral-response problems regarding women disciplining or terminating men; physical size differences between the manager and employee; race/age differences which some employees try to use as the "real" cause for their dismissals; and it helps to change the "danger dynamics" of already-difficult organizational interventions.

When Should We Worry?

To answer the previous irritated query of the manager who says, "Why do we have to concern ourselves with this person's problems?" consider this statement as a primary motivator:

Any disgruntled, destructive, or violent employee who *continues* to escalate his behavior; even when faced with progressive discipline, suspension, or termination, should cause alarm bells across the organization to ring.

Why? Faced with a heightened response by the employee it's time to assume his danger factor is rising. As Bill Murray said when faced with his first ghost in the movie "Ghostbusters," "Okay, the usual stuff's not working."

Here, the perpetrator-employee may be gearing up for one last act of violence as a final response to his failure as an employee and his self-perception of failure as a person.

Threat assessment expert Gavin de Becker, whose client protection list includes many of Hollywood's most notable people and studios, refers to disturbed people as following certain internal "scripts," which may "tell" them to prepare themselves to be violent.

Some warning signs that may signal the employee's onset toward "preparatory behavior" include: speaking about how the "end is near"; giving away possessions to family members; paying bills months in advance, especially for life insurance premiums; trying to making peace with other non-targets like family or love relationships; or otherwise exhibiting what witnesses later refer to as an "eerie calmness" prior to the incident.

Two cases illustrate these pre-attack behaviors in reality. Prior to his attack at the General Dynamics plant in San Diego, California, Robert Mack told his girlfriend to drive him to his termination hearing. On the way to the plant, he made statements like, "Take care of yourself and the house," and "Try to make a good life for yourself." He told her that she didn't have to wait around and that he wouldn't need a ride home.

A recently terminated perpetrator-employee in an Asheville, North Carolina multiple workplace homicide case gave all his possessions to his mother, including his clothing, before heading back to the plant. He had been fired for fighting in the employee breakroom, the culmination of three years of other threatening, confrontive, and assaultive behaviors.

Most employees in the 80 percent scenarios will usually take the bad news about discipline and within a short time, either decide themselves to change their behavior and save their job, or they won't. If they don't, they'll recognize they're subject to termination and may leave prior, or accept it when it arrives.

For those in the more threatening 20 percent group, no amount of counseling, discipline sessions, or threats of termination will force them or cause them to change their behavior. In fact, as the pressure from the organization increases, their potential to use immediate violence increases exponentially as well.

When progressive discipline has failed on every level, the employee moves himself from an irritating management problem to an organizational threat. It may be time to escalate the company's response to match the employee's potentially dangerous actions. This may include the need to file a workplace harassment order against the person, change security devices like door locks, initiate heightened security patrols and practices (posting his employee photo in the security office), or notifying law enforcement.

When Should We Call the Police?: Pre-and Post-Attack Behaviors

In July 1995, the City of Industry, California Post Office was the scene of an employee shooting. The suspect, a 59-year-old mail handler with decades on the job, shot and killed his supervisor, after hitting him during a fight minutes before.

With the concept of rising danger factors in mind, consider how this tragedy played itself out:

On the day of the shooting, the employee had argued vehemently with his boss (first warning sign). As the argument concluded, the supervisor turned to walk away to blow off steam. As he did, the employee struck him with his fist in the head (second warning sign; a crime of violence was just committed).

After other co-workers separated the men, the supervisor went to another part of the mail-handling facility to report the incident to his boss and to care for his injury. The employee prepared to leave the plant (third warning sign). In the employee parking lot, the employee went to his car and opened the trunk (fourth warning sign; he should not be allowed to leave prior to a police response).

He fished around in his car trunk and returned back inside the plant holding a paper bag (fifth warning sign; don't let disgruntled employees back inside, especially when holding an unidentifiable object). The employee walked around the work area until he found his supervisor (sixth warning sign; keep the victim-employee and the perpetrator-employee separated).

Finding his boss, he pulled a handgun from the bag and fired two shots, killing him. As he was being restrained by other employees, the man kept asking, "Did I get him? Did I get him?"

The employee in this case agreed to a plea bargain and accepted a sentence of 22 1/2 years-to-life for a federal second-degree murder charge.

While it's always easy to review these incidents in the clear light of hindsight, the fact remains that the two best intervention opportunities in this case came following the initial argument between the employee and his boss and the subsequent fight where the employee struck him.

To put it in succinct terms: Any time a crime of actual violence occurs in the workplace, it's time to call the police. If an employee is struck, punched, kicked, or injured in any manner by another, it should become automatically and without much debate, a police matter. When the police officers arrive, the organization's leaders should explain the situation, and the need for an investigation, a full report, and if necessary, an arrest of the perpetrator.

Granted, the arrival of the police make this scenario difficult under the best of circumstances, in this era of both the threat of workplace violence and the threat of civil suits directed at both the organization and individual managers, the police response helps to address the firm's due diligence requirements.

Even if the police make a determination that no report, investigation, or arrest is necessary in the situation, their presence offers documentable proof of management's concern for the legal rights of the victim-employee and the overall safety of eyewitness co-workers. If a civil case erupts later as a result of the incident, management can attest that the police were called, they took certain steps to determine the extent of the situation, they advised the victim-employee of his or her rights of citizen's arrest, and if so, they documented the incident on an official, court-approved report. (One of the immediate responsibilities of either the security or human resources manager is to obtain later a copy of any police reports for archival purposes.)

Since past violence may be an accurate indicator of future violence, the onset of a seemingly small act of workplace violence may serve as the instigator for other problems. In the City of Industry case, the gap between one act of employee violence and another was a matter of minutes; in other incidents, it might be days, weeks, or months. The presence of the police sends many positive, powerful messages to victims, perpetrators, and every other employee on the scene.

The Enforcement-Punishment Paradox

The increased use of law enforcement services to respond to acts of workplace violence should be part of an additional overall relationship between businesses and the police in general.

As noted before, the relationship between companies and the police is usually influenced by preconceived notions one group has about the other. Most police interventions or calls for service focus on the streets or in or near peoples' homes. When police officers go to a business, it's usually to take a burglary report, investigate a threat, or respond to a retail-oriented crime in progress like a robbery.

As such, they often believe that crimes inside large organizations are "handled by in-house security people, not us." And so because they may not have much contact with what seems like a nameless, faceless company, they don't make the connection to workplace violence prevention or awareness education through more interaction.

From their perspective, some managers and supervisors do believe that it is the function of an internal security department to investigate most workplace problems or crimes. With this mindset in place, it becomes easier to say, "That's why we have a security department.... let them do their jobs."

All this creates the following enforcement-punishment dilemma not unlike two baseball outfielders circling under a fly ball, both saying, "You take it! No, I've got it!" in the same breath.

Suppose a man goes into a grocery store and steals two bottles of liquor. When he is detained by the store security agents, he will be taken into the back room to await the arrival of the police. Before they arrive, the store security people will record his name, take his photograph and one of what he stole, and write their in-store incident report.

When the police arrive, they have several options, including: arrest the man and take him to jail for petty theft or write him a petty theft citation and release him at the scene. Later, the man will have to make a court appearance or risk a bench warrant.

Let's change this scenario in one way; suppose this time an employee of the grocery store is caught after stealing two bottles of liquor. What is the most common or usual response to this crime? The employee is made to return the items and is fired on the spot. What follows is usually a stern warning about never coming back to the store, or never asking for a reference. The employee turns in his or her uniform and name badge and leaves in shame.

What's missing from the second scenario that was in the first? Clearly, the presence and enforcement actions of the police. The only thing different between these two incidents of theft was the employment status of the participants. Why was the employee not subject to the same sanctions as the stranger? Is theft not theft, no matter who does it?

From our perspective in this textbook, consider a similar situation: A man comes into a convenience store and gets into a heated argument with the manager over buying beer after hours. Following the clash, the man punches the manager in the jaw. What just happened? A crime of violence was committed in the workplace.

At this point, the manager will call the police. If they get there when the suspect is still on the premises, they will detain him and advise the manager he or she can make a citizen's arrest. If the manager agrees, they will take the man to jail for battery or write him a battery citation for a later court appearance.

In the same convenience store, suppose an employee gets into a heated argument with his boss, the store manager, and punches him in the jaw. What is the most usual or most common response following this incident?

The store manager fires the employee on the spot, demands that he gives back his work shirt, and tells him that his last paycheck will be sent to him by the parent company headquarters. With that, the employee is sent out, told never to darken this door again, and that's the end of that.

Once again, why weren't the police called to investigate this crime of violence? What message does the missing police response send to other worried, future victim-employees who learn of these theft or violence incidents? What message does it send to other future perpetrator-employees, who want to know what might happen to them in similar circumstances?

In organizations that have a Security Department, they can and should conduct their own internal investigation into any criminal act, standing right alongside the police as they work. Company security should document the scene and serve as additional eyes and ears for responding police officers. The two groups should and need to work in harmony with each other, not in discord.

Again, as discussed during the previous section on the need to call police following workplace crimes of violence, the organization needs to send the right message: "We will use our written policies and procedures, the Labor Code, the Civil Code, and our state's Penal Code to enforce work rules, and educate and protect all of our employees from the threat of any form of serious crime or violence."

The Circles of Workplace Violence Victimhood

Some managers and supervisors are too quick to dismiss a punch to the face as somehow a minor incident of workplace violence, not calling for a police response or a serious investigation by the company. As one jaded manager I know put it to me, "C'mon! No one died, and besides, that's the way some people are..."

In a similar vein, some outsiders in other organizations as yet untouched by violence in the workplace or media members have viewed a criminal act like a robbery and subsequent homicide of an employee as somehow not a "true" act of violence in the workplace. "It's a robbery and a homicide. It's an unfortunate incident. But how is that 'workplace violence'?"

The short answer is that no one expects or deserves to be killed at work. When it happens to any employee of any organization from a small business owner to the hostess of a national restaurant, it is workplace violence.

Consider the impact upon the personal and working lives of the employees when incidents of serious injury or death take place, regardless if it was a disgruntled employee or a stranger who committed the act.

Let's examine this same robbery-homicide scenario in detail. We'll assume a woman is working behind the counter of a donut shop, one that is part of a national chain.

One late night, as she prepares to close the store, a man in a ski mask comes in brandishing a gun. Without a word, he shoots her in chest and as she slumps to the floor, he reaches across the counter and removes as much cash as he can carry from the register drawer. He leaves her to die at the scene.

Again, what is the impact of this event? If you draw concentric circles around the victim, who else is touched by this senseless crime?:

• the victim's family—who must now consider life without her.

• her co-workers—who look at this incident and cannot help but to put themselves in her place, as they wonder if they are next or if the store is still a safe place in which to work.

• the families of her co-workers—who worry about the safety and security of their loved ones who must still work at the shop.

• friends of either or both the employee and the co-workers—who grieve her death and worry about the safety of the others (and if they can continue to patronize the store in safety).

• the store manager—who must deal with his or her own grief, comfort terrified employees, and consider the unpleasantness of hiring a replacement employee.

- the store owner / franchisee — who worries about the security of his or her employees, the impact of this event on business, and whether this business investment is still worth the effort, in light of what can happen.

- the parent company executives — who must assist the store owner as they ask, "What happened? What can we do to make sure this doesn't happen at this or any other of our stores?"

- store vendors — who grieve for the employee and worry about their own safety as they service the store.

- customers — who may grieve for the employee if they knew her, who commiserate with the other employees, and wonder themselves if it's still safe to patronize the store.

One theme that runs through this collection of concerns is the need for others to guarantee or at least feel more comfortable about their own safety or the safety of others. This is both a human condition and normal response. We want to feel secure at work and when we shop or do business with other companies.

Consider these audiences and constituencies and their typical responses the next time you read or hear of a serious injury or death incident at any workplace. Too many people in organizations forget or ignore this ever-widening circle.

The Need For Pre- and Post-Incident Evacuation Planning for Workplace Violence Events

Every company should prepare emergency response and evacuation plans for potentially dangerous or life-threatening events like a fire, water or gas leak, a tornado, a hurricane, or an earthquake. It's time to add significant workplace violence events to that list of real disasters.

Back to the concept of due diligence, the company policy manual should include the steps to be taken in a serious workplace violence emergency. Many firms include these instructions near the pages describing the company's zero-tolerance policies, since they're so often related.

Realistically, a fistfight between two employees probably will not warrant a complete evacuation, but the presence of a man with a gun, a resulting homicide, any shooting incident, or any outburst by an employee or outsider armed with any weapon, should be met with a plan that verifies the safe removal of all surviving employees.

These plans should include the location of escape routes, common-area telephones (to help dial out to emergency services), safe areas (with steel or at least lockable doors), and the telephone numbers to be dialed in an emergency.

In stress, we revert back to how we have been trained. That helps to explain why when a recently terminated employee came back to an Illinois plant and started shooting at the employees, a foreman who had locked himself in his office could not dial the police from his telephone. With the sounds of gunfire in the background, he dialed 911, over and over, all to no avail. Finally, after several precarious minutes had went by, he remembered that he needed to dial "9" first to get an outside telephone line, and then dial 911 after hearing the dial tone.

We think we will know how to respond in crisis, but stress is the great demon of careful thought. This example illustrates why some firms post signs and stickers near the employee phones that say, "In Case of Emergency, Dial 9-9-1-1."

Workplace Violence Response Plans

Attorneys, risk managers, insurance company representatives, and others who must help support, protect, and later defend companies in court suggest these minimum standards for organizations to follow as part of an on-going response to threats or acts of violence in the workplace:

- the immediate notification of law enforcement agencies and rescue medical personnel, including instructions for all employees as to how to make contact outside the firm.

- the protection and isolation of any employees from further confrontations or attacks by an employee-perpetrator or outsider.

- the containment and protection of any workplace violence scene(s) for police officers and investigators first and in-house security managers later (who should serve in a police-company liaison position following the incident). This security employee also should determine from the police when it's possible to return the scene back to its original condition and then hire an outside firm to clean the area.

- the immediate creation of a secure and confidential critical incident debriefing area for employee counselors to use to meet with distraught or traumatized employees, co-worker witnesses, vendors, or customers.

- a company spokesperson who has been trained in advance to respond to media questions (away from the incident area or surviving employees) about both the situation and the firm's pre-and post-incident actions.

- the immediate notification of company legal, risk management, and insurance representatives to respond to the scene.

- grief and trauma recovery timeoff and the offer of crisis counseling for victim-employees, co-worker witnesses, vendors, or any customers who desire it.

- work with police and prosecutors to assist them in criminal investigations, prosecutions, or the service of protection orders in either employee-perpetrator or outsider crime cases or stalking; working with Personnel or Human Resources to initiate disciplinary sanctions or termination proceedings against employee-perpetrators.

- immediate, secure, and confidential access to EAP and psychological counseling programs to help every employees deal with post-incident trauma and lessen the possibility of serious, debilitating Post-Traumatic Stress Disorders (PTSD's).

- immediate contact, support, sympathy, and reasonable aid to victim-employees', and later to co-worker witnesses' families.

- continuing psychological support through the availability of follow-up counseling and debriefing sessions for all employees who desire them. This includes training managers and supervisors as to the ways employees may want to memorialize or remember victim-employees.

Workplace Violence Prevention Strategies

At this closing point in the text, it's time to review the contents with the hope that students of this book will continue with work in the related fields of understanding and controlling employee behavioral problems; practicing more diligent organizational security; protecting the psychological health of employees; and working to reduce violence in the workplace by reducing violence in society.

The following list highlights what has been covered throughout the book. Keep them in mind as you continue to form thoughts and opinions about past or new workplace violence cases, or plans and prevention strategies should you find yourself, the firm where you work, or will work at someday, facing the threat of workplace violence:

- **An admission that the problem exists**

    Violence in the workplace is not just a problem that affects cabdrivers or convenience store clerks; stockbrokers, vice presidents, and sales managers have fallen victim to killers' bullets. And the problem is more correctly defined as creating fear in the workplace by using threats, intimidation, vandalism, sabotage, assaults, or batteries against employees, either by other disturbed employees, customers, outsiders, or criminals. This makes the target for workplace violence much wider than originally thought.

- **Careful pre-employment screening and hiring practices**

    It's always easier to say no at the screening process than it is to remove an employee whose behavior is entirely inappropriate later on in the work relationship. Companies need to spend more time, effort, and dollars on thorough background checks, interview training for managers and supervisors, and legal advice to use during hiring times.

- **Zero-tolerance prevention policies**

    Informal, unwritten workplace violence policies aren't valid or applicable in an organization or more importantly, in a court of law. The organization must have written, enforceable zero-tolerance policies in place for all employees to read, understand, and be held accountable.

- **Management awareness of warning signs**

    Threatening, intimidating, coercive, or violent behavior is not usually difficult to recognize. The hard part is deciding what to do about it once it appears. Most managers and supervisors and their employees have excellent working instincts about what kinds of behavior are acceptable and what type scares them. Remember that the profile behaviors listed in this text are not a perfect crystal ball; only a stepping stone to further investigations by management as to possible or immediate interventions.

- **Management intervention into behavioral problems**

    Knowing about employee behavioral problems is critical; solving them is even more important. Many resources exist, both inside and outside the organization, to help concerned executives, managers, and supervisors, to set policy, enforce work rules, correct problems through discipline, termination or security measures. Workplace violence is not the problem of one single manager; it's the responsibility of the entire organization.

- **Fair and ethical treatment of employees**

The differences between a potentially violent employee who strikes out at people in the organization and one who does not often depends upon how that person was treated. Toxic companies, with unfair policies, harsh supervision, a punishment mindset, and a Theory X approach to the management and leadership of people, can bring out the worst in its employees. Nourishing firms treat everyone with fairness and dignity, whether during the hiring process or following a termination event.

- **Safe discipline and safe termination procedures**

Unusual employees call for unusual methods. It's time to change the usual one-on-one approach to the discipline or termination of employees with serious behavioral problems. Managers should rely more on the power, support, and insight of other people and departments in the organization, including EAP, Security, Personnel, and Human Resources.

Safe termination must include using specific violence-avoidance security policies—loose escorts, retrieving ID badges and security keycards—and the understanding that continuing problems with an ex-employee may call for the use of workplace harassment orders or help from law enforcement.

- **The continuing use of security policies, procedures, or devices**

Security and its dedicated practitioners don't get much attention, until, that is, both are sorely needed to assist with a difficult employee in a difficult situation. It's time to put more emphasis on the role of security policies, procedures, tools, devices, and the opinions of the management and guard personnel as to how to best protect the organization from attack by disturbed employees, stalkers, outsiders, or other criminals bent on harming the workplace.

- **Pre-established after-action plans**

Any firm who suffers through a serious workplace violence incident involving the injury or death of any employee, vendor, or customer will surely end up in a civil courtroom. By first accepting this as more than just a remote possibility, company leaders can start to draft and improve specific workplace violence emergency response plans, including the assignment of highly-specific duties, contact names and telephone numbers, and the need to build a relationship with outside consultants and psychologists or in-house EAP mental health counselors for on-scene help and intervention for every employee.

• **Courageous management**

Company representatives, executives, department heads, managers, and supervisors must be willing to do whatever it takes to recognize and prevent violence in the workplace, including thinking and acting outside their normal patterns; these are not normal situations.

In other words, since these are abnormal people acting in abnormal ways, the intervention practices into these situations and in these disturbed employees' lives requires the use of "abnormal" solutions.

Nearly every firm with more than one employee sits on a near 100 percent liability peg. The leaders must do everything possible to lower this liability factor and exhibit the necessary due diligence.

If I could speak to every executive, manager, or supervisor facing a potential or actual workplace violence problem, I'd suggest this:

• Have guts and trust them.

• Be creative, think outside the rule book for a safe, legal solution to the behavioral, security, or management problem.

• Work together in committees and teams, with other colleagues. Use the power of synergy.

• Know, use and pool all available internal and external resources.

• Create a safety and security protection mindset and workplace culture.

• Practice "if-then" thinking to protect yourself or others during any outburst of violence.

And if I could suggest only a few operational solutions for this subject it would be:

• stress-control classes for employees and supervisors

• anger management training for managers and supervisors

• anger management classes for employees

• better availability of outplacement services for downsized or terminated employees

• better availability and access for all employees to psychological services for work and personal problems

I realize much of what I've described in this book calls for the organization to become the "Intervener of Last Resort." These issues can be painful, expensive, hard to solve, and still fraught with the threat of injury or death to good people in the workplace. Until we recognize that crime and violence in the workplace is simply a mirror of crime and violence in society. To solve these problems as they erupt in the workplace, it is up to future generations of new leaders and their employees to address the root causes of violence, i.e. home problems, the lack of anger management or stress control training, inappropriate modeling, poor security plans, violent TV and movie shows, and non-stop media coverage of violence, etc.

Workplace violence does more than just start and end at work. Solving the problem of disgruntled employees at work must be related to solving the problems of disgruntled people in society. We have still more work to do on both fronts.

REVIEW/SUMMARY

This chapter discussed the need to change the usual ways managers and supervisors initiate discipline and termination events for employees with behavioral problems. It explained how and why to work with the police, especially following crimes of violence. Also, it outlined the post-incident dynamics of violence events, from assaults to homicides.

Future practitioners in the fields related to workplace violence and its prevention should look toward creating or supporting intervention solutions that protect everyone in the organization, legally, safely, and with regard to their psychological health as well.

APPENDIX A:
"SPILLOVER" CRIMES

A Case Study in Predicting the Threat of Domestic Violence In the Workplace

In the span of one week in April 1995, Albert Petrosky's wife told him that she no longer loved him, she was having an affair with a co-worker, and she wanted a divorce.

Within six days she was dead, shot at her Jefferson County, Colorado workplace by her enraged husband, who also shot and wounded her female friend, shot at an off-duty law enforcement agent, shot and killed her boss, and shot and killed a responding sheriff's sergeant.

We know what happened and why it may have happened; what we do not know is if it could have been prevented through more proactive security measures. This section outlines the Petrosky case from a variety of perspectives, in an attempt to help us learn from his deadly acts.

At age 35, Albert Petrosky began to feel more and more like a failure. A rarely-employed auto mechanic, he spent most of his time in a local Denver tavern, drinking, arguing, and often fighting with the other patrons. As he watched his life pass him by, he began to search for someone other than himself to blame. He chose his wife, Terry, 37, as the target of his resentment.

She worked as a service deli manager at a Jefferson County, Colorado Albertson's supermarket. She was well-liked by her co-workers, friendly to her customers, and deemed competent by her supervisors. Each of these traits only increased her husband's anger toward her. And while she may have had a good life at work, her home problems—namely those caused by Albert—began to mount.

On Saturday, April 22, 1995, Terry Petrosky reached her marital breaking point; what she would tell her husband would soon help him reach his as well.

Terry Petrosky began that afternoon by telling her husband that she was having an affair with a co-worker and wanted an immediate divorce. In a rage, he threw her on their bed and began choking her and hitting her with his fists. After he broke her nose, she tearfully agreed to sign a paper that surrendered all rights to their community property and gave him full custody of their 8-year-old son. She then fled their house in terror and spent the next days with friends.

By Monday, April 24, 1995, Terry Petrosky realized that although she had not reported his most recent domestic violence assault on her, it was time to take steps. She called in sick to work, and that day, applied for and received a temporary restraining order (TRO) against Albert.

Getting the restraining order was one thing; finding Albert to serve him was quite another. During the week that passed, court officers attempted to serve Petrosky, to no avail. He had left his house, moved in with his mother, and begun to prepare for a final showdown with his wife.

Terry Petrosky returned to work on Wednesday, April 26, and those who saw her facial injuries suddenly knew that her problems with Albert had escalated. He had called the store that day and asked to speak with her. One of her co-workers lied to him and said she wasn't working, to which he made the death threat, "That's it. I'm gonna take her out."

When Terry was notified of these threats, she met with her store director at Albertson's, Dan Suazo, 37, and told him of the previous battery and the impending restraining order against her husband. They discussed her continuing problems with Albert and he suggested she intensify her efforts to have authorities serve him with the TRO.

At that time, Albertson's had no formal training in how to effectively intervene in issues related to workplace violence or domestic violence at work. Since the Boise, Idaho-based company had no explicit policies or procedures regarding these events, the individual store directors relied on their own experiences and discretion to deal with unruly or violent customers, disgruntled current or former employees, or their spouses or partners.[1] The firm has since created a series of violence prevention programs.

In retrospect with the Petrosky case and others that have ended in workplace violence or death, we often learn in hindsight using this wait-and-see mode. In law enforcement or threat assessment circles, this approach is sometimes referred to the "observe and monitor" phase. What we know now is that while Terry Petrosky and her boss, Dan Suazo, were discussing what to do about Albert, he was preparing for a violent, final confrontation.

---

1. Telephone interview with Joe Venneman, Worker's Compensation Manager, Albertson's, Boise, Idaho, July 30, 1996.

As other workplace domestic violence homicide cases have illustrated, it's not unusual for the suspect to begin putting his "ducks in a row." While Denver authorities searched for him in vain to serve Terry's TRO, Albert was busy selling his van, his tools, his clothing, and most of his other possessions. He bought a new van—one he knew his wife wouldn't recognize—and shaved his head—a look he knew she despised.

He also gathered an arsenal of weapons, including a .32 caliber revolver, a 9mm semi-automatic pistol, an SKS assault rifle, and .50 caliber rifle.

On Friday, April 28, 1995, Albert Petrosky waited in the Albertson's parking lot for his wife to arrive for work. His van was parked near the only driveway entrance.

He watched as his wife's car entered the lot and drove near the front of the store. She was sitting in the passenger seat of her car, having agreed to loan it for the day to her friend, Misty Hudnall, 23.

As Hudnall stopped near the store's doorways to let Terry Petrosky out, Albert swerved his van near her and jumped out, armed with his revolver. He cursed threats at her and shot her in the lower back as she tried to flee inside. Half crawling and running into the store, Terry headed for cover near the store director's check-cashing booth near the doors.

Albert continued firing at her, now armed with his 9mm. He fired eight more shots at her as she tried to crawl away. Store director Dan Suazo looked out from his crouched position inside the booth just as Petrosky fired three fatal shots at him.

Albert Petrosky took a few seconds to survey his work inside the store and said nothing. Leaving the store, he saw Misty Hudnall, still driving Terry's car after she had doubled-back through the parking lot on her way out to the only exit. He fired four more 9mm rounds at her, striking the pregnant woman in the calf. As she sped away to head for a telephone to call the police, Petrosky got into his van and drove it to the highest point in the parking lot and wait for their inevitable arrival.

Sgt. Timothy Mossbrucker, 36, a father of six from the Jefferson County Sheriff's Office, drove into the store parking lot after witnesses relayed the news of Albert's attack to Sheriff's dispatchers. As he steered his police car toward Petrosky's position at the high point of the lot, Petrosky opened fire on him with the SKS assault weapon, hitting him with a 7.62 mm shot in the jaw.

This shot traveled a distance of over 300 feet, and yet Petrosky was still not finished. After spraying the parking lot and nearby store buildings with at least 15 other SKS rounds, he switched to a .50 caliber scope-mounted rifle, attached to a bipod so he could fire it from a prone ground position.

Petrosky fired three more .50 rounds at Sgt. Mossbrucker's patrol car as it slowly crashed to a stop.

An off-duty IRS agent, Robert O'Callaghan, was heading into the Albertson's store, when he saw Petrosky firing. He drew his own gun and after he exchanged several shots with the suspect, Petrosky quickly gave up and was subdued by a construction worker, who sat on him until more sheriff's deputies could arrive.

In the end, Albert Petrosky had shot and killed his estranged wife, her boss, and a responding law enforcement officer. He had shot and wounded Terry's friend, and shot at an off-duty law enforcement agent.

After a lengthy and emotional trial, he was convicted of his crimes. In a sad footnote to this incident, only two weeks before he was to be sentenced to several life terms, Albert Petrosky hung himself in his jail cell.[2]

With the usual understanding that we cannot perfectly predict the future and knowing in advance that our crystal ball is usually cloudy, we must ask and answer the question, "What can we learn from the Petrosky case?"

Case Study Question

From an organizational perspective, several prevention themes emerge from this case.

1. Discuss the critical, first-stage responses and then subsequent interaction and intervention steps for the following people or groups:

> the victim and her family and friends;
>
> the Albertson's facility;
>
> the Albertson's corporate headquarters, managers and supervisors in Human Resources, Security, and Employee Assistance;
>
> the local court system;
>
> local law enforcement;
>
> social services;
>
> state or federal legislatures.

---

2. In-person interview with Sgt. Randy West, Jefferson County Sheriff's Office, Golden, Colorado, July 18, 1996.

APPENDIX B

Domestic Violence in the Workplace: The Security Manager's Response to a Serious Off-the-Job Problem

The following section discusses the need for the security manager and his or her guard forces to take a more proactive, intervention-based, decision-making role in the company's policies and security procedures related to workplace violence and domestic violence in the workplace prevention.

What makes domestic violence such a pervasive workplace problem is that it ruins productivity and work performance for the victims. According to a 1990 study conducted by the Bureau of National Affairs:

> "Every year, companies lose anywhere from $3 billion to $5 billion in absenteeism, medical bills, employee turnover, and lost productivity because of domestic violence."[1]

Recognizing this problem when it is brought to the workplace by victims and suspects — whether they work together or not — starts with management awareness; first, recognizing that it exists, then, second, that management has a duty and obligation to protect domestic violence victims from further abuse — stalking, harassing phone calls, assaults that spill over from home to the workplace, etc., and third, that managers and supervisors should be aware of the warning signs of domestic violence abuse and know how to refer their employees to the proper EAP support, counseling services, social service intervention, or criminal justice help.

With domestic violence in the workplace becoming a visible issue, some firms have publicized their involvement in awareness and prevention campaigns. This list of concerned organizations includes Polaroid, Liz Claiborne, Ben & Jerry's, Reebok, Marshall's, VF Corp., and DuPont.

---

1. Staff written. *"Domestic Violence In the Workplace."* Bureau of National Affairs study, Washington, DC, 1990.

Managers and supervisors often express tremendous reservations when it comes to dealing with an employee's domestic violence problem that appears at the workplace.

It is *not* management's responsibility to play "marriage counselor" for the employee, take on her personal problems as their own, or otherwise lose their professional objectivity. It *is* management's responsibility to educate, empower, and empathize with the employee, by giving her the support and information she needs to help herself.

Much of what managers and supervisors learn about how and why domestic violence problems enter the workplace will come about from their own experiences, what they see in the media, and more importantly, what they can learn from the security manager.

Some employees, who would have never thought of burdening their bosses or co-workers with their problems, now see little reason not to drag everyone into their personal lives. In some cases, this may be a positive sign, largely because it can bring some of these things into the harsh light of reality where maybe the right kind of intervention will solve them.

This appendix section will seek to educate security managers as to the significant issues behind the domestic violence issue as it relates to the organization's employees.

Introduction to the Problem

In the past, domestic violence issues were usually handled by the police; they started at the victim and suspect's home and stayed there. Most people were too embarrassed or fearful to bring this problem to work with them. Thanks to the rising number of these kinds of cases, expanded media awareness about them, and the growing likelihood that people now feel less concerned about bringing their home problems to work, domestic violence is now an issue in the workplace. While the cases may still happen at home, the end result (the battered victim-employee) shows up at work with physical or psychological injures that cannot be ignored.

What we did at home and what we did at work used to be separated by a clear line of rights, roles, duties, and responsibilities. This is not the case today. People bring their problems to work now; they don't check them at the door.

People with ill children, eviction notices, or bankruptcies don't stop thinking about those things as they sit at their desks, counters, or assembly lines. An employee with a depression problem, a drug or alcohol addiction, or a violence problem at home will carry it to work.

What makes all of this even more disturbing is that some domestic violence suspects are not content to merely bother their victims at home; many of them are acting out their frustrations in public. Today we are seeing more and more examples of violence at home becoming violence at work.

These two problems—which used to be, for the most part, mutually exclusive, now go hand in hand more times than you might think.

Much of this has come because many suspects now realize they can continue to terrorize their victims even away from the home. Victim-employees (90% of whom are female) used to be able to get away from their batterers for at least an 8 to 10-hour period. This is no longer the case. Domestic violence victims get no peace from their tormentors, even at work. The suspect can control the victim even if she is on the job and away from her home.

There continues to be an alarming rise in the number of incidents where some male batterers have decided it's within their scope of power and control to take their home problems out in public and confront their partner at her workplace. This intervention requires expert help. The next section will discuss the following steps that should be considered by security managers and their officers.

Intervention Methods For Post or Impending Domestic Violence Workplace Incidents

Security managers and security officers should consider the following steps if they either witness a domestic violence incident on company grounds, i.e. a battery in the parking lot, or are given information about a previous incident from a manager or supervisor, or in some cases, from the victim herself. Understand, consider, and evaluate the following points:

• The victim has the right to request services from both in-house security and the local law enforcement agency.

Security officials should tell other managers and their respective employees that it's proper, desirable, and part of a legal requirement for the Security Department to document any incident that may affect the safety of the victim-employee, her co-workers, the company, or the company's various assets.

Further, the security manager should explain to the victim-employee that the police department will come on to company grounds and take reports or make arrests for domestic violence. Today, unlike in the past, most police agencies are now ordered by statute to document domestic violence cases, even if the injuries are not visible. In some states, like California, police are required to arrest a felony suspect (spousal abuse with minor or major injuries) even if the victim refuses to prosecute.

It's important that company property, although private, should not be seen as a safe haven for suspects. Further, any manager or supervisor who advises his or her employee to "take care of this on your own time" or "call the police when you get off work and are at home" should be educated as to how crime cases are investigated and the need for timely intervention by both the police and the Security Department. (If a company representative still won't listen to this logic, suggest that he call an attorney right away and start planning for an appearance in civil court. He will need to explain to a judge and jury why he denied a bona fide domestic violence victim access to the law.)

• Once security officers reach a victim of domestic violence (after it has taken place either at her home or later at her workplace), they should go out of their way to listen to her.

She may need or want to vent and when possible, the security officers should reassure her that they will attempt to do what they can to help her take care of the problem. This may require them to take her to a safe, discreet location in the facility, out of the view of other employees. It can be extremely stressful for a domestic violence victim to have other employees see members of the security department sorting through her family dirty laundry. The presence of a security officer and later, the police, tells most employees that something serious has happened and that the situation (and therefore, both the victim and the suspect) may be out of control.

Recognize that some of the anger the victim has for the suspect may be redirected at the responding security officers and then the police. They may be seen as the authority figures who cause the problem to escalate (by intervening in such a way that it causes her to believe she may lose her job, or have the suspect hurt her more in the future.) If the victim fears retribution from her partner or her employer, she may be uncooperative and fearful of any intervention by security officers or the police.

• On the other hand, security officers should resist the urge to wash out an incident report or otherwise discourage one to be filed with the police department.

In the interest of "corporate harmony," some frightened victims (and their employers) would much rather have the Security Department and the police forget the whole thing. Often, security or police arrival on the scene—in front of their bosses, co-workers, peers, and customers—can either lead the manager or the employee (or both) to want to change their minds and "not make a big deal out of it." This does little to help the victim-employee in the long run and it may let the suspect get away with a serious and destructive crime.

Recognize that this sense of fear and embarrassment is often due to the way a private matter has suddenly become public knowledge. As such, security officers should quietly escort the victim to a secure, confidential place to gather the information necessary to write a thorough incident report. If the facts of the case indicate the need for a security incident report, one should be written as a permanent company record. In any case, the responding police officers will be mandated by the Penal Code to write certain reports and document the event in a specific, permanent way. This is the case whether the domestic violence incident happened at the victim's home or in her workplace.

When the police arrive, security officers can brief the police and help them conduct their own investigation by giving them immediate access to the victim. Further, the Security Department's in-house report may also need to serve as an additional source of documentation for the police and it can have evidentiary value as well.

•Security managers and officers should never forget that the eyes of the company are upon them.

How the Security Department handles this particular incident at the workplace sends a strong message to the witnesses, co-workers, bosses, customers, potential or hidden domestic violence suspects, and anyone else who is on the scene and watching up close or at a distance.

A positive, professional, and empathetic approach not only comforts the victim, but it tells other people that, "Yes, our organization and our Security Department really does care about domestic violence, no matter where it happens." This kind of observation pays obvious dividends. It makes for better witness statements, it leads to more cooperation from management and the employees, and it may give the police that extra piece of information they need to intervene and help to solve the problem. Lastly, it tells other people—who may be gauging the Security Department's response and comparing it to domestic violence issues in their own lives— that this is a serious, significant off and on-the-job problem.

• Security managers and officers should never forget that in the future, the eyes of the victim's attorney may be on them as well.

Serious workplace problems have a tendency to end up in court. In cases of workplace violence through domestic violence, expect to see the company's incident report again as a piece of evidence. In a "failure to intervene/failure to protect" lawsuit against the victim's employer, attorneys from both sides will scrutinize the security and police reports, looking for information gaps, mistakes, or other wedges to use as leverage for themselves or against the other party. Some of that leverage could be aimed right back at the Security Department, especially if the security manager was told or learned about some critical information that didn't get into either report. The old saying in police work still holds true: "If it's not in the report, it's as if it didn't happen at all."

- The security manager should make it a point to teach other managers and supervisors how to safely and effectively intervene into the aftermath of domestic violence situations that end up at work.

Just as law enforcement and the criminal justice system have intervened in these kinds of problems, businesses have to intervene as well. It's no longer possible to ignore these situations that start at home and get brought to the work place. There are a number of things company managers and supervisors can do to shield the victim from continuing work-related domestic violence problems and help them stay productive (and employed). This includes referral to the company's EAP office, help in getting a restraining order, referral to legal, psychological, medical, or counseling services, and help guiding the victim through the criminal justice system.

One end of the domestic violence spectrum involves workplace harassment by phone. Harassing, threatening, or otherwise "crank" phone calls offer a way for the suspect to control or terrorize the victim from anywhere he happens to be near a phone.

In one case, a man called the office where his girlfriend worked every 10 minutes—like clockwork—for the next eight hours. And in Tokyo, a man was arrested for making 6500 crank phone calls a month to his former boss who had fired him. At one point, he made 1200 calls per day.

If security officers respond to this kind of problem inside the company, there are some immediate steps they can take to try and stop the problem and offer some relief to the victim (who may be in jeopardy of losing her job) and to the company manager (who worries—rightly—that this problem can hurt the business). Consider the following action steps to deal with phone harassers; these can be initiated by the security manager or responsible security officers:

- Call the suspect and tell him to stop.

    As one sociologist puts it,

    > "The chronic phone harasser needs to be confronted and threatened with legal action by an authority figure. Often, these people can't solve their problems face to face, so they choose the phone as a way to get nearer to their victims. They are scared of confrontation. In many cases, all it takes is for an authority figure to say, 'I know who you are. I know what you've been doing and I'm telling you right now that it had better stop or we will do what it takes to have you arrested and prosecuted.'"[2]

- Call the suspect's parents, friends, or other important people in his life and have them tell him to stop this behavior.

    Often, the victim knows the suspect's circle of family and friends and can provide information to the Security Department and the police. Sometimes, asking other people to put him on notice about these calls will force him to stop this behavior.

- The employer can help the victim and the company get a restraining order that forbids the suspect from calling the victim at home or work.

    In California, the recent creation of the "Workplace Harassment" order now allows companies to either help their employees get a Temporary Restraining Order (T.R.O.) or list the firm as the "victim" along with the victim-employee.

- Security managers can advise the company or the victim to sue the suspect in Small Claims Court.

    Most judges are sympathetic to this case because they know what effect it can have on a business. With the dollar limit in many states now at $5,000, this can put a financial hurt on the suspect. If he fails to go to court, the plaintiff will win by default and can start an aggressive collection process.

    Otherwise, he'll have to come to court and explain to the Small Claims commissioner why he made so many calls and why it didn't cause the business or the victim to lose money or time.

    While harassing phone calls may be one of the most common domestic violence-related workplace problems, the security manager may have to han-

---

2. Interview with Nancy Smith, California State San Marcos University, Social Behavior Department, April 2, 1995.

dle incidents that have a stronger likelihood of violence. Here, the suspect may wish to continue to terrify or injure the victim and it is up to the Security Department to develop safe and legal intervention and protection methods.

The paradox here is that the victims or potential victims of these incidents may still continue to see the presence of security officers and later, the police, as a threat to their jobs and future safety. The victims may respond to security officers and police differently because the eyes of their workplace are upon everyone concerned. The manager may or may not welcome the presence of security officers or police officers on the site—because their arrival indicates to all that something has gone wrong with the management status quo. Co-workers, customers, and other bystanders may or may not understand why they are on the scene; their level of help and support may depend upon their relationship with either the victim or the suspect and how they perceive the Security Department's or the police department's handling of the problem or not.

Lastly, the arrival of security officers or the police at the workplace may cause the suspect in a domestic violence or workplace violence-related case to do all kinds of irrational, violent, or dangerous things. The way victims and suspects react to the presence of security may vary from: subservient, as in, "Thanks for coming by, Mr. Security Officer. I'd be glad to tell you all about it."; to suspiciously hostile or uncooperative, as in, "Don't interview, interrogate, or mess with me in front of my boss or co-workers," to murderous, as in, "My job is my life and if you or anyone tries to take that from me, I'll have nothing to lose."

With regard to domestic violence in the workplace, here are some possible scenarios (already mirrored by recent real-life incidents across the country). In each case, consider first the Security Department's response to this kind of call, then make some judgments about the victim's state of mind (and likely reactions), and more importantly, the suspect's frame of reference to the crime and intervention by security officers or the police.

• Security officers respond to an incident at the victim's workplace; the suspect does not work there.

In this instance, the victim's feelings with regard to the location of the event are in near complete opposition to the suspect's. In other words, she's probably very worried about the stability or future of her job and he couldn't care less. In fact, in many cases, he may have chosen to attack her in some way at her workplace—both physically or psychologically—because he knows how much damage he can cause her.

Security officers' efforts should be guided by their desire to protect the victim from further harm from the suspect and then from further embarrassment from her boss or co-workers. The Security Department's goal should be to foresee and then attempt to prevent the likelihood of future confrontations with the suspect, i.e. help her get a Temporary Restraining Order, suggest security precautions such as posting the suspect's picture at the guard posts, transfer the victim to a less visible position or location, etc.

If the suspect is still on the scene, the police should be notified immediately. Their arrival may solve the problem if he can be arrested for trespassing, violation of a TRO, warrants, drug or alcohol use, etc. The security manager may be able to assist the police to get the suspect out of the area using any legal means at their disposal. Security officers telling the suspect to leave the premises probably won't work. For the batterer who attacks, threatens, or confronts (or re-confronts) his victim at her workplace, the issue has become an extension of the "power and control" mindset he is trying to create with her. Here, the police should be called in to remove the suspect from company property before he can cause problems there.

In these potentially volatile situations, the employee's manager should not say to the victim, "You two should go talk things out in the parking lot," or "Can't this wait until your coffee break or lunchtime?" Besides the obvious danger in this, other potential or on-going "hidden" victims will watch what the company and the Security Department does with their own situations in mind; other future or current batterers or harassers will do the same.

• Security officers respond to an incident at the victim's workplace; the suspect works there as well.

These incidents can be tricky for a variety of reasons, most of which have to do with job security and money. In one case where a female battery victim co-owned a small printing business with the male suspect, they were financial partners in the company and had a boyfriend-girlfriend relationship which obviously went from home to work and back again.

While this woman clearly didn't want to be hit, her options were limited. A TRO was not feasible; a misdemeanor arrest by the police for battery only left her with double the work and more business and personal problems; throwing in the towel, selling out her half, or otherwise quitting the shop would leave her in bad financial straits. What could she do? Information, education, referral, and support is probably the best solution the criminal justice system can provide.

These kinds of problems are more common than most security managers might first think. When the suspect and victim are tied to the same establishment for their paychecks, their emotions may cause or force them to make decisions they might not otherwise make at home. When the victim has to face the suspect at home and on the job, the Security Department's and the police department's response may be limited to how much information they can gather from any witnesses, rather than the victim, who may fear retaliation, not just from her partner, but from the employer as well. These cases can be doubly difficult, since some people will lie, deny, or leave rather than tell what really happened to them at work, on the way to work, or near work.

The key to handling these victim-suspect workplace incidents is to recognize the impact of the company's actions on all parties—the victim, the suspect, the witnesses, the co-workers, and the employer. Security officers need to use discretion, tact, careful steps, and not let any of these people or groups talk them out of the right, legal thing to do.

A crime is a crime is a crime, especially when it comes to domestic violence. The fact that the participants work together should not change the legality of it.

- Security officers assist the police with an incident at the suspect's workplace; the victim does not work there.

This is common in police follow-up calls, where they arrive to take a report at the victim's home and then go to the suspect's workplace to make an arrest or to gather more information for their report. When they or the security officers enter the suspect's "domain," he will probably exhibit one of three behaviors: complete submission ("I feel just awful about what happened."); wary or hostile indifference ("I don't appreciate you coming around here and messing with me at my job."); or escalating or immediate violence ("No one is gonna take me out in front of my friends, my boss, or from the place where I earn my money!")

This last one is the most dangerous and the most difficult, especially if the signs of either or both of the other two exist as well. In any event, if an arrest is in the cards, security officers and the security manager should stand by to assist the police with the remote possibility that his friends on the job might not take kindly to their attempts to remove him from their circle. This is especially true in domestic violence situations where the suspect has successfully rationalized this current crime or any past ones to his friends on the job. If he gets them to buy into his standard claim that "she made me hit her," then the police could have a fight on their hands from many different sides.

If a batterer at work has earned a trip to jail, suggest to the police that they get him out of earshot and eyesight of his friends, boss, and co-workers. The security manager may want to quietly explain to a supervisor what has happened and then allow him or her to report the incident to inquiring co-workers only on a need-to-know basis.

As with the previous scenario, handling suspects in their workplaces calls for an increased amount of safety and awareness. As strange as it sounds, the suspect may be more concerned about saving his job, saving his reputation, and saving "face" more than with anything related to his marriage or dating relationship. His response may seem completely out of the ordinary to observers, but it might make perfect sense to him.

- Security officers respond to an incident at the suspect's workplace; he has either just lost his job or is likely to face serious discipline or termination.

A large number of disturbed people will lash out in their workplaces following a discipline meeting or a termination hearing. The pages of our newspapers are filled with incidents where disgruntled employees or newly-fired workers came back and took out their frustrations with their fists or their guns.

Any response by security or the police to a post-incident domestic or workplace violence crime should come with the knowledge that in the worst cases, these suspects have nothing more to lose.

For the psychologically-impaired employee, thoughts of suicide, murder, or more typically, a deadly combination of both, are not far from the surface. If he knows the police have come to arrest him and that this will either cause his termination or add to his problems following his termination, anyone could become the focus of his rage.

There is an old and cynical saying among some men in this world: "If you have the choice between a good job and a good woman, take the good job; you can always get a good woman." The people who sincerely believe this statement may fight harder in order to protect their jobs than they would in order to save their marriages. There are men out there who operate under the life-guiding principle that says, "My job is who I am. My work and my career—not my wife or my house, or my kids—is what defines me as a MAN. If I don't have my job, then I must not be a man. No one is going to interfere with that."

Don't assume that the suspect who sees security officers or the police coming to take him out of his livelihood will go along without a fight. He may truly believe that while his marriage or relationship may be replaceable, his job or career is not. For the highly-disturbed employee, any attempts to remove him may be the last straw in a life that he has already decided is not worth living.

Proactive Problem-Solving

The problem of workplace domestic violence is complex and highly emotional. It demands a total organizational approach. Following the discovery of any bona fide domestic violence threat to any employee, consider the following intervention steps as well:

Use the power of early intervention—Often in certain low-level threat cases, the best defense is a strong offense. Use the size, strength, and resources located in your organization to your advantage. Taking steps to confront the behavior of a known perpetrator, especially if he is an employee of the organization, can ward off problems before they intensify.

This further sends the right message to the victim-employee that the organization, and specifically, the Security Department, cares about her safety and welfare, as well as that of her co-workers. Other observers—known as "fencesitters," for their potential future involvement in similar domestic violence situations as either a victim or a perpetrator—will also look at the organizational response and weigh it against their own perceptions of what is a positive, determined intervention.

Take the initial threats seriously—In cases where the employee's spouse or partner has started making multiple telephone, e-mail, voice mail, or in-person threats, it's critical to see them as valid. While they could range from harmless pranks to deadly warnings, you need to view the occurrence of each one somewhere along a threat management spectrum. Gauge your response based upon your review of the threat contents, facts or other information provided by the victim-employee or informed co-workers, and the perpetrator's history, if known.

These can be highly emotional events and psychologically damaging to the victim-employee and her surrounding co-workers. When we don't pay them proper heed, we send the wrong message to the recipients and may in fact, encourage the perpetrator to continue his threat campaign.

The frequency, type, intensity, and violence potential of the threats should be your early guide and an indication to meet with several people or groups inside your organization, including human resources, personnel, legal, and employee assistance.

Get threat assessment help—In these days of rampant civil and even criminal liability, i.e. California's new "Be a Manager, Do the Wrong Thing, Go to Jail" law, you need to demonstrate due diligence in your threat assessment activities. It's no longer enough to review the case and make an educated guess based upon training and experience. Courts are taking a dimmer view to the "we meant well" defense. When the threat situation turns serious, contact bona fide threat assessment professionals—typically psychologists, psychiatrists, or highly-trained behavioralists with specific violence and/or law enforcement training. Don't wait to bring their expertise into the case.

Use proactive employee protection steps—The Albert Petrosky case presents an imminent threat of serious violence, which sadly, came to pass. In workplace cases where the perpetrator makes himself known and follows with visible, terroristic threats, it's time for aggressive movements designed to protect the victim-employee and her equally-frightened co-workers.

This can include transferring the victim-employee to another department or company location; helping her get a Temporary Restraining Order to protect the organization, or using what many states are now developing, a "workplace harassment" protection order, where the company shares victim status with the employee.

Communicate with all guard shifts—Miscommunication can turn deadly. Make sure you or your staff verbally briefs every member of the guard force on what they need to know about the case, the victim, the suspect, and the appropriate security responses. Don't rely on memos, standing orders, log notes, or other written commands that may not get read in time or at all. Take prescribed precautions: posting the perpetrator's photograph and vehicle description in a private "eyes-only" location in the Security Department; meeting with key representatives of the Human Resources Department for legal or labor law advice; and assigning security officers to monitor the victim-employee when near company facilities and parking lots.

Continue to assess and tighten access control policies—As we have seen in recent cases, domestic violence suspects can be quite vigorous and diligent in their efforts to gain access to their partners. They often bring the mind of safecracker to their task of gaining access to your facility and attacking their target. You need to look hard to close any loopholes that will allow any unauthorized people into any doorway, window, ramp, or gate in the building.

Work with law enforcement early and often—Making threats of violence is a crime in every state, and depending upon the degree, is a felony as well. Call in law enforcement help at the patrol and detective levels to help document these incidents with reports. Use your local civil procedure resources to get TRO's and workplace harassment orders with and for the victim-employee and urge that these papers get served as soon as possible.

Insist on follow-up activities from police investigators. If the case seems serious, don't take, "We're too busy" as the only answer from a detective. Keep in contact, provide new information when you can, and ask for updates and important notifications, i.e. when the suspect is arrested or released from custody.

Continually educate and empower the victim—Keep in constant contact with the victim-employee, filling her with information, reassuring her fears, and encouraging her to cooperate with your department, police authorities, and others who want to both help her solve her own problems and stay secure, both physically and psychologically.

From an organizational perspective, there is safety in numbers and safety in size. You have a number of resources, departments, divisions, and experts in many fields at your disposal, both inside and outside the company. Put these people and service groups to work, helping you attempt to solve the problems created by workplace threats or employee-related domestic violence.

Conclusions

Domestic violence and the workplace go together like drunk driving and car accidents; there is a built-in cause-and-effect relationship between the problems people face at home and those they bring with them to work. Security officers and the police may become the intervener of last resort. A Bureau of National Affairs report reiterates the growing concern some companies have for domestic violence:

> "Prompted by publicity from . . . high-profile cases and by new public-awareness campaigns and legislation, U.S. companies are beginning to realize that domestic violence is a business issue and it affects the bottom line."[3]

Not every incident that brings security officers face to face with domestic violence victims or suspects at work will end in problems, confrontations with security, injuries, violence, or worse, but the precedents have already been set. Crimes at home have now become crimes at work. Security managers, their officers and department, and the entire organization now have a legal duty to intervene in these problem areas, specifically

---

3. Staff written. *"Domestic Violence In the Workplace."* Bureau of National Affairs study, Washington, DC, 1990.

when they affect the work performance and work productivity of the victims, their co-workers, and others associated with the organization.

Today, the employer, the Security Department, and later, the police department, has no choice but to intervene in some of the off-the-job problems some people bring to work. While it's not possible to fully protect every domestic violence victim at her work, security managers can work with the employer to educate, empower, and support the victim-employee, and help the criminal justice system to intervene, arrest, prosecute, incarcerate, and follow-up. It's critical—especially in the early stages of any work related domestic violence incident—that the company officials exhibit due diligence in their efforts to assist any victim of a serious crime, even if it did not take place on company property. To do anything less is to be seen as insensitive at the least, and harmful at the worst.

Recommended Reading List

The following list is not meant to be all-inclusive, but it should serve as a good starting point for further reading and research. These books look at occupational violence, homicide, crimes at work, criminal behavior, human resource issues, and the psychology of violence.

Parenthetically, there are many dangers in creating a list of related works. Critics and the other authors will either suggest that the writer has ignored similar works in the field or that the writer has somehow stolen from these works. I have tried to do neither.

Albrecht, Steve. Crisis Management For Corporate Self- Defense: How to Protect Your Organization In a Crisis. New York: AMACOM, 1996.

My book examines what I referred to as P.I.E. problems - attacks on or by a company's products, image, and employees. If the subject of workplace violence is one single tree, this book looks at the whole forest of potential corporate problem areas.

Baron, S. Anthony. Violence in the Workplace. Ventura, CA: Pathfinder Publishing, 1993.

Baron was one of the early authors in this field.

Bartol, Curt R. Criminal Behavior. 4th edition, Englewood Cliffs, NJ: Prentice Hall, 1995.

Long a standard in many criminology and sociology courses, Bartol's text offers an excellent psychological, biological, and social look as to why people commit the crimes they do.

Coleman, James William. The Criminal Elite: The Sociology of White Collar Crime. 2nd edition. New York: St. Martin's Press, 1989.

A good discussion of white collar, business-specific crime.

Darden, Christopher. In Contempt. New York: HarperCollins, 1996.

The early part of this effort from a member of the O.J. Simpson prosecution team looks at the Nicole Brown-Ron Goldman murders from the killer's point of view.

De Becker, Gavin. The Gift of Fear: Survival Signals That Protect Us From Violence. New York: Little, Brown, 1997.

De Becker is one of the leading threat assessment experts in the country. He has developed a software package—MOSAIC—to identify risk behaviors in perpetrators of workplace violence, domestic violence, and stalking.

Douglas, John and Olshaker, Mark. Mindhunter: Inside the FBI's Elite Serial Crime Unit. New York: Scribners, 1995.

Douglas served as an early adopter of homicide suspect profiling for law enforcement purposes. This book highlights many of his most successful cases and features his comments about his interviews with a number of famous and infamous serial criminals.

Goleman, Daniel. Emotional Intelligence. New York: Bantam Books, 1995.

This bestseller offers a new context for measuring intelligence, and places it into a thought-provoking discussion of our most serious social problems.

Grote, Dick. Discipline Without Punishment. New York: AMACOM, 1995.

This book serves as the bible for the human resources concept of progressive discipline. Grote offers an excellent counseling and coaching progression that helps managers and supervisors deal with difficult employee behavioral problems.

Hamper, Ben. Rivethead: Tales From the Assembly Line. New York: Warner Books, 1986.

An excellent window into the blue-collar world of a General Motors assembly plant. Written in a witty, profane, and highly informative manner, this book highlights the hostile and even violence-prone relationship between employees and management. Hamper's sense of humor makes this book shine.

Hickey, Eric W. Serial Murderers and Their Victims. Belmont, CA: Wadsworth Publishing, 1997.

A new and well-researched book in this subject and field.

Katz, Jack. Seductions of Crime. New York: Basic Books, 1988.

This text offers a compelling discussion as to the "whys" of crime, which may be more common than we would like to imagine.

Kinney, Joseph. Preventing Violence At Work. Englewood Cliffs, NJ: Prentice Hall, 1995.

Kinney did much of the early statistical work and research on workplace violence. This book is a culmination of effective intervention steps without a lot of distracting case studies.

Labig, Charles. Preventing Violence in the Workplace. New York: AMACOM, 1995.

Labig is an organizational psychologist. This brief book offers a practical discussion on downsizing and large-scale terminations.

Mantell, Michael and Albrecht, Steve. Ticking Bombs: Defusing Violence In the Workplace. Burr Ridge, Illinois: Irwin Professional Publishing, 1994.

This was the first nationally published book on workplace violence. We created a total intervention process for the problem—pre-employment screening and hiring, counseling and intervention methods, to discipline and termination. Mantell is a leader in the field of on-scene crisis counseling, having worked at the San Ysidro, California McDonald's massacre and the Edmond, Oklahoma Post Office shootings.

Norris, Joel. Serial Killers. New York: Anchor Books, 1988.

An early work on this subject; the author offers a detailed profile at the end of the book.

Reiss, Albert J. and Roth Jeffrey A. Understanding and Preventing Violence. Washington, DC: National Academy Press, 1993.

Sprouse, Martin. Sabotaging the American Workplace. Pressure Drop Press, San Francisco, CA: 1992

A disturbing and thought-provoking book. Sprouse collected the accounts of sabotage, theft, vandalism, and other crimes from the employees who committed them.

Wheeler, Eugene D. and Baron, S. Anthony. Violence in Our Schools, Hospitals and Public Place. Ventura, CA: Pathfinder, 1994.

An industry-specific book on violence problems at some of our public businesses and organizations.

ABOUT THE AUTHOR

Steve Albrecht is a business author, seminar leader, speaker, and management consultant from San Diego, California. He has been featured over 75 times in national newspapers, magazines, radio, and television as an expert in workplace violence awareness and prevention.

He is currently a Ph.D. (ABD) candidate in management, with an emphasis on employee behavioral problems and human resource issues. He holds a Masters Degree in Security Management from Webster University, where he was named the "Outstanding Graduate of the Year." He has a B.A. degree in English from the University of San Diego.

He is the Managing Director for Albrecht Training & Development, which offers seminars and consulting services in employee behavior problems, workplace violence prevention, security management, threat assessment, and crisis management.

Steve is also an adjunct professor of criminal justice for Central Texas College (in association with the United States Navy) and for National University in San Diego, California.

He has been in the training profession since 1985 and is certified as a Professional in Human Resources (PHR) from the Society of Human Resource Management (SHRM). He is also a member of the American Society for Industrial Security (ASIS); the Association of Threat Assessment Professionals (ATAP); the American Society for Training and Development (ASTD); the Western Society of Criminology (WSC); and the Academy of Criminal Justice Sciences (ACJS).

He has been with the San Diego Police Department since 1984, both as a regular officer and now as a reserve sergeant. He works part-time as an investigator in the SDPD Domestic Violence Unit, and has handled over 1,000 cases since 1993. He is a member of the San Diego District Attorney's Stalking Strike Force.

Steve is the author or co-author of ten other books, including: *Crisis Management for Corporate Self-Defense* (AMACOM), and the first nationally published business book on occupational violence, *Ticking Bombs: Defusing Violence In the Workplace* (Irwin).